olent Histories

Cultural Identity Studies

Volume 8

Edited by
Helen Chambers

PETER LANG
Oxford · Bern · Berlin · Bruxelles · Frankfurt am Main · New York · Wien

David Gascoigne (ed.)

Violent Histories

Violence, Culture and Identity in France from Surrealism to the Néo-polar

Pop

PETER LANG

Oxford · Bern · Berlin · Bruxelles · Frankfurt am Main · New York · Wien

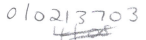

Bibliographic information published by Die Deutsche Bibliothek
Die Deutsche Bibliothek lists this publication in the Deutsche National-
bibliografie; detailed bibliographic data is available on the Internet at
‹http://dnb.ddb.de›.

British Library and Library of Congress Cataloguing-in-Publication Data:
A catalogue record for this book is available from The British Library,
Great Britain, and from The Library of Congress, USA

ISSN 1661-3252
ISBN 978-3-03910-317-1

© Peter Lang AG, International Academic Publishers, Bern 2007
Hochfeldstrasse 32, Postfach 746, CH-3000 Bern 9, Switzerland
info@peterlang.com, www.peterlang.com, www.peterlang.net

Printed in Germany

Contents

6

Acknowledgements

The editor would like to express his warm appreciation of the generosity of the Carnegie Trust for the Universities of Scotland in supporting the publication of this volume. Thanks are also due to Christine Gascoigne for her invaluable proofreading skills, and to the staff of the St Andrews University Library for their unfailing helpfulness.

DAVID GASCOIGNE

Introduction: France's Violent Histories

This volume is designed as a contribution to the study of the textual representation of and reflection on violence in twentieth-century France, and the traces recorded in both fictional and non-fictional writing by the violent events and upheavals of that century. Like two other volumes in this series, it owes its origins to a selection of the papers presented at the international conference on 'Violence, Culture and Identity' held in the University of St Andrews in 2003 under the auspices of the University's Institute for European Cultural Identity Studies.

The contributions presented here focus on the period since about 1920, marked initially by movements such as surrealism or international socialism which were born of, or strengthened by, the reactions to the slaughter of World War I. We then set out to trace, both through the lens of a number of major writers and thinkers of the period and in the more popular recent genre of the *néo-polar*, some of the resonances and fissures left by the wounding experiences of Occupation and decolonisation in the French psyche, both individual and collective.

In sketching out, in the very broadest terms for our purposes, the formative historical context over this period in France, it is perhaps useful to identify three phases of cultural and ideological reaction to violence which correspond to the aftermath of World War I, the Occupation and the wars of decolonisation, especially the Algerian conflict, respectively.

France's toll of casualties in World War I was particularly grievous – over 1.3 million dead and about three million wounded[1] –

---

1   'Of all the great powers in the war', writes one historian, 'no other country mobilised on such a vast scale as France or suffered such a high rate of casualties'. Seen as a proportion of those enlisted (16.5 per cent) or of the total

and, as in World War II, much ground fighting took place on French soil. The horrific slaughter to which the lists of names on every village war-memorial in France bear witness to this day had an impact on the national consciousness beyond the immediate economic and social implications. Many were impelled to question those attitudes which were seen to have led to the war, and this dissatisfaction was instrumental in reinforcing those strands of avant-garde French culture which defied establishment norms in a search for sweeping renewal. Surrealism, characterised by Peter Read here as a 'post-traumatic movement', developed a passionate challenge to the post-Enlightenment faith in science, rationality and technological control as the keys to human progress and personal fulfilment. For these cultural dissidents, the subversive inner forces of desire and imagination, including (at least in theory) the capacity for a more spontaneous, individualist violence, were there to be mobilised against the stifling political, moral and sexual conservatism which had given birth to the dehumanised, mechanistic Armageddon of the trenches. The principles and the polemic which fuelled the Surrealist movement retain to this day, as Peter Read shows, a remarkable power to inflame intellectual controversy in France.

Another, more explicitly political and collective, kind of reaction to the Great War was the increasingly potent impetus towards a revolutionary transformation of French society and its values. The intense clash between the extreme left- and right-wing versions of this vision of renewal found particular expression in conflicting French reactions to the violence of the Spanish Civil War. Malraux's fictions, spanning a tumultuous period from 1928 to 1942, offer a telling personal barometer of the evolving shifts of focus: from the fascination with heroic-tragic individualist violence to the requirement for disciplined collective action in pursuit of an equitable socialist society, and then from advocacy on behalf of a Communist-controlled

population (3.4 per cent), French losses outstripped those of Britain, Germany, the Austro-Hungarian Empire, Russia or Italy. See Stephane Audoin-Rouzeau, 'The French Soldier in the Trenches', in Hugh Cecil and Peter H. Liddle (eds), *Facing Armageddon: the First World War Experienced* (London: Leo Cooper, 1988), 221–9 (pp.221, 223).

anti-Fascist struggle in Spain to the overriding need to defend the values and culture of France itself, and of mankind in general, against the threat of Nazi barbarism.

The experience of Occupation in what have come to be known as the Dark Years of 1940–1945 confronted the civil population with acutely difficult choices, morally and politically. It generated painful divisions within the social fabric of the nation, from the leadership right down to the most local level of *quartier*, village or family. It does not now seem over-dramatic to describe these five years of internecine tension and strife as a national trauma. It not only provoked the often uncontrolled score-settling of the *épuration* at the Liberation, but left a distressing legacy of anger, bitterness and guilt with regard to official and unofficial French collaboration with the Nazis and complicity in the deportation of French Jews. Following the weaknesses and shortcomings of the governments of the Third Republic regimes in the pre-war period, national consciousness was dealt a succession of blows: the devastating military defeat of 1940, the humiliating armistice, and the subsequent crimes against humanity committed under the aegis of an apparently legitimate and initially widely supported Pétainist *Etat Français.*

While pride in the Resistance and the euphoria of the Liberation enabled many to retain and emphasise only the positive features of the wartime experience, the weight of all that had been done in the name of France nevertheless contributed to perhaps the greatest crisis since 1871 as to what France stood for. The solidity of its culture, its values and its sense of collective identity was thrown into doubt, in an acute crisis of confidence and status which de Gaulle saw it as his vocation to combat. While the German people faced a more pressing need to understand and come to terms with the moral and political catastrophe of this period, a process recognised and encapsulated in the term *Vergangenheitsbewältigung* ('overcoming the past'), the requirement for a French version of this same recognition and reckoning was, for all kinds of reasons of political expediency, only patchily and often reluctantly taken on board by the French establishment. The consequence of this refusal, in many instances, to investigate the atrocities committed by French citizens against other French citizens and to identify those responsible for authorising or carrying them out produced a kind of generational split which emerges clearly from a number of the later studies in this volume. In the work of a Prix Goncourt winning writer such as Patrick Modiano as well as in the popular crime fiction of the Série Noire, we find characters of the post-war generation irreconciled to – even haunted by – the crimes and injustices of the Dark Years. The rampart of concealment or willed forgetfulness which they encounter throws into uncertainty their allegiance to the society of which they are part, or even to their immediate family and its history. The writing gives expression to their need for clarity and closure in this inheritance of trauma, and often more explicitly to a political demand for a new order of transparency and justice, representing a challenge to a political system seen, even today, as inherently conditioned by an ethos of continuing complicity and corruption.

The dissident strand of writing and thinking which sought to disrupt public complacency about the legacy of the Occupation was given a distinct boost, even before the upheavals of May 1968, by the increasing opposition to France's colonial wars in Indochina and especially in Algeria. The savagery of the struggle against the F.L.N. in Algeria, involving the covert but extensive use of torture, was gradually investigated and publicised in the 1960s. As Margaret-Anne Hutton and Alan Morris show, some writers, looking back as far as the Dreyfus affair, saw a disturbing link between the anti-Semitism of the French conservative Right which had colluded in the deportations of Jews to the death-camps on the one hand and what they saw as the racism underlying the ruthless struggle against Algerian independence on the other. The process of decolonisation was arguably harder to accept, and consequently more demanding, for France than for Britain, for a number of reasons. These include the French colonial policy of close political and cultural integration with the motherland, the relative proximity of the North African colonies and the undertakings of support given to the numerous French settlers there. Once again, however, a phase of history including humiliating military defeat (Dien Bien Phu) and the official underwriting of abjectly inhumane violence in the name of the national interest served to swell the questioning of French values by a sceptical post-1968, post-Gaullian generation. What one might call the politicisation of the genre of noir fiction was both a sign of the debate engaging with a wider public and a remarkable feature of the Gallicisation of a genre borrowed from American popular culture. This sector of literary production, aimed at a broad audience, found its counterpart and some ideological nourishment in ongoing intellectual analyses and controversies, from Sartre and Camus onwards, around the construction of the ethnic Other within French cultural consciousness. This body of reflection on an acutely sensitive area of concern gave French writing a significant role in what has been a very international field of debate deriving from questions posed both by the Holocaust and by the travails of decolonisation.

Memory, Witness, Reflection

As the foregoing discussion suggests, the representations of violence commented on here can be related, almost without exception, to the perception or memory of this context of war or collective violence. The writing may be discursive, as in Sartre's *Réflexions sur la question juive* and Genet's article on Chartres Cathedral, or fictional as is the case for most other texts discussed in this volume. Our contributors have, however, focused on fictions which either inhabit and shed light on war or massacre, as in the narratives of Malraux or Sebbar, or seek to interrogate the origins, realities and implications of such episodes in retrospect, as in Daeninckx or Amila. Issues involving the disparity between individual memory and public commemoration of war and violence surface frequently. David Platten shows how Jean Amila's anarchist revolt against militaristic nationalism is reflected in the opposition between two quite different modes of commemoration: the official versions which consolidate establishment power and the passivity of the mass, and the very unofficial, subversive versions and individual counter-rituals enacted by Amila himself and by his characters. Margaret-Anne Hutton suggests how texts of this kind contribute to a contemporary memory culture, which can serve to revalorise what has been suppressed, and even, more progressively, to anticipate a more ethical political order for the future.

The writer's mode of operation can be designed to lay bare the scandal of politicians' involvement in what is shameful (Thierry Jonquet on Georges Marchais, Didier Daeninckx on Maurice Papon), and thereby to arouse the reader's indignation, or at least stimulate a more critical observation of the political scene. Alternatively, as in the case of Camus or Modiano, the focus may be on registering the movements of a particular consciousness. In Camus's *L'Hôte*, explored by Toby Garfitt, we experience the scene through the awareness of Daru, a Frenchman charged with escorting an Algerian prisoner. We soon become aware, however, that, as in *La Peste*, the fictional situation is constructed by Camus as a vehicle for moral and political reflection, exploring the sensitive node of a problematic encounter between a Frenchman required to act as an unwilling jailer and an Algerian prisoner, at a time in which the colonial power-relationship governing this situation is in deep crisis. Written a decade or so later, Modiano's first three novels represent a similarly anxious reflection on a critical period, as they weave patterns of fantasy, black humour and loss around the uncertain memories and imaginings of his fictional alter egos haunted by the darker sides of the Occupation. These early texts have by now been much analysed, but Dervila Cooke shows how resonances of this dimension of obsession still haunt Modiano's much more recent fictions: evidence of their tenacious survival in his writing, as perhaps more generally in the French psyche.

Violence: Issues of Definition

As many well-filled library shelves attest, violence has become a widespread, even obsessive, subject for analysis in our culture, with a proliferation of discourses derived from many different disciplines: history, anthropology, psychology, sociology, semiotics, philosophy, theology among others. As one commentator typically concludes:

> there is no well-demarcated, widely accepted concept of violence. On the contrary [...], 'violence' is a term that suffers from conceptual devaluation or semantic entropy.[2]

A series of textual studies of the kind presented here, which may draw on any one or more of the discourses mentioned, can thus be un-apologetically flexible and multi-faceted in its approach to the topic. Such an approach is a proper response, in the view of Michel Maffesoli, to what he calls the 'polyphonic' aspect of violence:

> Il n'est pas possible d'analyser la violence d'une manière unique, de la prendre comme un phénomène unique. Sa pluralité même est l'indicatrice privilégiée du polythéisme des valeurs, de la polysémie du fait social dont il a été question.[3]

Nevertheless, while accepting this polyvalence of the notion of violence, it is worth noting some key issues in the debates around this term. Some commentators seek to counter the over-promiscuous use of the term by restricting it to the indisputable sense of direct physical injury of people or material damage to objects.[4] Many commentators,

2 Philip Schlesinger, *Media, State and Nation. Political Violence and Collective Identities* (London: Sage Publications, 1991), 5.
3 'It is not possible to analyse violence in just one particular way, to treat it as one single phenomenon. Its very plurality is highly indicative of the polytheism of values, of the polysemy of the feature of society in question'. Michel Maffesoli, *Essais sur la violence banale et fondatrice* (Paris: Librairie des Méridiens, 1984), 14.
4 Schlesinger (p.7) lists a number of such closely circumscribed definitions. The political scientist John Keane moves in the same direction, arguing that violence is best understood as 'the unwanted physical interference by groups and/or individuals with the bodies of others' which consequentially suffer pain,

however, implicitly or explicitly extend the scope of the concept to include oppressive psychological pressure exerted by one individual against another, such that it damages the well-being of the object of that pressure. Further, since such non-physical acts or attitudes of domination or aggression are often driven by cultural norms or models (of ethnicity, gender, sexual orientation, religious allegiance and so on), this application of the term 'violence' can readily be further extended to include the active presence of hostile constructions of the Other underpinning the cultural behaviour of a group or indeed the ideological structure of a whole society. Sartre's representation of Jewish identity as being constructed largely in response to anti-Semitic prejudice, analysed by Kirsteen Anderson, is a pertinent example (although in his case, as she shows, it touches on far-reaching personal issues of identity and ethics). The textual representations of violence, or reflections upon it, presented in these pages will often traverse all three of these levels of physical aggression, psychological intimidation and cultural oppression which frequently co-exist and reinforce each other. This is one sense in which violence is (to re-use Maffesoli's term) polyphonic.

Violence and Culture

To extend the idea of violence to include the impact of collective constructs of cultural identity is, however, to raise a number of further issues around the notions of social order and of difference. The word 'violence' is generally used in a pejorative sense. As a description of an action it is more often deployed by the person or group subjected to the action or by a witness to it than by the perpetrator(s). It carries the implied judgement that the action in question is reprehensible.[5] This

damage or death. See John Keane, *Reflections on Violence* (London and New York: Verso, 1996), 66–7.

5   See David Riches, 'The Phenomenon of Violence', in D. Riches (ed.), *The Anthropology of Violence* (Oxford: Blackwell, 1986), 1–27 (p.3).

implied evaluation, however, rests on an assumption about the (il)legitimacy of any particular act of violence. Max Weber defined as one of the essential properties of the State its 'monopoly of the legitimate use of violence within a given territory', and by extension its control over decisions regarding the legitimacy or otherwise of acts of violence. However, as Philip Schlesinger points out:

> one of the immanent possibilities of the state's monopoly of violence is the transgression of [the] legal frameworks which in theory act to limit its arbitrariness. It is at this point that we speak of states becoming terroristic, or of employing techniques (such as torture) whose use they themselves would wish to deny, dissimulate or euphemise.[6]

Insofar as State violence is exercised in the defence of 'public order', judgement upon it (and even our choice of the term 'violence' to describe it) will depend, not only on whether it is appropriate to the situation and proportionate in its degree, but more fundamentally on our assessment of the values of the 'order' which is thereby being defended. In texts studied here, the violence legitimised by World War I generals against deserters, by the Vichy government against Jews and others, or by the colonial authorities in Algeria against the insurgents are all contested. This in turn raises the question of the circumstances under which violence may properly be deployed to oppose, reform or overthrow a regime or a social 'order' perceived as unjust or inhumane. My own essay on Malraux's fiction, tracing a particular cluster of images in successive works, looks at how cultural icons can change in their exemplary significance from negative to positive, depending on a shifting assessment of the political and cultural 'orders' or values which they are seen to symbolise.

This relativisation of the concept of violence problematises the relationship between violence and culture, two of the key terms of this volume. In one sense, violence, and the particular signifying forms it takes, is always likely to be rule-governed and meaningful in terms of

---

6   Schlesinger (p.9), from which the quotation from Max Weber is also taken. The texts by Daeninckx and others discussed by Margaret-Anne Hutton and Alan Morris are precisely designed to function as antidotes to such denial, dissimulation or euphemism on the part of the authorities.

the culture in which it is embedded. Acts of extreme collective violence, such as the massacre of Algerians in Paris discussed by Margaret-Anne Hutton, are, to quote the anthropologist Neil White-head, in cultural terms:

> very meaningful, recalling the histories that shore up the conflicts in which the antagonists are engaged, forcing the nightmares of the past into the waking realities of the present.[7]

Such resurgence of the past into the present is apparent in a number of the texts under discussion here. Alan Morris directs our attention to Thierry Jonquet's *Les Orpailleurs*, in which an investigation of recent murders leads back to a literal 'unearthing' of the horrors of the Hitlerian death-camps, while Dervila Cooke traces more subtle in-scriptions of this grim heritage in Patrick Modiano. However, as Whitehead further observes:

> violence certainly marks the limit of the cultural order. Moreover, this limit is a highly unstable border, beyond which the lack of meaning and the denial of sociality lurk constantly. At the same time, this very instability is the source of the cultural possibilities for violence to remake and redefine the cultural order itself.[8]

This last positive view of violence as a potential instrument for cultural renewal is developed further by Maffesoli. Violence, he argues, is a natural by-product of difference. Heterogeneity engenders violence, but it is also a source of vitality, whereas homogeneity, while more peaceable, is potentially deadly. This stultifying effect is apparent when violence becomes the monopoly of some over-arching authority. Violence can, however, be utilitarian, constructive of new order: it can carry a call for a new rationality or a return to roots (religious reform, or political revolution). It is part of what he calls, borrowing a phrase from Duvignaud, 'la dialectique vivante de l'im-aginaire et de l'institué', the tension between the perception of what is

---

7   Neil L. Whitehead, 'Cultures, Conflicts and the Poetics of Violent Practice', in
      N.L. Whitehead (ed.), *Violence* (Santa Fe: School of American Research Press
      and Oxford: James Currey, 2004), 3–24 (p.10).
8   Ibid., 8.

in place and the imagining of how things might be ordered otherwise.[9] This principle evokes both the Surrealists' rallying-cry of 'l'im-agination au pouvoir' ('Let imagination rule'), taken up by student activists in 1968, and the aspirations of revolutionaries from both left and right. Peter Read outlines some of the friction between the political and cultural-libertarian aspects of this fervour for violent renewal within the Surrealist movement. Elsewhere, the response explored here to the regressive violence of government-sponsored atrocities takes the form, for the authors concerned, of a would-be creative violence of anger, indignation and (sometimes) satire refined through the narrative construction and style of writers such as Jonquet, Sebbar or Daeninckx. Their aim is to reaffirm the possibility of an 'order' different from what they see as the corruption and hypocrisy of the existing political establishment.

Violence and Identity

The issues we have outlined so far have tended to focus on violence in its relation to the institutional and the collective, and have been viewed largely as an expression of social and cultural tensions. A quite different perspective is opened up by asking the age-old question as to whether violence is innate in the human psyche rather than simply culturally conditioned. Freud sees the tendency to destruction, aggression and cruelty as a fundamental component of the life of the psyche,[10] and Malraux's writing about abjection will often suggest

9 More literally, 'the living dialectic between the imaginary and the established'. See Maffesoli, 14, 25.

10 'men are not gentle creatures [...]; they are, on the contrary, creatures among whose instinctual endowments is to be reckoned a powerful share of ag-gressiveness. As a result, their neighbour is for them not only a potential helper or sexual object, but also someone who tempts them to satisfy their aggres-siveness on him, to exploit his capacity for work without compensation, to use him sexually without his consent, to seize his possessions, to humiliate him, to cause him pain, to torture and to kill him. *Homo homini lupus*'. See Sigmund

how fascist or reactionary forces seek to exploit these primitive and deeply embedded tropisms in human beings of fear, insecurity and hostility to the Other, or what he calls 'the beast within us'.[11] Nietzsche, who exerted a powerful influence on early twentieth-century French thought and not least on the young Malraux, had sought to cut through this Gordian knot of moral anxiety by identifying an ideal, elite category of beings to whom such considerations did not apply. Nietzsche saw in morality a conspiracy of the weak to contain the strong, a debilitating structure which must be destroyed if vital energies were to be released. A paragraph heading in *Human, All Too Human*, 'Morality as the self-division of human beings', encapsulates this Nietzschean position. The final sentence of this paragraph reads: 'In morality, people treat themselves not as *individuum* but as *dividuum*', suggesting that moral introspection serves to undermine any robust strength of identity.[12] A capacity for cruelty and violence is an intrinsic component of the Nietzschean hero's drive towards an exceptional destiny. For him, pleasure is achieved through 'the excitation of the feeling of power by an obstacle', through 'the will's forward thrust, and again and again becoming master over that which stands in its way'.[13] André Gide, in *Les Caves du Vatican* (1914), offers an ironic slant on this notion of a superior human being who can place himself beyond moral accountability. The story tells how the young Lafcadio, under the influence of his Mephistophelian companion Protée, aspires to commit a meaningless murder, an 'acte

Freud, *Civilization and its Discontents*, trans. J. Riviere, ed. J. Strachey (London: Hogarth Press, 1982), 48. The Latin tag, from Plautus, translates as 'Man is a wolf to man'.

11   This line of thinking will lead Malraux to define humanism as the will to oppose such dark forces of the psyche: 'L'humanisme, [...] c'est dire: "Nous avons refusé ce que voulait en nous la bête [...]"' ('Being a humanist [...] is saying: "We have rejected what the beast within us wanted"'). See A. Malraux, *Les Voix du silence* in *Œuvres complètes* (Paris: Gallimard, Bibliothèque de la Pléiade, 1989–), IV, 899.

12   Friedrich Nietzsche, *Human, All Too Human*, trans. Gary Handwerk (Stanford: Stanford University Press, 1997), 59 (§57).

13   Nietzsche, *The Will to Power*, trans. W. Kaufman and R.J. Hollingdale (New York: Vintage, 1968), 347, 370 (§§658, 696). The sexual implication of this idea is made explicit in §699.

gratuit' (gratuitous act) which by its very purposelessness would be both indecipherable to the authorities and proof of his independence of any restrictive moral or social code. Actually committing the murder, however, proves to be a messy and uncontrolled business and, like Dostoevsky's Raskolnikov in *Crime and Punishment*, Lafcadio has finally to retreat from his claim to amoral autarky and return to a more humble and responsible posture. Similarly, Sartre's much less light-hearted short story 'Erostrate' depicts a self-absorbed sociopath who, from his unshakably superior vantage-point, sets out to shoot down in the street as many of the despised herd of humans as he can. His enterprise ends even more ignominiously than Lafcadio's.[14] As early as 1927 the youthful Malraux also recognises both the attraction and the negativity of the Nietzschean influence: 'Si Nietzsche trouve tant d'échos dans des cœurs désespérés, c'est qu'il n'est lui-même que l'expression de leur désespoir et de leur violence'.[15] The heroes of his early novels seek to assert their domination by achieving total control, by force of will, of both their own minds and bodies and those of others in situations of extreme violence. The experience of ordeal and struggle leads them nevertheless to recognise the limitations, and the fragility, of a strategy based wholly on individual power exercised in a moral vacuum.

The Nietzschean perspective on violence as a spontaneous expression of an individualist elite is questioned and modified not only by writers of fiction but in a significant current of French political thought. Georges Sorel, compiling his *Reflections on Violence* (1908) in a decade when Nietzsche was very much in vogue, takes the German thinker's idea of a kind of exemplary warrior class and redeploys it in a quite different ideological context. He reminds us that, beyond the oft-quoted rhetoric of the 'blond beast' and his occasional natural Dionysiac bestiality, Nietzsche cites as historical

14 'Erostrate' was published as part of a collection of stories under the title *Le Mur* (Paris: Gallimard, 1939).

15 'If Nietzsche finds so many echoes in desperate hearts, it is because he himself is simply the expression of their despair and their violence'. See André Malraux, 'D'une jeunesse européenne', in *Ecrits* (Les Cahiers verts, 70) (Paris: Grasset, 1927), 133–53 (p.139).

exemplars 'l'aristocratie romaine, arabe, germanique ou japonaise, les
héros homériques, les vikings scandinaves'.[16] Sorel seizes in particular on the Homeric paradigms exemplifying (in Nietzsche's words)
'la gaieté terrible et la joie profonde que goûtent [les héros] à toute
destruction, à toutes les voluptés de la victoire et de la cruauté'.[17] For
Sorel, these heroic traits had found fresh expression in French history,
in the French Revolution and in Napoleon. He went further: 'Je ne
suis pas de ceux qui regardent le type achéen, chanté par Homère, le
héros indompté, confiant en sa force et se plaçant au-dessus des
règles, comme devant disparaître dans l'avenir'.[18] Where Nietzsche
goes wrong, in Sorel's view, is in seeing such values and such a noble
philosophy of action as inapplicable to the proletariat. Sorel's project
is to promote the inspirational myth of the general strike as an
instrument of political revolution, to encompass the destruction of
capitalism and of the inequities of the class system. Sorel thus adopts
Nietzsche's heroic view of violence, but radically redirects it towards
a collective, ethically disciplined crusading politics of anarcho-
syndicalism, informed by a Marxist critique of bourgeois capitalism.
Moreover, Sorel saw such a revolution as the indispensable means to
re-establish a moral regeneration within society, founded on 'les
vraies *valeurs de vertu*' which were based on the family rather than on
organised religion: 'le respect de la personne humaine, la fidélité

16   'the aristocracy of Rome, Arabia, Germany, Japan, *the Homeric heroes*, the
      Scandinavian Vikings'. Georges Sorel, *Réflexions sur la violence*, 2nd edn
      (Paris: Rivière, 1910), 334. The italics are Sorel's. The English translation by
      T.E. Hulme (revised) can be found in Sorel, *Reflections on Violence*, ed. J.
      Jennings (Cambridge: Cambridge University Press, 1999), 231. Sorel is here
      quoting Nietzsche, *On the Genealogy of Morality*. See e.g. the translation by M.
      Clark and A.J. Swensen (Indianapolis and Cambridge: Hackett, 1998), 22.
17   'the terrible gaiety and the profound joy which [the heroes] tasted in des-
      truction, in all the pleasures of victory and of cruelty'. See Sorel, *Réflexions*,
      335 (*Reflections*, 231). The quotation is again taken from Nietzsche, *On the
      Genealogy of Morality* (22–3).
18   'I am not among those who consider Homer's Achaean type, the indomitable
      hero, confident in his strength and putting himself above rules, as necessarily
      disappearing in the future'. Sorel, *Réflexions*, 338 (*Reflections*, 233).

sexuelle et le dévouement pour les faibles'.[19] This moral prescription, derived from Proudhon, could hardly be less Nietzschean.

A vigorous and radical debate around the relationship between violence and individual identity was thus already well advanced by the start of the period covered in the essays presented in this volume. My concern in what precedes has been to elucidate some aspects of the fraught climate of thought in France deriving from these debates. Some appreciation of this context is helpful in understanding the diverse reactions being explored here to the various conflicts and political crises in France. Nietzschean heroic individualism is variously subverted by Sorel, satirised by Gide, and presented as a tragic impasse by Malraux, and the pendulum in the interwar decades swings towards a conception of violence as an instrument of collective change rather than as the self-assertion of the privileged individual. The issue of individual responsibility, however, refuses to go away, with the spirit of Dostoevsky as well as Nietzsche informing the debates in the writings of Gide and Malraux. Alongside the discourse of communists, anarchists and terrorists, Malraux's major fictions from the 1930s, *La Condition humaine* and *L'Espoir*, include voices which articulate the problematics of a Christian position in the context of commitment to violent change. Several decades later, the legacy of Christian thought and civilisation will still be the troubled focus of passion and self-analysis. This is particularly apparent in Camus's *L'Etranger* where a man drawn unthinkingly into an act of murder feels impelled to define himself in opposition to the Christian ethos of guilt and forgiveness as much as against the parody of human justice which he has undergone. As Toby Garfitt shows, however, Camus's later story 'L'Hôte' sketches an encounter with the Other which is now characterised by generosity and by a Girardian spirit of the necessity of sacrifice and atonement. This posture of humility on the part of the coloniser is dramatically complemented by Genet's pungent articulation, analysed by Mairéad Hanrahan, of an aggressive, alienated, third-world view of Chartres Cathedral as a questionable

---

19 'the true *values of virtue* [...]; respect for the human person, sexual fidelity and devotion to the weak'. Sorel, *Réflexions*, 340 (*Reflections*, 234). The italics are Sorel's.

monument to an imperialist French Eurocentric culture. Yet, as I show in my own essay, that very edifice had been for Malraux in 1941 the epitome of the precious values at stake in the anti-Fascist struggle. Caught in such polarised spotlights, the currents of violence eddying around a high symbol of European civilisation thus articulate the tension between the perceived need to dominate the Other in order to effect necessary change or renewal, and the need to recognise the Other in its fullness in order to create an indispensable space of acceptance and tolerance.

In our discussion of culture above, we noted an anthropological view that violence marks the highly unstable frontier of the cultural order. The same tension and instability can be posited with regard to the relationship of violence to individual identity. Erich Fromm sees human nature as based on a series of existential contradictions, being both body and mind, embedded in nature yet transcending it, impelled to live yet aware of death – the list could be much extended. These dualities serve to set up a 'state of constant disequilibrium' which distinguishes humans from animals. While, in a given situation (Fromm suggests), a state of relative stability may be provisionally achieved, man's ability to change his environment, and thereby himself, means that sooner or later imbalance and uncertainty reassert themselves. It is this prevailing state of disequilibrium, insecurity and tension which, he argues, accounts for the recurrence of violence, whether destructive or creative.[20] France's history in the twentieth century, and the discourses that have emerged from it, provide a particularly striking testimony to this tectonic instability.

20   See Erich Fromm, *The Anatomy of Human Destructiveness* (London: Jonathan Cape, 1974), 225–6.

Language as Violence, Language Against Violence

Given that this volume is essentially a study of texts rather than actions – or, one might say, of texts *as* actions – it seems appropriate to conclude this introduction with some remarks on the multiple relations between language and violence.

Language itself can, of course, be the instrument and servant of violence. Verbal abuse of an individual or group is often the prelude, or accompaniment, to physical abuse. A familiar feature of such discourse is the use of terms which present the object(s) of attack as less than human. The innate reluctance of most human beings to kill a fellow-member of the same species can be circumvented by dehumanising the victim – not calling him by any proper name – and by euphemising the vocabulary of killing.[21] In Zygmunt Bauman's view, as summarised by Helmut Kuzmics, the one pre-condition for mobilising ordinary people to commit mass crimes is that 'identification with other human beings breaks down. Once the latter turn into impersonal, inanimate objects of ideological, national or political antagonism all ethical inhibitions against the limitless use of violence will be swept away'.[22] In this process, the violence of language is used to simplify and exacerbate an us/them mentality and thus aggressively to reinforce a particular group identity, such as an ethnic or national one. As Keane astutely observes:

> At the heart of nationalism – and among the most peculiar features of its grammar – is its simultaneous treatment of the Other as everything and nothing.

21   Ibid., 121. Fromm cites as examples the wartime substitution of the epithets 'Huns' or 'les Boches' for Germans, or the American soldiers' parlance, in Vietnam, where 'killing opponents' becomes 'wasting the gooks'.

22   See Helmut Kuzmics, 'Violence and pacification in Norbert Elias's theory of civilization', in Helen Chambers (ed.), *Violence, Culture and Identity: Essays on German and Austrian Literature, Politics and Society* (Oxford: Peter Lang, 2006), 27–46 (p.37). Kuzmics refers to Bauman's *Modernity and the Holocaust* (Ithaca: Cornell University Press, 1989). Bauman calls this process of denying the human status of adversaries 'the social production of moral invisibility' (*Modernity and the Holocaust*, 24–7).

The Other is threatening, a menace to the Nation's way of life – but also inferior rubbish, unworthy of respect or recognition.[23]

One implication of this kind of discourse is that, just as much as physical attack, it aims to deprive the Other of any power of discourse or even right of utterance. As Keane further observes, the (at least temporary) effect of violence is to reduce potentially speaking and peacefully interacting subjects to the level of mute objects. It displaces verbal communication and denies it.[24] Where language is itself deployed in the service of such dehumanisation and denial of dialogue, it is being used to mutilate itself, and to impair its own power of free expression, exchange and understanding. Henrik Pedersen, in his essay on the German 'Red Army Faction' (more generally known as the Baader/Meinhof group), emphasises the theatricality of the terrorist act. Researchers into terrorism (he reports) commonly view it in terms of communication theory. 'The terrorist […] lets his "gun speak". The act of terror can be viewed as a speech-act, an extension of political discussion by other means'.[25] As Pedersen briefly acknowledges, however, it is perilous to gloss over in this way the crucial distinction between the verbal and the non-verbal. The fact is that terrorism, like any act of physical violence, betokens a denial of verbal expression, and most often a despair of the capacities of language to express or resolve human anguish or conflict. The maintenance of a civilised society based on laws, treaties and agreements requires the recognition of access to language by all parties, respect in its formulation, and understanding and acceptance of its complexity as a signifying system.

The essays which follow demonstrate in a number of ways how language can provide the necessary counterpoise to individual and collective experiences of violence. The texts under discussion seek to investigate and understand the origins of violent events, to articulate the moral or political problematics which inform them, to locate

23   Keane, 127.
24   Ibid., 69.
25   Henrik Pedersen, 'Terror on the stage: the German 'Red Army Faction' (RAF) as political performance', in H. Chambers (ed.), *Violence, Culture and Identity*, 327–42 (p.330).

responsibility for them or to trace the scars they leave behind. In doing so, they jostle the reader into uncomfortable awareness of difficult issues at stake and of scandals which cry out for resolution. Their capacity for disturbance is an index of the recreative power of language, subversive of complacency and reminding us of our fundamental disequilibrium. As Maffesoli puts it, 'la parole donc est cette irruption dangereuse qui rompt la sécurité de l'institué'.[26] It is a salutary violence.

---

26 'Speech, then, is that dangerous irruption which breaks down the security of what is established'. See Maffesoli, 67.

PETER READ

French Surrealism and *la démoralisation de l'Occident* in 1932 and 2001

The rhetoric of violence in Surrealism became the focus of sharp controversy in France after a provocative article on the subject, by Jean Clair, was published in *Le Monde*, dated 22 November 2001. Clair denounced the Surrealists as enemies of Western civilisation and precursors of al-Qaida. His article provoked a series of rapid ripostes, some of which the newspaper published, and then a lengthier response from Régis Debray. I intend to suggest some parallels between this debate and events in 1932, when Louis Aragon was attacked for publishing a violent poem entitled 'Front rouge', and a raft of intellectuals came to his defence. Engaging with the arguments deployed in these debates will also allow me to investigate how far the rhetoric of violence, and the controversy it causes, are relevant to what might be called French cultural identity.

Jean Clair is a renowned essayist, art historian and exhibition curator. The name Jean Clair is, however, a pseudonym, used by Gérard Régnier, a cultural administrator who holds the Civil Service rank of *Conservateur général du patrimoine*, and was also until recently Director of the Picasso Museum in Paris.[1] His article in *Le Monde* was entitled 'Le Surréalisme et la démoralisation de l'Occident' ('Surrealism and the Demoralisation of the West', though 'démoralisation' here also means 'corruption').

The article was inspired by circumstances specific to that moment. On the one hand, there were two blockbuster Surrealist exhibitions, in London and Paris. The London exhibition, at Tate

---

1   Gérard Régnier retired as Director of the Picasso Museum in 2005, the year in which he also curated the exhibition 'Mélancolie: Génie et folie en Occident' at the Grand Palais, Paris and the Neue Nationalgalerie, Berlin.

Modern in autumn 2001, entitled *Desire Unbound*, displayed Surrealist works from 1920 to the present day, and showed how love and
sexual desire fostered Surrealist creativity. The Paris exhibition was
then being prepared for its March 2002 opening, at the Centre Pompidou. Entitled *La Révolution surréaliste*, curated by Werner Spies, it
would define Surrealism as a predominantly aesthetic art movement,
whose exquisite artefacts were laid out in symmetrical rows and
panels.[2] The overall effect of the two shows was a stunning vindication of the prodigiously creative Surrealist imagination.

On the other hand, on 11 September 2001, just before the two
Surrealist exhibitions, came the terrorist attack on the Twin Towers.

Jean Clair's essay proposes a connection between these con-
trasting events on opposite sides of the Atlantic. He quotes violently
anti-Western statements from Surrealist writings of the 1920s, mainly
by Louis Aragon, who in a 1925 magazine proclaimed:

> D'abord nous ruinerons cette civilisation qui vous est chère, où vous êtes
> moulés comme des fossiles dans le schiste. Monde occidental, tu es condamné à
> mort. Nous sommes les défaitistes de l'Europe [...]. Nous nous liguerons avec
> les grands réservoirs d'irréel. Que l'Orient, votre terreur, enfin, à notre voix
> réponde. [...] Que l'Amérique au loin croule de ses buildings blancs.[3]

2   *Desire Unbound*, curated by Jennifer Mundy, at Tate Modern (20 September
     2001–1 January 2002), then Metropolitan Museum of Art, New York (6
     February–12 May 2002), displayed an eclectic range of works, from the 1920s
     to the present day, including many by Surrealist women, linked by the theme of
     eroticism. It also included an extensive display of manuscripts, letters, drawings
     and lyrically inscribed books. *La Révolution surréaliste*, curated by Werner
     Spies, at the Centre Pompidou (6 March–24 June 2002), was similarly dazzling,
     but more classically conceived. Focusing on the heroic interwar years, it was
     dominated by dozens of exquisitely finished works by recognised masters,
     symmetrically aligned. Considering that the subversive spirit of Surrealism was
     thus effectively denied, an enterprising group of malcontents replaced the
     official leaflet guide with multiple copies of an unauthorised facsimile which
     emphasised Surrealism's anti-fascist, anti-capitalist and anti-clerical credentials.
     The illustrations represented some of what had been omitted from the show,
     including works by women and Czech artists. On these events, see Michael
     Löwy, 'Surréalisme pas mort, sauf à Beaubourg', *Le Monde*, 28 juin 2002, 16.
3   Louis Aragon, 'Fragments d'une conférence', *La Révolution surréaliste*, no.4,
     15 July 1925, 23–5. 'First we will ruin this civilisation you hold so dear, in

Clair refers to Breton's notorious 1929 statement that 'L'acte sur-réaliste le plus simple consiste, revolvers aux poings, à descendre dans la rue et à tirer au hasard, tant qu'on peut, dans la foule'.[4] He also cites a 1929 Surrealist map of the world, in which the scale of countries and continents was distorted to match their relative interest. New Guinea is thus much larger than Australia, the Mediterranean disappears, Afghanistan is hugely expanded, and North America is reduced to Labrador, Alaska and Mexico, with mainland United States abolished.[5]

According to Jean Clair, the Surrealists have for too long benefited from critical immunity. His own youthful admiration for the Surrealists was misguided, for he now knows they were irreparably tarred with the Stalinist brush. Furthermore, they were pro-Oriental, anti-Western, armchair terrorists. According to Jean Clair, Surrealist dreams came true in Manhattan on 11 September 2001.

Le Monde received a spate of replies to Jean Clair, and published three of them. The debate spilled into various Surrealist and other websites and inspired three books. The first, entitled *Jean Clair ou la misère intellectuelle française* (*Jean Clair or French Intellectual Penury*), published in February 2002, contains Jean Clair's original essay, followed by a collection of ten pro-Surrealist replies addressed to *Le Monde* by artists, writers and other citizens. Jean Clair then

which you are embedded like fossils in schist. Western world, you are condemned to die. We are the defeatists of Europe [...]. We will join forces with the great reservoirs of unreality. May the Orient, which terrifies you, finally answer our call. [...] May far-off America collapse from its tall, white buildings.'

4   A. Breton, *Second manifeste du surréalisme* in *Œuvres complètes* (Paris: Gallimard (Pléiade), 1988–), I, 782–3 (hereafter abbreviated to *O.C.*). 'The simplest Surrealist act consists in going down into the street, guns in hand, and shooting at random, for as long as possible, into the crowd.'

5   Anon., 'Le Monde au temps des surréalistes', *Variétés*, Special Issue: 'Le surréalisme en 1929', June 1929, 26–7, in José Pierre (ed.), *Tracts surréalistes et déclarations collectives* (Paris: Le terrain vague, 1980–1982), I, 94–5 (hereafter abbreviated to *T.S.*). For a discussion of this map, see Elza Adamowicz, *Ceci n'est pas un tableau. Les écrits surréalistes sur l'art* (Lausanne: L'Age d'Homme, 2004), 111–41 (chapter 3, 'Cartes du monde surréalistes: au-delà de l'exotique?').

published, in May 2003, a book-length development of his anti-Surrealist 'J'Accuse', entitled *Du surréalisme considéré dans ses rapports au totalitarisme et aux tables tournantes* (*On Surrealism and its Relationship with Totalitarianism and the Occult*). This was followed in July 2003 by Régis Debray's reply to Clair's article, in a 47-page pamphlet entitled *L'Honneur des funambules* (*The Honour of Tightrope Walkers*).[6] I intend to focus here on the original article and the replies it provoked.

The collective response of the *Misère intellectuelle française* writers, in tones that range from consternation to sarcasm and acerbic hostility, indicates the extent of visceral loyalty Surrealism continues to inspire. The painter and radio art critic Bruno Mathon compares Clair's position to the pro-Americanism of cultural and political commentator Bernard-Henri Lévy; the poet, critic and ex-Surrealist Alain Jouffroy places Jean Clair in the Western supremacist, anti-leftist tradition of *L'Action Française*, Vichy and the Front National; Annie Le Brun, similarly evoking a petit-bourgeois right-wing mindset, refers to his 'répugnant poujadisme'. Clair's presentation of evidence is seen as 'faussaire et manipulateur' ('fake and manipulative' –

6   Jean Clair's article first appeared in a special Supplement, headed 'Guerre éclair, doute persistant', containing articles on the American intervention in Afghanistan, in *Le Monde* of 22 November 2001. In reply to Clair, *Le Monde* published a letter from Etienne Lesourd, headed 'Des Surréalistes chez Ben Laden?' (2–3 December 2001, 21); and articles by Surrealist-affiliates Annie Le Brun ('Clarté de Breton, noirceur de Clair') and Alain Jouffroy ('Venimeuse attaque') (both 8 December 2001, 18–9). The three books are: Malek Abbou et al., *Jean Clair ou la misère intellectuelle française* (Paris: Association des amis de Benjamin Péret, 2002) (anthology containing Clair's article and texts by M. Abbou, Claude Courtot, Pablo Durán, Renaud Ego, Giovanna, Jean-Michel Goutier, Alain Jouffroy, Etienne Lesourd, Bruno Mathon and Pierre Vandrepote. It does not include Annie Le Brun's article); Jean Clair, *Du surréalisme considéré dans ses rapports au totalitarisme et aux tables tournantes. Contribution à une histoire de l'insensé* (Paris: Mille et une nuits and Fondation du 2 mars, 2003); Régis Debray, *L'Honneur des funambules. Réponse à Jean Clair sur le surréalisme* (Paris: L'Echoppe, 2003). On Clair's book, see also Roger-Pol Droit, 'Recette pour rater un pamphlet', *Le Monde des livres* (13 June 2003), p.V; and Philippe Forest, 'Jean Clair, du surréalisme', *Artpress*, 292, July–August 2003, 62.

Malek Abbou), and the word 'contrevérités' ('falsehoods') recurs (Malek Abbou, Claude Courtot, Pablo Durán). Given his undoubted erudition, Clair's arguments can only amount to a 'travestissement volontaire' ('wilful travesty' – Renaud Ego), 'délire falsificateur' ('falsifying delirium' – Le Brun), and 'totale mauvaise foi' ('utter bad faith' – Giovanna).

Other contributors point out that Duchamp and Picasso, on whom Clair is a specialist, are both tellingly absent from his essay, because they would have refuted his arguments (Malek Abbou). As Picasso was a 'fellow traveller' alongside Aragon, Breton and, according to Clair, Ben Laden, the Picasso Museum must logically be a terrorist lair; Clair should therefore resign as its Director (Annie Le Brun, Renaud Ego, Pierre Vandrepote).

In *L'Honneur des funambules*, Régis Debray marks his territory by stating that he has no personal axe to grind, either against Clair or for Surrealism. He is not, for example, one of those who were up in arms over the recent sale and dispersion of the contents of Breton's flat. He considers the Jean Clair affair, however, to be more than a storm in a teacup, mainly because he sees Clair's attack on Surrealism as symptomatic of current widespread intolerance towards all forms of non-consensual and unconventional thinking. Clair, he suggests, has thus allied himself, intentionally or not, with forces intent on demonising or demolishing any sign of opposition to the Western imposition of worldwide ideological hegemony. Debray unfortunately reduces the whole Surrealist movement, international and heterogeneous, to the single figure of André Breton; but he also addresses all the issues that disturb Clair, including Surrealist exploration of the occult and the irrational, and others not raised by the Cartesian art historian, such as Surrealist tribunals and expulsions, or Breton's stance during World War II. Debray's response to Clair thus expands into a brilliantly written and tellingly documented tribute to the diffuse, quicksilver spirit of Surrealism, and to a poet who shunned television, never stooped to writing novels, never came near a Nobel Prize, and whose polymorphic imagination could never be enclosed in the rigidly ideological positions that Clair attributes to him.

One example of fundamental differences between the two sides in this argument is that whereas Clair projects Surrealist writing forward into the context of 2001, his adversaries tend to refer back to the historical and cultural context in which it was produced. Debray, Abbou and others recall how young Surrealist anger was fuelled primarily by first-hand experience of warfare and combat in the trenches. Clair fails even to mention World War I, which for the Surrealists and their generation was *the* formative experience.

Significantly, Jean Clair's argument largely relies on edited extracts from polemical writings by Aragon and Breton. These were the Surrealists who were most acutely involved in military action in World War I: Aragon was buried three times by explosions, and was decorated for bravery; Breton was a front-line stretcher-bearer, a dangerous and harrowing job, during the bitter winter of 1916. It is no coincidence that during the post-war period, their language was, even among Surrealists, particularly angry and anti-nationalistic. Surrealism was a post-traumatic movement. Furthermore, during the two decades following the Armistice, the Surrealists increasingly sensed and feared the approach of another great war. Debray and Abbou recall that, with oracular prescience, Breton declared in 1925, '(Je) sais ce que me réserve l'année 1939' ('I know what awaits me in 1939').[7]

Surrealist forebodings were exacerbated by the fact that they were operating in a climate of venomous hostility, fostered by increasingly virulent nationalist groups. Jean-Michel Goutier, in an impressive contribution to *La Misère intellectuelle française*, recalls how, in the 1920s, there were demands in the press (in *Comœdia* and *La Liberté*, for example) that Surrealists be 'severely punished' or 'shot'. He also recalls the first screening, in Paris in 1930, of Dali and Buñuel's film, *L'Age d'or*: the League of Patriots and the Anti-Jewish League ransacked the cinema, slashed Surrealist paintings and destroyed books displayed in the foyer. They then fomented a press campaign which resulted in a French distribution ban being imposed a

---

7   A. Breton, 'Lettre aux voyantes', *La Révolution surréaliste*, no.5. in *O.C.*, I, 910. Elsewhere he refers to 'la période pro-fasciste que nous traversons' (*Misère de la poésie* (March 1932), in *O.C.*, II, 12).

week later, a ban that remained in place until 1981.[8] In comparison, Surrealist resources and actions seem moderate.

Clair castigates the Surrealists for being pro-Oriental, anti-Western. In reply, Annie Le Brun points out that dreams of the Orient as an imaginary alternative universe have been an integral part of Western sensibility since the eighteenth century (a tradition enhanced in Surrealist eyes by the writings of Nerval and Rimbaud). Her arguments may be extended by reference to the contemporary context. For example, in 1927 *La Défense de l'Occident* was the title of a book by xenophobic *Action Française* activist Henri Massis, anthologising his 1924 and 1925 press campaign against Semitic and other supposedly Eastern influences. Such campaigns encouraged the Surrealists to take a clearly adversarial position and, in opposing prevalent Western values, to emphasise not only their allegiance to the Russian Revolution, but also the attractions of a largely mythical, anti-materialist Orient. The Surrealists thus tended to use the terms 'Asia' and 'the Orient' to characterise a state of mind capable of envisaging alternatives to the positivist, nationalist and rationalist parameters of Western thought and organisation: 'En Europe même qui peut dire où n'est pas l'Orient? Dans la rue, l'homme que vous croisez le porte en lui: l'Orient est dans sa conscience'.[9] When he equates Surrealist anti-

8   See the collective Surrealist tract *L'Affaire de "L'Age d'or"*, January 1931, in *T.S.*, I, 188–93. In 1929, Buñuel had declared that *Un Chien andalou*, far from being 'beau' or 'poétique', 'n'est qu'un désespéré, un passionné appel au meurtre' ('is nothing other than a desperate, passionate call to murder') (L.B., '*Un Chien andalou*', *La Révolution surréaliste*, no.12, 15 December 1929, 35).

9   Collective declaration, 'La Révolution d'abord et toujours!', *L'Humanité*, 21 septembre 1925, in *T.S.*, I, 54–6. 'In Europe itself, who could say where the Orient is not present? The man you meet on the street carries it within him: the Orient is in his mind'. Examples of differing connotations of 'the Orient' within Surrealism include the *Manifesto of Surrealism* (1924), where Breton invokes the anti-realist aesthetic of oriental story-telling, as in the *Tales of 1001 Nights*, epitomising the 'merveilleux' (*O.C.*, I, 320); Antonin Artaud's 'Lettre aux Ecoles du Bouddha' and 'Adresse au Dalaï-Lama', where the East is envisaged as the distant home of his own spiritual and metaphysical aspirations (*La Révolution surréaliste*, no.3, 15 April 1925, in *T.S.*, I, 37–8); Aragon's poem 'Front Rouge', which refers to 'le bourbier occidental' ('the Western quagmire'), and where the East is certainly the Soviet Union (*T.S.*, I, 459–65). See

Western, pro-Eastern statements with modern al-Qaida terrorism Jean
Clair is, to say the least, being strikingly reductive. He reduces the
East to Islam, and Islam to terror. Several of his critics further suggest
that, given Surrealism's 'definitive atheism', any comparison with
Islamic fundamentalists is patently absurd (Claude Courtot, Jean-
Michel Goutier, Annie Le Brun).

After the Great War, the Surrealists were far from isolated in
seeing Western Civilisation as morally bankrupt. The overtly political
dimension of Surrealist references to the Orient was reinforced by the
movement's opposition to France's increasingly drastic repression of
colonial unrest, notably during the Moroccan campaign ('la guerre du
Rif'), which in 1925 inspired the Surrealists' ill-fated alliance with the
French Communist Party. It is also worth recalling that in 1924 Paul
Eluard had visited Indochina and witnessed at first hand the realities
of French colonial rule. He twice sailed close to Poulo Condore, the
penal colony that was the local Devil's Island and just one outpost of
France's extensive Gulag Archipelago. His experience heightened
Surrealist sensitivity to that part of the world and to colonial injustice.
The movement reacted vehemently, for example, to the French
campaign of military and judicial violence which was unleashed after
an uprising in Yen-Bay, near Hanoi, in February 1930. The guillotine
was a major tool of colonial control and, according to Robert McNab
in his excellent book on Surrealism and Indochina, 699 people were
executed there without trial during 1930, including 50 in Yen-Bay. By
the end of 1932, 'the number of political prisoners in Indochina stood
at about 10,000. Another 10,000 are estimated to have been killed and
50,000 more to have been deported'.[10] The Surrealist periodical *Le
Surréalisme au Service de la Révolution* was a focus for campaigning

also, Marguerite Bonnet, 'L'Orient dans le surréalisme: mythe et réel', *Revue
de littérature comparée*, no.216, October–December 1980, 411–24; Norbert
Bandier, *Sociologie du surréalisme 1924–1929* (Paris: La Dispute, 1999), 193–
207 ('Le mythe de l'Orient dans le champ intellectuel et son usage par les
surréalistes').

10   Robert McNab, *Ghost Ships. A Surrealist Love Triangle* (New Haven and
London: Yale University Press, 2004), 212. McNab documents journeys to
Indochina by Max Ernst, Paul Eluard and his wife Gala in 1924, and the
literary, artistic and political consequences in Surrealism.

against France's tropical penal colonies, and the first issue, in July 1930, featured an article on the Yen-Bay bloodbath in which Eluard asserted that 'Il n'y a que deux races dans le monde: celle des oppresseurs et celle des opprimés',[11] before listing the names and professions of some of those executed. Subsequent issues listed further executions and deportations and highlighted how 'des milliers et des milliers meurent lentement à l'île Poulo-Condore, dans les innombrables geôles de Hanoï, de Saigon'.[12] The Surrealists systematically sided with the colonised against the colonisers, a position which may, of course, be interpreted as 'anti-Western'. Their revolutionary zeal was, however, grounded in an unflinching assessment of the current state of French and international politics. Bruno Mathon and Alain Jouffroy point out that France is only now starting to confront colonial atrocities which the Surrealists campaigned against from the 1920s to the 1960s. As Malek Abbou puts it, the West was corrupted and demoralised, not by Surrealism, but by colonialism, the holocaust, Hiroshima and Nagasaki, the Cold War balance of fear, and the 'free world's' treatment of Third-World countries.

Annie Le Brun notes how slyly Clair smears Surrealism as anti-Semitic. In his article, this charge is brief and unsubstantiated; Clair may be thinking of an anti-Semitic cliché in Antonin Artaud's 1925 'Lettre aux Ecoles du Bouddha' ('Letter to the Schools of Buddha') (*T.S.*, I, 38). Collective guilt is thus inferred from the words of a single, one-time member of the group. The charge is further discredited when one considers how the Surrealist theory of *Amour fou* resulted in a constellation of Jewish-Gentile couples. Robert McNab lists over a dozen such alliances, from André Breton and Simone

---

11 'There are only two races in the world, the oppressors and the oppressed'. Paul Eluard, 'Yen-Bay', *Le Surréalisme au Service de la Révolution*, 1, 1930, 8.
12 'thousands are dying slowly on Poulo Condore and in the countless prisons of Hanoi and Saigon'. Anon., 'Le Haut du pavé', *Le Surréalisme au Service de la Révolution*, 2, 1930, 21. The Surrealists also distributed tracts calling for a boycott of the 1931 Colonial Exhibition in Paris (*T.S.*, I, 194–5, 198–200). In April 1947, after French artillery bombardment of Haiphong produced thousands of casualties, the first collective Surrealist tract to be published following André Breton's return to France was entitled *Liberté est un mot vietnamien* (*Liberty is a Vietnamese Word*) (*T.S.*, II, 27–8).

Kahn, André Masson and Rosa Makles, to Max Ernst and Peggy Guggenheim. According to Salvador Dali, Elena Diakonova, known as Gala, perhaps the most powerful of all Surrealist muses, who moved from Eluard, to Ernst, to Dali, was also Jewish.[13]

For the pro-Surrealists, however, Clair's claim that Surrealism was tainted by Stalinism seems particularly galling and incongruous. Annie Le Brun states categorically that Breton was never a Stalinist, and she recalls how, after joining the French Communist Party in 1927, he spent several years struggling against ideological directives. He was expelled from the Communist A.E.A.R. (Association of Revolutionary Writers and Artists) in 1933 for slandering the Soviet Union, and split definitively with the Party in 1935. His anti-Stalinist positions lost him some of his closest friends, including Aragon in 1932 and Eluard in 1938, both of whom chose the Communist Party over Surrealism. Breton was one of the few French intellectuals to denounce the Moscow show trials, as early as 1936 (Le Brun, Giovanna), and publicly to criticise Picasso for his silence after the Soviet invasion of Hungary in 1956 (Jouffroy). Debray, in turn, reminds Clair that Breton was resolutely anti-Stalinist well before the likes of Gide, Malraux or Koestler and before many French scientists and academics, and emphasises Breton's subversive consistency: in 1925 against the Rif campaign, in 1960 against the Algerian War; for Trotsky, against Stalin; for blacks, against whites; for Hopis, against yuppies; for tribal charms, against stone angels and crosses. Breton stands for the oppressed, against the oppressor.

Perhaps most far-reaching, however, are questions on the moral and political responsibility of creative writing, raised by Pablo Durán. Durán locates the key to Jean Clair's argument in the phrase 'Les mots sont responsables: il leur est répondu' ('Words count: they have been answered'). Clair seems to suggest that any pronouncement, spoken or

---

13   According to Robert McNab, this phenomenon may be explained by Surrealist attitudes to travel and displacement, combined with the distinctive sense of cultural identity enjoyed by European Jews: 'It is their detached point of view as outsiders, with its irony and self-awareness, that chimed with the *dépaysement* the Surrealists valued. The vibrations of *dépaysement*, of a life lived elsewhere, must therefore account for the reciprocal group seduction of the founders of Surrealism and of their Jewish partners' (McNab, 249, note 263).

written, may be held responsible for subsequent acts and events. So the works of Mayakovsky and his Russian avant-garde comrades paved the way for Soviet persecutions and massacres. Artists and writers should watch their step, says Clair, and work within acceptable moral parameters. As Régis Debray points out, if we accept the strictures proposed by Clair, and his theory of cause and effect, then we must expunge not only Surrealist visions of falling skyscrapers, but also, for example, whole passages from St John of the Apocalypse and the Old Testament, where the towering hubris of Babylon is brought crashing to the ground.

Against Clair's censorious arguments, Pablo Durán, for his part, defends artistic autonomy, recalling Breton's insistence on freedom of expression, and that the creative imagination is necessarily independent of moral and political pressures and servitudes. It is here that the recent Surrealist violence controversy comes closest to one of Surrealism's most celebrated battles, known as 'L'Affaire Aragon'. The focus of that campaign was a poem entitled 'Front Rouge', published by Aragon in January 1932, in an anthology entitled *Littérature de la Révolution mondiale* (in *T.S.*, I, 459–65; *O.C.*, II, 29–39).

Aragon's poem is designed on a pattern of cumulative, climactic momentum, progressing from a chic Paris restaurant (Maxim's) in 1930, to scenes of insurrection in the working-class East End of the city, to heroic views of the Soviet Union, to cosmic visions of 'Révolution Universelle'. Dialectical materialism marches on feet 'magnifiques comme la violence' ('as magnificent as violence'); 'L'éclat des fusillades ajoute au paysage / une gaieté jusqu'alors inconnue' ('Bursts of gunfire add to the landscape / a previously unknown gaiety'); 'Les yeux bleus de la Révolution / brillent d'une cruauté nécessaire' ('The blue eyes of Revolution / shine with necessary cruelty'). The imagined uprising in Paris is accompanied by cries such as 'Descendez les flics' ('Kill the police'), or 'Feu sur Léon Blum' ('Shoot Léon Blum').

Aragon was consequently prosecuted for incitement to mutiny and murder, charges which carried a possible five-year prison sentence. The case provoked public displays of support for Aragon from the French and Belgian Surrealist groups, and from a broader range of intellectuals and writers. André Gide and Romain Rolland sympathised with Aragon, but stated that a writer must have the courage of his convictions and admit the consequences of what he has written. For Romain Rolland, 'Nos écrits sont nos armes. [...] Au lieu de les renier, nous sommes tenus de les revendiquer'. He recognised that words have consequences, but saw French justice as hypocritical: the writings of Charles Maurras, founder of *L'Action Française*, inspired the murder of socialist peace campaigner Jean Jaurès in July 1914, but Maurras was never prosecuted. For Gide, there should be no impunity for writers: 'La pensée est aussi dangereuse que des actes. Nous sommes des gens dangereux. C'est une honneur que d'être condamné sous un tel régime'.[14]

Aragon had in fact, from late 1930, moved irretrievably away from Surrealism and towards pro-Soviet Communism. Breton nevertheless led the pro-Aragon campaign, probably hoping to slow his comrade's slide towards Stalinism. Breton co-authored a collective tract, *L'Affaire Aragon* (*T.S.*, I, 204–5), which attracted three hundred signatures, and followed this with his own more expansive statement, entitled *Misère de la Poésie* (*Penury of Poetry*) (*T.S.*, I, 208–22; *O.C.*, II, 3–27). Breton's arguments are very different to Gide's and Rolland's, and seem particularly relevant to the Jean Clair polemic.

In *L'Affaire Aragon*, Breton recognises that 'Front Rouge' fervently represents the way things will be on the day revolution comes, but denies that the poet is thus inciting any individual to commit a crime. More fundamentally, however, he opposes any judicial interpretation of poetry, because judges are unqualified for

---

14   Rolland: 'Our writings are our weapons. [...] Rather than denying them, we must stand by them'. Gide: 'Thought is as dangerous as acts. We are dangerous people. It is an honour to be condemned under a régime like this one'. For Gide's and Rolland's responses, see *T.S.*, I, 465–6; *O.C.*, II, 39–42. Belgian Surrealists, including Magritte and Mesens, also issued a statement denouncing bourgeois hypocrisy, which trumpets Liberty, but clamps down on freedom of expression as soon as it attacks the status quo (*La Poésie transfigurée*, 30 January 1932, in *T.S.*, I, 206–8). Other tracts were *Paillasse! (Fin de l'Affaire Aragon)*, signed by Paris Surrealists in solidarity with *Misère de la Poésie*; *Protestation*, by a larger group of Belgian Surrealists, writers and artists; *Certificat*, by Paul Eluard; *Autour d'un poème*, by Maxime Alexandre and Pierre Unik. See *T.S.*, I, 223–34.

such a task, and any attempt to establish correspondence between the letter of poetry and the letter of the law is illegitimate. For Breton, a poem conforms 'par définition aux lois d'un langage exalté' ('by definition to the laws of exalted language'), and so is not to be taken literally. Any literal reading falls far short of the full significance of poetry; poetry cannot be judged in the same way as texts which aspire to what, in *Misère de la Poésie*, he calls the 'expression *exacte*, autrement dit *mesurée* et *pesée* de la pensée' ('*exact* or, in other words, *measured* and *weighed* expression of thought'). With this in mind, he recalls how in 1924 he had stated that, whatever its content, a poet could no more be prosecuted for a Surrealist poem than he could for his dreams. In the first *Surrealist Manifesto* he had, indeed, in the context of automatic writing, claimed that a poet in the dock would be no more responsible for a shocking Surrealist text than the judge facing him (*O.C.*, I, 344).

In *L'Affaire Aragon*, Breton states that, given historical circumstances, the deepest feelings of a twentieth-century poet can hardly be anything other than violent. He also makes it clear that he does not particularly like 'Front Rouge', which he describes as 'poétiquement régressif' ('poetically regressive'), because it harnesses poetry to Soviet propaganda. Breton was committed to social and political activism, but always insisted that poetry is never a means to an end, and must never sacrifice its deep, shifting and multifarious nature to a pedagogical or propagandist cause. This essential position would later be reflected in Surrealist objections both to stirringly patriotic Resistance poetry and to the Soviet-approved aesthetics of Socialist Realism.

In 2001, Pablo Durán contrasts Breton's position with the arguments used by Jean Clair. He suggests that Clair's reading of Surrealist texts is consistently moralising, literal and reductive, treating lyrical writing as if it were ideological analysis. Just as Clair misrepresents Surrealist use of the term 'the Orient', so he misreads the Surrealist world map, implying that the shrinking of mainland United States and the expansion of Afghanistan make the Surrealists antiAmerican and pro-Taliban. The Surrealists, in fact, magnified those lands which might offer cultural and spiritual alternatives to Western norms and values. For Régis Debray, this alternative atlas, reversing global hierarchies and domination, is as prophetically relevant today as in 1929.

While Jean Clair's essay chooses not to engage with Surrealist art and poetry, his response to written and graphic expression is strangely literal and anachronistic. What other conclusions can we draw from the Jean Clair Affair?

Firstly, beyond the specific issue of Surrealist violence, it demonstrates the continuing importance of the printed word in France, and the fact that there is still dialectical debate around cultural, political and philosophical issues. The Surrealists saw themselves as fighting a war against fatalism and the prevailing drift of history. Clair opposes their stand, but the response to his essay shows that there are French writers and intellectuals who continue to resist the mould of consensual vacuity and conformism. Parts of the French media, including *Le Monde*, continue to give space to such analytical and polemical statements by writers, academics, philosophers and func-tionaries. Clair and Debray publish charge and counter-charge, and the French tradition of the concerned and campaigning intellectual, dating back to Voltaire, is thus perpetuated.[15]

Secondly, as the 1932 Aragon Affair demonstrates, the debate on violence in Surrealist discourse is not new, and the critical immunity imagined by Clair is a myth. Indeed, both Sartre and Camus famously crossed swords with Breton, and more recently, Bernard-Henri Lévy saw fit to criticise Surrealist violence in his book on French intel-lectuals, *Les Aventures de la liberté*.[16] Régis Debray argues that

15   Jean Clair's 2003 book on Surrealism is itself sponsored by the *Fondation du 2 mars* which, in the book's Postface, is defined as a gathering of 'intellectuals, trade unionists, militants, researchers and, more widely, of citizens concerned about civic affairs [...] of varied sensibilities, from Communists to Gaullists', founded to promote intellectual debate in the face of increasing ideological and media conformism.

16   For Sartre on Surrealism, see 'Situation de l'écrivain en 1947', in *Qu'est-ce que la littérature?*, *Situations* II (Paris: Gallimard, 1948), 202–29. See also Camus's two open letters, headed *Révolte et conformisme*, published in *Arts* in October and November 1951 (A. Camus, *Essais*, ed. R. Quilliot, L. Faucon (Paris: Gallimard, Bibliothèque de la Pléiade, 1965), 731–6). Camus's 'Catch-22' conundrum on revolt and revolution may be tested against Surrealist political trajectories: 'Le révolutionnaire est en même temps révolté ou alors il n'est plus

Surrealism has always been a target for the intellectual establishment
of whatever colour, whether it be the Vichy government that banned
Breton's books because 'l'auteur est la négation de la Révolution
Nationale' ('their author is the antithesis of the National Revolution');
the French Communist Party writers, who always treated the Surrealists as bourgeois individualists; or the voices of currently ascend-
ant conservatism, who smear Breton as a Stalinist.

Jean Clair's intervention is indeed part of what Régis Debray
refers to as an ongoing 'conservative revolution'. For Clair, Surrealism could only be acceptable as a purely aesthetic movement,
close to the version displayed by Werner Spies in the *Révolution
surréaliste* exhibition. Surrealism always aspired, however, to
reconcile poetry and life, to show that action can be the sister of
dreams. Some will argue that the predictable failure of such aspirations necessarily led to the despair that breeds nihilistic violence,
and indeed several Surrealists committed suicide. This in no way
nullifies Surrealism's life-affirming legacy and the continuing vitality
and relevance of its artistic and philosophical achievements. Surrealist
discourse, in all genres, is dominated by constant references to poetry,
love and liberty, and Breton would often use the phrase 'ne pas
démériter' (meaning 'not be unworthy of' or 'live up to') to encapsulate Surrealist morality: 'ne pas démériter de l'amour', 'ne pas
démériter de l'aventure humaine' (*O.C.*, III, 517, 575). The Surrealist
challenge is thus to live up to love, to live up to life. Surrealism
provides a model for a definition of human dignity which, in appropriately secular terms, ennobles both human potential and life
itself.

révolutionnaire, mais policier et fonctionnaire qui se tourne contre la révolte.
Mais s'il est révolté, il finit par se dresser contre la révolution. [...] Tout
révolutionnaire finit en oppresseur ou en hérétique' ('The revolutionary must at
the same time be in revolt or no longer be a revolutionary, but rather a
policeman and a state employee who turns against revolt. But if he is in revolt,
he ends up opposing the revolution. [...] Every revolutionary ends up as an
oppressor or a heretic' (*L'Homme révolté*, in *Essais*, 651). See also Bernard-
Henri Lévy, *Les Aventures de la liberté: une histoire subjective des intellectuels*
(Paris: Grasset, 1991).

Clair's selective and jaundiced interpretation of Surrealism ultimately leads us back to the importance of context and of imaginative
empathy. Just as the French Revolution cannot be discredited by
selective focus on the excesses of the Terror, so the edited passages
cited by Jean Clair in no way diminish the achievements of Surrealism. The lyrical rhetoric of violence and terror was one jagged
aspect of Surrealism during a specific period. As we have already
seen, it was inspired by front-line experience of World War I and
continuing outrage in the face of a flagrantly inequitable world order,
and increasing nationalism and militarism during what the poets
rightly perceived as the build-up to other conflagrations, in Europe,
Indochina and North Africa.

Such considerations finally lead me to suggest that Surrealist
rhetoric was also inspired by the language of a previous generation.
Politically, their rhetoric recalls the days when Marx and Bakunin
vied for radical hearts and minds, when *fin-de-siècle* anarchists revered Ravachol and Emile Henry as secular saints. Surrealist discourse
was equally, however, shaped by literary models, and by the example
of writers from that same earlier period who similarly abhorred the
predominant social and cultural values of their day, from Lautréamont
to the Huysmans of *A rebours*, 'de Rimbaud à Mallarmé, de Saint-Pol
Roux à Marcel Schwob, de Darien à Jarry...' (Annie Le Brun).

The young Surrealists also looked further back, beyond Ravachol
and Rimbaud, to Robespierre and Sade. In 1925, and again in 1936,
the Surrealists proclaimed 'Il n'y a pas de liberté pour les ennemis de
la liberté', a formula taken directly from Robespierre.[17] In 'Front

---

17   'There can be no liberty for the enemies of liberty'. Collective declaration,
      'Ouvrez les Prisons. Licenciez l'Armée', *La Révolution surréaliste*, 2, 15
      janvier 1925, in *T.S.*, I, 34; collective tract, *Arrêtez Gil Robles*, 20 July 1936, in
      T.S., I, 301. Similar references to the French Revolution include, for example,
      Breton's support in 1922 for a revolution 'aussi sanglante qu'on voudra [...]. Il
      ne serait pas mauvais qu'on rétablît pour l'esprit les lois de la Terreur' ('as
      bloody as you like [...]. It would be no bad thing if the laws of the Terror were
      re-established in our minds') ('Caractères de l'évolution moderne', *O.C.*, I,
      305); or the phrase 'Il faut aboutir à une nouvelle Déclaration des droits de
      l'homme' ('We have to achieve a new Declaration of the Rights of Man'), on
      the front cover of *La Révolution surréaliste*, no.1, 1924.

Rouge', Aragon's historical perspective also reached back, via the anarchist martyrs Sacco and Vanzetti, and the funeral of Jaurès, to the French Revolution, seen as the matrix of all popular insurrections. Surrealist revolutionary rhetoric is thus rooted in the eighteenth century and refers, most notably, to the 1793 *Déclaration des droits de l'homme et du citoyen* (*Declaration of the Rights of Man and the Citizen*), whose thirty-fifth and final article states: 'Quand le gouvernement viole les droits du peuple, l'insurrection est pour le peuple, et pour chaque portion du peuple, le plus sacré des droits et le plus indispensable des devoirs'.[18]

The Surrealist brand of libertarian values and creativity thus carried into the twentieth century a prestigious literary and cultural tradition. Their conception of politics was particularly marked by the decisive role of civil strife and insurrection in modern French history. The myth of liberation through political violence was, in their eyes, legitimised by reference to the French Revolution, promoted by French Republicans as the founding act of the nation, and to the rhetoric of Robespierre, Saint-Just and the 1793 Committee of Public Safety.

The Surrealists held to their vision of 'La Planète sans Visa', a world without frontiers (*T.S.*, I, 268–9). Surrealist rhetoric of anger and violence nevertheless grew out of a radical tradition which is an integral part of France's very specific national identity. In conclusion, it could thus be argued that Jean Clair fails to recognise how much French culture and identity are rooted in revolutionary mythology and indebted to expressions of resistance and dissent. Such a view is itself too reductive and comfortable, however, as it tends to normalise revolt and assimilate Surrealism (alongside Pataphysics, Dada, Lettrism and Situationism) into a reassuring cultural mainstream. Surrealist art and writing, whatever their cultural and political ancestry, remain so potently and pervasively disruptive that they resist being categorised, neutralised and rehabilitated. They thus incidentally and magnificently confirm that while culture is the norm, art is the exception.

---

18   'When government violates the rights of the people, insurrection is for the people, and for every section of the people, their most sacred right and their most indispensable duty'.

David Gascoigne

André Malraux's *musée imaginaire* of Violence

For André Malraux, the third and fourth decades of his life, which were also the third and fourth decades of the twentieth century, became a period of crucial confrontation with violence, both in its most brutal contemporary actuality and as a locus of urgent intellectual, political and moral debate. From being an observer of the violent political turmoil in the Far East, he moved to active service with the International Air Force supporting the Republican cause in Spain, until this was overwhelmed by the superior technology of the Italian and German forces of the Fascist alliance. He would see military action again both in the fall of France and in the Resistance forces at the Liberation. The theatres of war in which he was involved thus moved ever closer to home, and the debates which this involvement provoked in his thinking and writing became no less intense as the perspective moved from a left-wing internationalist stance to that of a crusade to defend liberal European and French culture and values from the threat of totalitarianism. These debates found immediate expression in the speeches he made at meetings of anti-Fascist intellectuals and on speaking tours to rally support for the Spanish Republican cause. More enduringly, however, they also formed a core part of the existential questioning at the heart of his fictional writings, from *Les Conquérants* of 1928 through to *Les Noyers de l'Altenburg* of 1943.

Numerous critical studies have sought to analyse the evolution of Malraux's political and metaphysical interrogations, and to reach a view about the essential consistency or inconsistency of the values he defended. Rather than replicate that enterprise, this essay will seek to plot a different route through some of the fictions of André Malraux, a route that will take us from Turkey to Moscow to Spain, to end in Chartres Cathedral. The markers on this journey will be a particular

and revealing cluster of images which form part of what one might
term (redefining for our purpose one of Malraux's own concepts) his
musée imaginaire,[1] the fund of recurrent images which, consciously or
otherwise, inform his literary expression.

The point of departure is a relatively little-known early and rather
fantastical Malraux text, entitled *Royaume-farfelu*, which he wrote in
his twenties, and which was published in 1928, the same year as *Les
Conquérants*. The opening paragraph of *Royaume-farfelu* exemplifies
its surreal, incantatory exoticism:

> Prenez garde, diables frisés: de pâles images se forment sur la mer en silence;
> cette heure n'est plus la vôtre. Voyez, voyez: en face des tombeaux des lieux
> saints, les veilleurs remontent lentement les horloges qui mesurent l'éternité
> aux sultans morts – les papes et les antipapes dorés se poursuivent dans les
> égouts déserts de Rome; derrière eux rient sans bruit des démons à la queue
> soyeuse qui sont les anciens empereurs [...] – un roi qui n'aime plus que la
> musique et les supplices erre la nuit, désolé, soufflant dans de hautes trompes
> d'argent et entraînant son peuple qui danse... et voici qu'à la frontière des deux
> Indes, sous des arbres aux feuilles serrées comme des bêtes, un conquérant
> abandonné s'endort dans son armure noire, entouré de singes inquiets...[2]

---

1   'Le musée imaginaire', translated as 'museum without walls', is the term
    Malraux uses to signify that fund of works of art and cultural icons which is
    characteristically embedded in the collective consciousness of our culture and
    which is nourished in particular by the diffusion of photographic repre-
    sentations of these artefacts. It is the title he gave to the first of the three
    volumes of his *Psychologie de l'Art* (Geneva: Skira, 1947–1950), subsequently
    revised as *Les Voix du silence* (Paris: Gallimard, 1951), his major work on the
    cultural significance of art.

2   'Watch out, you curly-haired devils: pale visions are forming over the sea in
    silence; your hour has passed. See, see: in front of the tombs of the holy places,
    the watchmen are slowly rewinding the clocks which measure out eternity for
    the dead sultans – the gilded popes and antipopes are pursuing one another in
    the deserted sewers of Rome: behind them comes the noiseless laughter of
    silky-tailed demons who are the emperors of old [...] – a king who now enjoys
    nothing except music and torture wanders desolate through the night, blowing
    high silver trumpets and leading his people in a dance [...] and see where, at the
    frontier of the two Indies, beneath trees with leaves as dense as a pack of beasts,
    an abandoned warrior falls asleep in his black armour, surrounded by nervous
    monkeys [...]'. Malraux, *Royaume-farfelu*, in *Œuvres complètes* (Paris:

Here, in a landscape littered with the death-stricken remnants of a glorious but dying civilisation flicker strange survivals of life: the slow clock-winders, a flurry of gilded popes, one-time emperors transformed into silky-tailed demons, the sadistic king leading his people in an aimless *danse macabre* and, in a final image of decay and lost power, an abandoned warrior slumbering amidst the monkeys. Everything in this catalogue of images bespeaks disintegration, defeat, loss of energy and purpose. As the text proceeds, we come to understand that the 'pâles images' here described are hallucinatory apparitions seen through the eyes of the narrator and his companions, who are on board a ship drifting helplessly toward a hostile Turkish city. This city is described as one of 'inhuman architectures', shaped like crustaceans and mushrooms. On reaching the city, the narrator is soon arrested, placed in solitary confinement, and finally drafted into the Moghul's army, which is on its way to attack Ispahan. As this army moves on Ispahan it is greeted by a melancholy spectacle: the retreating Prince Vlad of Transylvania has hanged all his prisoners, and their bodies, now reduced to skeletons in rusty armour, are still displayed, adding a sense of threat to the prevailing atmosphere of decay. As the army lays siege to Ispahan, the narrator speaks of an inner voice which he can hear: the voice, he says, of one of the faceless demons of the ruins which inhabit our own bodies. This voice spells out a warning:

> [...] tu ne te souviendras pas d'Ispahan, car Ispahan est gardée par les Bêtes. Sa couronne d'abandon saura la délivrer de tes compagnons de mauvaise fortune et de leurs officiers voués à une fin immonde. Rien ne prévaudra contre ceux qui naissent du sable; leur image règne parmi les constellations.[3]

Gallimard, Bibliothèque de la Pléiade, 1989–), I, 317 (hereafter abbreviated to *O.C.*). All translations are my own.

3   'You will have no memory of Ispahan, for Ispahan is guarded by the Beasts. Its corona of surrender will save it from the hands of your companions in ill-fortune and their officers doomed to a dreadful fate. Nothing can prevail against those who are born out of the sand; their image reigns among the constellations'. *O.C.*, I, 331. The Pléiade edition reads 'gardée par les bêtes', but I have taken the liberty of restoring the capital letter ('Bêtes') found in preceding editions from the author's lifetime: see Malraux, *Œuvres complètes* (Geneva: Skira, 1945), V, 148, or *Œuvres* (Paris: Gallimard, 1970), I, 334. The

And, sure enough, defeat by this conspiracy of inhuman forces is indeed imminent:

> La ville était calme; autour des mosquées volaient des pigeons et des tourterelles. Mais les décombres que le départ des lézards teignait en rose étaient noirs, ce matin, absolument noirs. Tout à coup, comprenant à la fois la terreur des animaux et la signification de cette large tache qui s'avançait vers nous, je hurlai: 'Les scorpions! les scorpions!' Tous se ruèrent sur les terrasses. En quelques minutes ce mot, et la vue de l'immense nappe frangée de pinces nous soulevèrent d'une telle épouvante que l'armée se décomposa: en un vaste tourbillon, emportant officiers et princes, la terreur nous lança hors du faubourg, dans un tumulte d'armes, de clameurs, de hennissements... La démence, tout à coup surgie, jetait à poignées cette multitude aux vautours des déserts, comme des grains.[4]

We can note that this assault of scorpions emerges from, and is indissociable from, the ruins and mosques of the ancient city. The first city where the narrator was imprisoned earlier was, we recall, a city of crustacean shapes, and that 'profil de crustacés' is here echoed in the scorpion horde with its similarly baleful 'nappe frangée de pinces'. The scorpions seem to stand for the sub-human, the triumph of the bestial. The text's opening showed us a warrior falling asleep in his armour, in a state of surrender to the forest 'aux feuilles serrées comme des bêtes' with its tribe of monkeys. The scene is a vivid allegory of the exhaustion of the human will, and especially of the will to resist. Here in this last quotation describing the rout which is the climax of the narrative, the 'Bêtes', in the shape of scorpions, are the

symbolic emphasis bestowed by the capital letter seems quite apposite in context.

4   'The city was calm; around the mosques flew pigeons and doves. But the ruins, which were usually tinted pink once the lizards had gone, were black that morning, absolutely black. Suddenly, understanding in an instant the terror of the animals and the significance of that large dark patch which was advancing towards us, I screamed: 'Scorpions! Scorpions!'. Everyone rushed onto the terraces. In a few minutes that cry, and the sight of that vast mass fringed with pincers, swept us up in such horror that the army broke ranks: in a great whirl, sweeping away officers and princes, terror pitched us out of the city's confines, in a tumult of arms, shouting and whinnying [...] Madness, surging up in an instant, was scattering this multitude in handfuls to the vultures of the deserts like so much grain'. *O.C.*, I, 333.

terrifying adversaries, inspiring instinctive and overwhelming panic. Indeed they could be read as simply externalisations of the monsters of the sub-conscious – the demon who warns of them is an inner voice (a 'demon who lives in our own bodies'), and the attack of the scorpions is presented more as a nightmare vision than as a tangible external event. The instrument of doom is finally not so much the scorpions themselves as the inner irrational, superstitious horror they evoke, increasingly emphasised in the words *l'épouvante, la terreur, la démence*. The meaning of the terse warning in the second quotation now becomes clear: 'Ispahan est gardée par les Bêtes. *Sa couronne d'abandon* saura la délivrer...' This parable suggests how a powerful, long-established culture, even if moribund, is capable of savage violence to put down any effort to overthrow it, and its efficacy is based on its ability to conjure up and exploit the most primitive reflexes of abjection, dehumanisation and surrender in any who seek to challenge it.

It is instructive to bear this scenario in mind in moving on to consider a novel published in 1935, which is also not highly rated in the Malraux canon, *Le Temps du mépris*. At the opening of the novel, Kassner, a German communist militant, has been arrested by the Nazi security forces and is in prison, where he faces the imminent prospect of brutal interrogation and torture. Among his most immediate memories is that of the last meeting of his clandestine Communist cell. They had gathered in an antique shop, where his attention was caught by a pile of Orthodox Church icons, vestments and ornaments. A second memory he has is of a scene he glimpsed as he was being driven to the prison: a gang of painters singing as they repainted the shopfront of a paint shop, 'as multi-coloured as Red Square', he thinks to himself. Now in a Nazi prison, in his mind beset by waves of panic and terror, these images, both associated with Russia, recur and combine to compose a kind of symbolic nightmare, a nightmare accompanied, in his fevered imagination, by an Orthodox plainchant going round and round in his head:

La vitrine bariolée du marchand de couleurs qu'il a vue après son arrestation devient l'église Saint-Basile avec ses oignons multicolores, au fond de la Place Rouge; et, comme si les croix et les encensoirs de l'antiquaire, tout son déballage d'étoles et de dalmatiques montaient de terre, les coupoles toutes semées d'étoiles de cuivre d'un couvent-forteresse appareillent dans la nuit sous leurs croix doubles et tout leur gréement de chaînes dorées chargées de pigeons et de corneilles; au-dessous, une ville contre-révolutionnaire pourrie d'ex-votos, de jouets et de pèlerinages, vieille Russie dont la mystique ensanglantée masque mal les corps des partisans pendus aux cloches.[5]

As this waking dream continues, the priests of his imagination launch an attack on the partisans:

> Les popes sortis du tertre commencent à avancer, dalmatiques et tiares sous les croix et les bannières, et une irréalité sans limites anime ce Trésor en marche [...]. Ils approchent en chantant avec une haine indignée la psalmodie [...] qui retombe sur des frissonnements de feuilles comme des fuites de bêtes [...].[6]

Between *Royaume-farfelu* and *Le Temps du mépris*, between 1928 and 1935, European politics had undergone a drastic change with the inexorable rise of Fascism, and with it Malraux's involvement in anti-Fascist political campaigning. While the fantastical *Royaume-farfelu* takes place outside any precise history or geography, *Le Temps du mépris* is set in 1930s Germany, and is unambiguously a parable of the anti-Fascist struggle in Europe generally. Nevertheless, in this resolutely contemporary narrative, carrying a sense of political commitment which is a far cry from the fantasy exoticism and dream-like detachment of the earlier text, we find Malraux re-mobilising

---

5   'The gaudy window of the paint-shop he saw after his arrest becomes St Basil's church with its multicoloured onion-shaped domes, behind Red Square; and, as though the crosses and thuribles from the antique shop, all its jumble of stoles and dalmatics were leaving the ground, the cupolas of a convent-fortress, studded with copper stars, set sail into the night beneath their double crosses and all their rigging of gilded chains laden with pigeons and crows; below, a counter-revolutionary city rotten with pious plaques, playthings and pilgrimages, that Russia of old whose blood-stained mystique does little to conceal the bodies of the partisans hanged from the bells'. Malraux, *Le Temps du mépris* in *O.C.*, I, 798.

6   'The priests emerging from the mound begin to advance, dalmatics and tiaras beneath the crosses and the banners, and an unbounded unreality seems to be driving forward this marching Treasure-house [...]. As they approach they sing chants of indignation and hatred [...] which fall back on the rustling leaves like creatures scuttling away [...]'. *O.C.*, I, 799.

much the same vocabulary of images. The parallels are striking. The tombs of holy places of the earlier text's opening and the mosques of Ispahan which launch the devastating scorpion attack become here the pointed domes of Saint Basil's church. The gilded popes and anti-popes evoked at the outset of *Royaume-farfelu* become the aggressive priests, the 'marching treasure-house' of Kassner's nightmare. The 'pincer-edged mass' of the scorpions prefigures this eccelesiastical horde bristling with crosses and banners. The hanged prisoners of prince Vlad of Transylvania are transmuted into the bodies of Russian partisans hanged from the church bells. In *Royaume-farfelu* a king with a taste for music and torture leads his subjugated people in his aimless wandering. Here music, the music of Orthodox chant, is again, in Kassner's fevered mind, obsessively associated with sadistic authority and the imminent threat of torture and subjugation.

There is one important overall difference to be noted: *Le Temps du mépris* is a more optimistic text, in that this sinister coalition of political and psychological forces is not allowed to prevail. Kassner, encouraged by secret messages of solidarity from a fellow prisoner, successfully resists the pressure, and escapes to Prague to fight again. The margin of his victory is, however, a narrow and precarious one, and the narrative powerfully suggests that the struggle for human dignity will always be threatened by the temptations of passivity, surrender or dehumanisation, by 'les Bêtes', by forces of debasement acting within the mind as well as outside it.

This struggle, using very much the same vocabulary of images, will again manifest itself in certain episodes in Malraux's Spanish Civil War novel, *L'Espoir*, dating from 1937. In an episode very near the end of that novel, the Communist Manuel, a senior officer in the Republican army, arrives at a village church. The church has been requisitioned and transformed into a garage for captured lorries, parked in the nave among the smashed chairs and guarded by a militiaman. However, Manuel discovers to his surprise that the chancel has been left intact, on the instructions of the local Revolutionary Committee, out of respect for the workmanship of the décor:

> Le regard de Manuel, pas encore accoutumé à l'obscurité, s'arrêtait à un fouillis doré qui tremblait dans l'ombre au-dessus du portail comme un incendie

immobile: des anges, hérissés de pieds en l'air, emplissaient le mur tout entier, autour de tuyaux en sifflets: des orgues extraordinaires.[7]

Manuel, who used to play the organ before the war, decides to try the instrument out:

> Il commença à jouer: le premier morceau de musique religieuse qui passa dans sa mémoire, le *Kyrie* de Palestrina. Dans la nef vide le chant sacré se déployait, raide et grave comme les draperies gothiques, mal accordé à la guerre et trop bien accordé à la mort; malgré les chaises en débris, et les camions, et la guerre, la voix de l'autre monde reprenait possession de l'église. Manuel était troublé, non par le chant, mais par son passé. Le milicien, ahuri, regardait le lieutenant-colonel qui se mettait à jouer un chant d'église.
> 'Alors ça va, il marche toujours bien, le truc' , dit-il quand Manuel cessa de jouer.[8]

The undertone of hostility in the militiaman's comment is the hostility of present commitment for past passivity, the hostility of the revolution for the trappings of anachronistic authority. The implication is that, for this soldier and to some extent for Manuel himself, Manuel's playing of a Palestrina Kyrie is a treacherous revival of the church's old function, and thus a sinister reanimation of the power of a theocratic establishment. It is described as 'too much in tune with death', and thus redolent of surrender rather than of struggle. In this perspective the golden tangle of the angels bristling round the organ-pipes recalls the gilded popes of *Royaume-farfelu*, or the gaudy paraphernalia and the 'gilt chains' of the Orthodox church in *Le*

---

7   'Manuel's gaze, not yet accustomed to the dimness, settled on a tangle of gold which was flickering in the shadow like a motionless fire: angels, their feet bristling outward, filled the whole wall, around the fluting of the pipes: an extraordinary church organ'. Malraux, *L'Espoir*, in *O.C.*, II, 421.

8   'He began to play: the first piece of religious music which came to his memory, Palestrina's *Kyrie*. Down the empty nave the sacred song unfolded, grave and austere like gothic draperies, out of tune with the war, and only too well in tune with death; despite the smashed chairs, and the lorries, and the war, the voice of another world was reclaiming the church. Manuel was troubled, not by the music but by his own past. The militiaman, flabbergasted, was staring at this lieutenant-colonel who had started playing a piece of church music. "All right, then, so that thing still works O.K.," he said when Manuel had finished playing'. *O.C.*, II, 422.

Temps du mépris. Thus we can observe that the residual power invested in these symbols of autocracy is still perceived as a threat, although at nothing like the level suggested in *Le Temps du mépris*. Malraux's hero Manuel is here shown at a moment of temporary military success, a man in command, who can flirt with these latent powers with impunity, even as he exorcises them by converting churches into lorry parks and convents into barracks. Nevertheless, his attitude is interestingly ambivalent: 'Manuel was troubled', we are told, 'not by the music, but by his own past'. The 'autre monde' to which he gives voice in playing the organ is not just the other world of religious piety and ecclesiastical power, it is the whole world of non-violent peacetime culture for which he feels some nostalgia, and a sense of loss. This suggests a more nuanced position on Malraux's part, a shift away from earlier works where ecclesiastical architecture and paraphernalia simply embodied and activated a hated and dehumanising ideology. This shift in Malraux's authorial position points to a tension between his twin vocations: he was on one hand an advocate of and participant in armed struggle, but on the other he was a passionate explorer of the arts, preoccupied with the mystery of how certain supreme artefacts have the power to speak to us seemingly beyond the vagaries of history and cultural change. Here, in *L'Espoir*, music and gilded angels are no longer wholly on the side of the enemy, as they were in *Le Temps du mépris*. They cannot be reduced to an ideological function.

Malraux's final work of fiction, *Les Noyers de l'Altenburg*, was written between 1940 and 1942 and first published in 1943. Part III of the novel relates the experiences of the narrator's father, Vincent Berger, in an earlier war, in 1914–1918. Being from Alsace, in-corporated into Germany since 1871, he found himself fighting on the German side of the Eastern Front. In the following passage, Berger is in the presence of a German scientist, Professor Hoffmann, who is expatiating enthusiastically on the efficacy of a new poison gas he is planning to launch against the Russians, a weapon which, he thinks, gives his side a decisive edge in the arms race. We are not directly given Berger's reaction to this chilling technical discourse on mass extermination, but that reaction is suggested indirectly in this passage, where Berger is gazing distractedly out of the window:

Il [mon père] passait devant la fenêtre [...]. Au delà du jardin, les bulbes et les
croix d'une église orthodoxe brillaient dans le soir au fond de la grande place en
pente. Mon père sentait la Russie autour de lui, moins à cause des coupoles
violettes et dorées qu'à cause des très anciens pavés de cette place bosselée
[...]; au-delà des roses-thé couleur des routes, l'invincible passé russe était seul
vivant dans le soir et le silence suspendu de la guerre. La voix du professeur
énumérait les qualités et les défauts du phosgène, et mon père ressentait la
profondeur du monde slave jusqu'au Pacifique.[9]

It is striking that those very gilded domes which haunted Kassner in
Le Temps du mépris are no longer seen by Vincent Berger as part of
the threat of a vicious reactionary power. Although Vincent, like
Manuel, is still wary of recognising their cultural potency, they are
nevertheless, along with the worn paving stones of the rugged square,
a manifestation of that depth of Russian culture and history which is
threatened by the new inhumanity of a science devoid of morality or
of any sense of the value of cultural identity.

Elsewhere, *Les Noyers de l'Altenburg* recounts the experiences
of Vincent Berger's son, the narrator of the text. He has a similar
moment of insight in another war, World War I, and in another church
rather closer to home, Chartres Cathedral. The novel opens with a
prefatory section headed 'Chartres, 21 June 1940', as young Berger
lies wounded after the fall of France, amongst a mass of defeated and
humiliated French troops herded into the basilica:

Je ne reconnais pas le vaisseau de la cathédrale: les carreaux qui ont remplacé
les vitraux de la nef l'éventrent de lumière. Au-dessous, dans les chapelles, les
verrières étroites comme des colonnes de jour tremblent du haut en bas, sous le
grondement marin des chars allemands qui déferlent. Semblable aux prisonniers

9   'He [my father] moved by the window [...]. Beyond the garden, the bulbs and
     crosses of an orthodox church were gleaming in the evening light behind the
     great sloping square. My father sensed Russia all around him, less because of
     the purple and gold cupolas than because of the uneven cobbles of this very
     ancient square [...]; beyond the tea-roses, of the colour of the roads, the
     inextinguishable Russian past was the one thing alive in the silent evening
     suspense of the war. The voice of the professor was spelling out the qualities
     and defects of phosgene gas, and my father was caught up in the depth of the
     Slavic world, stretching right to the Pacific Ocean'. Malraux, *Les Noyers de
     l'Altenburg*, in *O.C.*, II, 705.

blessés qui me précèdent, à ceux qui me suivent, je suis fasciné par le sol couvert de ce que nous croyions ne jamais revoir – de paille. Dans la nef déjà pleine semblent trembloter sous le jour vacillant des soldats qui ouvrent des boîtes de conserve ensanglantées [...]. Nous nous jetons sur les gerbes dont les épis frémissent, eux aussi, de la trépidation des chars jusqu'aux limites de la Beauce...[10]

The leitmotif of this passage is fragility and hurt. As the tanks roll past outside, everything is trembling – the windows, the straw, even seemingly the figures of the soldiers themselves. The cathedral itself, 'pierced through with light', is wounded like the soldiers it shelters.[11] As Berger looks up at the great Gothic arches, we register how much the significance of this recurrent motif of church architecture has changed. Malraux is now, in 1941–1942, writing in a context of the threat to his homeland and to European civilisation. Accordingly, the monuments of the Christian past are no longer placed under the sign of reaction and oppression to be overthrown in the name of dignity and the revolution. Rather, they are part of what is under attack from a Fascism hostile to humane culture and blind to the value of a *patrimoine* now seen as infinitely precious.[12]

10   'I do not recognise the cathedral nave: the panes which have replaced the stained glass are piercing it through with light. Below, in the side-chapels, the tall windows like pillars of light are trembling from top to bottom, from the churning roar of the steady waves of German tanks rolling by. Like the wounded prisoners who come before me and those following behind me, I am fascinated by the floor, covered with what we thought we would never see again – with straw. In the already packed nave, the flickering light picks out the tremulous vision of soldiers opening bloodstained tins of rations [...]. We slump down onto the sheaves; the ears of corn too are trembling from the vibration of the tanks rumbling on towards the furthest limits of the Beauce [...]'. *O.C.*, II, 621.

11   The stained glass had been removed to a place of safety at the onset of hostilities.

12   In an earlier article I develop a fuller analysis of this novel in the context of the wartime situation. See David Gascoigne, '*Les Noyers de l'Altenburg*: Malraux and 1940', in Anthony Cheal Pugh (ed.), *France 1940: literary and historical reactions to defeat* (Durham: University of Durham Modern Language Series, 1991), 35–45. I suggest there that Malraux sees Chartres as a symbol of human, rather than specifically French, culture. The narrator, hearing a German soldier speak of Bamberg, refers to that city's cathedral as 'la Chartres allemande' ('the

From this very selective guided tour of particular sites in Malraux's densely suggestive topography, two points emerge strongly. Firstly, we can observe the shift which takes place across this sequence of texts in the relationship between the ideological and the aesthetic. For the mid-century writers of Malraux's generation, the connection between art and politics was arguably the most urgent and contentious issue, and close comparative analysis of samples of text can reveal how, even at the microcosmic level of the use of a certain set of images linking art and violence, Malraux's position changes. He can be seen to move from a position first of elegiac, poetic detachment, then to one of quite hard-line ideological dialectic, to end with a revaluation of art as having a unique permanent significance, as manifesting some fundamental human value which transcends the violent actuality of human affairs. Such comparative analysis also brings into sharp focus the way in which a particular stock of images, a pre-rational *musée imaginaire*, is subject to ever-changing representation and interpretation in a radically shifting context of meaning. These images speak of the direct link which Malraux insists on between the relics of art and history on the one hand, and our deepest inner impulses and needs on the other, a link which he sought to probe and articulate to the end of his life. They speak too of that other key Malraux concept of metamorphosis, the mysterious power of a given image or set of images to provoke quite different cultural reactions across time without its significance ever being exhausted.

Les Noyers de l'Altenburg would turn out to be Malraux's farewell to fictional writing. Henceforth, his powers of description and imagination would be placed at the service of large canvases of autobiography or his own brand of art history. He was, it seems, no longer interested in the imaginative investment in fictions focused on the local violences of political conflict. The Chartres episode already suggests an epic broadening of focus which will lead logically on to his reflections on the whole human heritage of art and culture and its supreme importance, and to his ideal job as Minister of Culture under de Gaulle, tasked with promoting a sense of French national identity

German Chartres') (*O.C.*, II, 622). Even in France's darkest hour, Malraux resists taking up a purely patriotic, nationalist view of the conflict.

(as well as intercultural awareness) through cultural education and diffusion. The violence which most concerns him now is the metaphorical violence by which a great artist can reshape our view of the world. Manuel, Kassner and Vincent Berger all struggle physically against the forces which oppress them and their fellow-combatants, but Malraux finds in artistic 'conquest' an equivalent but more universal and abiding triumph:

> L'accusation de la condition sociale mène à la destruction du système par lequel celle-ci se fonde; l'accusation de la condition humaine, en art, à la destruction des formes qui l'acceptent.[13]

In the analogy offered here, revolutionary politics, challenging and dismantling oppressive social structures, provides the paradigm for the gesture of artistic creation, remoulding the forms of culture itself. In this formulation, artistic action, like political action, defines itself as revolt, as a striving for liberation from passivity and subordination to the status quo. In the great masterpieces we discover that:

> l'artiste, par sa lente conquête, s'y est si puissamment libéré de sa dépendance, qu'elles [les œuvres] apportent à tous ceux qui entendent leur langage le plus persuasif écho de sa libération.[14]

Malraux's credo is thus that art can make manifest the triumph of the heroic individual, transcending the limits of the artist's historical and cultural circumstances, and thereby bringing an exemplary glimpse of liberation to mankind. The final section of *Les Voix du silence* proclaims that this conquest is a cumulative one, in which each individual artist makes a particular contribution to the wider struggle of humanity against all that oppresses it:

13 'The indictment of social conditions leads to the destruction of the system on which these are based; the indictment of the human condition, through art, leads to the destruction of the forces which are accepting of it'. Malraux, *Les Voix du silence* in *O.C.*, IV, 783–4.
14 'the artist, by his slow conquest, has in these works liberated himself so powerfully from his dependency that they bring to all those who understand their language the most persuasive echo of liberation'. *O.C.*, IV, 702.

David Gascoigne

[...] la victoire de chaque artiste sur sa servitude rejoint, dans un immense déploiement, celle de l'art sur le destin de l'humanité. L'art est un anti-destin.[15]

The rhetoric of political and social violence – victory over servitude, destruction, conquest, liberation – is now redeployed to convey the dynamic force of a more macrocosmic and metaphysical vocation, a kind of cultural salvation. In this advocacy of the ahistorical power of art, Malraux finally strives to align individual achievement and the collective struggle of mankind, and to transform the gesture of violence into a symbol of creativity and humanity. To the cathedral of art is given the power to envelop and give value to all.

15   '[...] the victory of each artist over his servitude merges, in a vast outspreading, into that of art over the destiny of mankind. Art is an anti-destiny'. *O.C.*, IV, 897. Malraux uses the general term 'destin' (destiny or fate) to denote all the deterministic forces that govern and limit human life and action.

KIRSTEEN ANDERSON

Sartre and Jewishness: From Identificatory Violence to Ethical Reparation

Réflexions sur la question juive, published in 1946, offers Sartre's assessment of the options for Jewish identity in an often hostile, non-Jewish, liberal democratic environment, and in this essay he elects deliberately to focus on the French Jew in the period leading up to World War II. He argues that Jewish identity is mainly a response to the hostility of the Gentile community, that it is the construction of anti-Semitic prejudice.[1] In the course of his argument Sartre claims that Jews have no history, share no religious bond other than a purely symbolic or ritualistic one, and lack a sense of community. This thesis appears to do considerable violence to the integrity of Jewishness, as some of the earliest reviewers of his text noticed and as later critics have continued to argue.[2] This article seeks to explore possible reasons for Sartre's apparently reductive early account of Jewish

1   *Réflexions sur la question juive* (Paris: Gallimard, 1946); hereafter *Réflexions* in the text. English translation by George J. Becker: *Anti-Semite and Jew* (New York: Schocken Books, 1965). Sartre is not alone in this judgement. Isaac Deutscher discusses the view that it has been the Jewish tendency to separatism that has provoked anti-Semitism, and that this anti-Semitism in turn keeps Jewish identity alive. See Deutscher, *The Non-Jewish Jew* (Oxford: Oxford University Press, 1968), 47.

2   It is noteworthy, however, that there have been few substantial accounts of Jewish identity by a Jew which propose a positive alternative. Susan Suleiman challenges Sartre vigorously in 'The Jew in Jean-Paul Sartre's *Réflexions sur la question juive*: an Exercise in Historical Reading', in Linda Nochlin and Tamar Garb (eds), *The Jew in the Text. Modernity and the Construction of Identity* (London: Thames and Hudson, 1995), 201–18. Daniel and Jonathan Boyarin offer one of the few positive interpretations of Jewish identity in 'Diaspora: Generation and the Ground of Jewish Identity', *Critical Inquiry*, 19 (1993), 693–725. See also Emmanuel Levinas, *Difficile liberté* (Paris: Albin Michel, 1963).

identity. The broader context for this discussion is the unfinished
project that tormented Sartre's thinking throughout much of his life,
namely, his attempt to elaborate an ethics and, within this, to resolve
the question of how violence should be accommodated.

Réflexions is premonitory: it establishes the problematic of
otherness as difference in Western critical thought. It is also a brave
text in the context of the then recent Holocaust and of the resurgence
of anti-Semitism in France immediately after the war. It is impas-
sioned and generous in its intention which explains its largely
favourable reception at the time of publication. It is also highly
ambiguous and seems, on certain points, strangely ignorant of Jewish
experience. Until fairly recently *Réflexions* appears to have been one
of the least-mentioned of Sartre's texts. Critics ignore or skirt round it
as though the relationship between mainstream Western identity and
Jewishness was something of a black hole, an amnesiac point, too
problematic and provocative to merit attention.[3] Sartre had the
courage to at least attempt to address the painful complexity of this
situation. My aim in referring to the ambiguities of *Réflexions*,
therefore, is not to cast doubt on the fundamentally humanistic project
underpinning it, that is, to alert the European Gentile community to its
responsibility to embrace difference in its midst, in its own self-
interest. It is rather to clarify an entanglement of the personal and the
political which leads Sartre to do violence to the very individuals
whom he is exhorting the broader public to save, and to jeopardise his
own credibility as a philosopher of freedom.

At the end of his life, in the contentious interviews with Benny
Lévy published under the title *L'Espoir maintenant*, Sartre returns to
the question of Jewishness in an altogether more positive vein.[4] In the
broader context of whether violence can further the cause of fraternity,
he envisages a new stage in the becoming of humanity, in which

3   A Special Issue of *October*, 87 (Winter 1999) devoted to Sartre's *Anti-Semite
     and Jew* is one of the few publications to confront the text head on.
4   Jean-Paul Sartre and Benny Lévy, *L'Espoir maintenant: les entretiens de 1980*
     (Lagrasse: Verdier, 1991); English translation by Adrian van den Hoven: *Hope
     Now. The 1980 Interviews* (Chicago and London: University of Chicago Press,
     1996). Cited hereafter as *Ent* and *Int* respectively.

human solidarity will be realised on the model of the Jewish ethical community. Thus, in a somewhat ironic reversal, the philosemite who contributed, albeit unwittingly, to the disempowerment of Jewish identity in the 1940s through his ambiguous portrayal of what constitutes a Jew, later locates the salvation of his own ethical identity and that of the human community in a specific utopian vision. We shall all live as 'Jews' – use the power of ethics to contribute to revolution – in the new world order that we can, collectively, bring into being.

It takes virtually forty years to accomplish this move from ambivalence to insight. In the process, death and resurrection provide thematic connections between *Réflexions* (1946), *Les Mots* (1954/1963) and *L'Espoir maintenant* (1981).[5] The deaths of many Jews and (metaphorically) of an earlier Sartre, in the mid-century, lead to a rebirth of Jewish identity (the State of Israel) and of a later ethical Sartre. This transition from disempowerment to valorisation of Jewish identity can also be read as going beyond a specifically Sartrean preoccupation to acquire symptomatic status as part of the unfolding negotiation between the European ethical consciousness and its Other, around the focus of violence.

Sartre was strongly drawn to the idea of Jewishness over an extended period of his career; he wrote and spoke a great deal about the Jews and Israel until the end of his life.[6] Two possible, and connected, explanations of this closeness suggest themselves. First, the Jews and Sartre share a problematic sense of their identity. The complex derivation of Jewish identity – language, culture, religion, historical circumstance, genealogy – has challenged definition throughout time; similarly, the question of personal identity is a recurring preoccupation throughout Sartre's life and writing. In his self-characterisation in *Les Mots*, he chooses to represent Poulou, his child subjectivity, as experiencing a sense of exclusion from the norm, a feeling of rootlessness (*Jean sans terre*), the conviction of bearing

5   *Les Mots* (Paris: Gallimard, 1964); trans. by Irene Clephane, *Words* (Harmondsworth: Penguin, 1967).
6   Michel Rybalka gives a thorough survey of these writings in 'Publication and Reception of *Anti-Semite and Jew*', *October*, 87 (1999), 161–82.

an unwanted and unwarranted destiny and an acute sensitivity to the fit between individual self and collective body of society.

Secondly, it is quite possible that Sartre felt drawn to Jewishness, perhaps unconsciously at the outset, because of the parricidal aspect of the anti-semitic characterisation of Jewish identity. The Jews, in the mytho-cultural memory of the West, are the people who have dared successfully to challenge the Law of the Father, something which Sartre, in the textual imaginary of his *œuvre*, repeatedly dreams of achieving. Their alleged killing of Christ can be interpreted as effacing the power of the Father, of the Christian God. In the Sartrean imaginary, a violent act is often the prelude to a new world order, destroying the massive inertness of being-in-itself and opening up a space for being-for-itself. Various enactments of the violent event which humiliates or destroys the father in order to make self-affirmation and freedom possible for the son recur throughout his work.[7] In part because of his own problematic relationship to violence in the context of identity formation, in part because of the horrific predicament of contemporary Jewry at the time he was writing, Sartre's early depiction of the Jew in *Réflexions* cannot allow this parricidal component of the stereotype to be accentuated and he therefore downplays its heroic potential. He is perhaps frightened of his own attraction to violence, as well as being aware of the risks that the Jewish community runs because of its association, in the cultural imaginary of the West, with that self-asserting and foundational act of symbolic violence.

The magisterial monologue of *Les Mots* reminds us that we live in a universe of words. My concern is not, then, to arrive at some unattainable 'truth' about Sartre but to understand better how questions of identity and identification are addressed in his work for the light that this may shed on the relationship of the Western con-

---

7   Sartre's drama, in particular, explores various enactments of the violent confrontation between father and son, God and human subject, which accompanies the attempted emancipation of one consciousness from the controlling power of another consciousness or absolute. See, for example, *Les Mouches/The Flies* (1943); *Les Mains Sales/Dirty Hands* (1948); *Le Diable et le Bon Dieu/The Devil and the Good Lord* (1951); *Les Séquestrés d'Altona/The Condemned* (1960).

sciousness with its Jewish Other. Sartre's theory and fiction signal that, as subjectivity evolves, both masculine and feminine identificatory positions are envisaged as problematic. In *Réflexions* Jewish identity is portrayed as almost entirely reactive and dependent. In his eagerness, laudable in itself, to discredit any essentialising definition of Jewish identity, Sartre ends up denying Jews any possibility of authentic agency, access to effective history or self-determining cultural reality. Obeying the same logic as is implied in the philosophical structure of *L'Etre et le néant*, the Jew in Sartre's analysis makes himself a fascinating object for the gaze of the desiring anti-Semitic subject. He is variously depicted as passive, humiliated, victim, insecure and, more restrictively, as masochistic and even self-destructive.

How is the reader to make sense of this highly subjective, imaginary projection whereby Sartre violates the particular lived reality of individual Jews, robbing them of their freedom and of their responsibility for creating and living out their Jewishness both individually and collectively?[8] The best explanation is that Sartre unthinkingly allows his own unresolved difficulties with identification, later to be shaped into the self-portrait of *Les Mots*, to contaminate his critical portrait of the Jew. Sartre's conception of human relations as mutually sado-masochistic, centred on an intrinsic violence born of conflictual identity, forms the basis on which his more specific reflections on Jewish identity are developed. His interest in Jewishness, which began with the psychological study of the young anti-Semitic Lucien Fleuret in 'L'Enfance d'un chef',[9] was pursued, still relatively uncritically, in the context of his activity as a committed writer, at the time of the Holocaust. *Réflexions* was intended as an essay and never received the degree of elaboration and self-reflexiveness of, for instance, *Les Mots*.

---

8   A partial answer is that Sartre's text was, as he himself acknowledged, hastily drafted without any preliminary reading, 'à partir de rien, à partir de l'anti-sémitisme que je voulais combattre' ('based on nothing, based on anti-semitism, which I wanted to combat') (*Ent*, 74 / *Int*, 103). This cannot, however, adequately account for the disabling image of Jewishness conveyed by the Sartrean portrait.

9   'L'Enfance d'un chef' ('Childhood of a Leader') was published in a collection of stories by Sartre entitled *Le Mur* (Paris: Gallimard, 1939).

At the time Sartre developed his thesis on the subjugated identity of
Jews, therefore, his own identity was still, as will be argued here,
problematically in thrall to both masculine and feminine identificatory
positions.

Réflexions is thus, at one level, a naive and unreflective projection of Sartre's unconscious onto the Jewish predicament. His
psychological state, if we allow ourselves to be seduced by the
virtuoso imaginative logic of *Les Mots*, involves a painful awareness
that he, as child-subject, lacks definition and has no comfortable
identificatory position to call his own. The dynamic of identification
in many of Sartre's psycho-critical studies (on Baudelaire, Flaubert,
Genet, for example) depicts the emerging masculine subjectivity
caught between the Scylla of a castrating father and the Charybdis of a
differently castrating mother whose excessive tenderness threatens the
subject with feminisation. The evolving subject's desire for an effective identity faces an impasse since it lacks any model to imitate:
either path – the masculine or feminine identificatory position – is
blocked by the threat of destruction. Relating this specifically to *Les
Mots* we see, on the one hand, how the petrifying gaze of his
grandfather Karl, as God the Father, paralyses the child Poulou's
initiatives and projects; and, on the other, how the bond between
Poulou and his mother is shown as both threatened by severance (the
cutting of his hair) and complicitous – his mother is relegated to
infantile status within the family.

In this framework both agency and dependency become problematic. To be an autonomous, active self is to occupy the masculine
position as defined by Karl – massive, crushing, authoritative, absolute, beyond the reach of dialogue or negotiation. It also means
being on the side of History (in Karl's case, representative of
bourgeois historical determinism). Conversely, to be dependent – and
this is true of Poulou and his mother – appears equally threatening; it
implies vulnerability, being overwhelmed by the care, the love or the
controlling instinct of the Other. Poulou and his mother, in different
ways, find themselves relegated to the margins of power. According to
Sartre's interpretation of how the individual self negotiates its
insertion into culture in *Les Mots*, identity can only be conceived of
empoweringly if the subject is actively and self-affirmatively engaged

in History viewed as a shared ideological project. Poulou's desperate
search for a destiny conveys the conditioning power of this idea. A
lack of self-definition, or an inability to subscribe to this transcendent
conception of the socio-historical norm, is interpreted as passivity or
dependence. A certain intertextual echo can be heard here: the un-
assailable monotheism of Karl's prejudice re-enacts the stonelike
impermeability of the anti-Semitic consciousness in the opening
section of *Réflexions*. Similarly, the infantilised status of Poulou's
mother, who fails to achieve independence from the authoritarian
familial situation, reiterates the passivity and dependence of the Jew in
the third section. This point will be raised again later in relation to
Sartre's alternative, non-violent, diasporic identity for the West as a
condition of cultural survival.

Karl epitomises transcendence as the combined embodiment of
God, bourgeois ideology and collective History. He has so totally
colonised Poulou's inner world that the latter is alienated from any
sense of self-possession, driven into the exile of his imaginary world.
The anti-Semite in *Réflexions*, a parallel amalgam of Christian dogma,
bourgeois *Weltanschauung* and traditional history, is depicted as
having so poisoned Jewish consciousness by myth and prejudice that
the Jew is banished from his birthright, the right to his own identity as
concrete particularity. In the portrait Sartre paints of the relationship
of anti-Semite and Jew in 1946, achieving authenticity in existentalist
terms is shown to be a virtually unattainable ideal. Sartre here
strangely seems to align himself with Karl: what the logic of the
argument implies, but cannot state openly, is that the only way for
Jews to be authentic is through active, virile engagement with the
hostile situation which European Jewry faces, in other words by
becoming violent. Assert yourself, make a name for yourself in
History even if you have to suffer anti-Semitic violence and die for
your beliefs – this is the same fantasy of martyrdom as underpins *Les
Mots* and just as unliveable in reality. Identity formation, it seems, can
only derive from conflict, yet the subjectivity that is asserted through
violence runs the risk of being destroyed by violence. Thus the text's
explicit stance is that inauthenticity – avoidance of direct conflict,
refusal of violence – is the predominant model of Jewish behaviour.

Jewishness in *Réflexions*, therefore, appears as elusive, lacking historical definition and embeddedness, awaiting transformation through transcendence which would rescue it from an abject position and enable it to achieve integrity or wholeness. In Sartre's imaginary, it is unconsciously fantasised as porous, holed, requiring penetration and transformation by an active principle – the Gentile consciousness, the Socialist revolution, the unfolding of History in the Hegelian scheme of things. Why might this be so? The reason seems to lie in a parallel between this view of a defective Jewish identity and Sartre's notorious representation of the feminine. In several of his psycho-critical biographies Sartre reveals, through analysis of his case studies, how a loving relationship with the (m)other appears as devirilising, a threat which must be resisted.[10] A passage from *L'Etre et le néant*, focusing on the female genitals as a gaping opening which exerts a considerable force of fearful attraction, points to where the threat may lie:

> l'obscénité du sexe féminin est celle de toute chose *béante*; c'est un *appel d'être*, comme d'ailleurs tous les trous; en soi, la femme appelle une chair étrangère qui doive la transformer en plénitude par pénétration et dilution. Et inversement la femme sent sa condition comme un appel, précisément parce qu'elle est 'trouée'.[11]

Perhaps the anxiety which we sense in this confession of what the female other may represent for the male subject – an incomplete being, because full of holes, which threatens the integrity of the perceiver – expresses not only something of Sartre's fear of being engulfed by a voracious vagina but equally something of Western culture's anxiety about the Jew as Other. For both Sartre, in terms of

10   Andrew N. Leak, *The Perverted Consciousness. Sexuality and Sartre* (New York: St Martin's Press, 1989), 52. I am indebted to this study for the psychoanalytic insights which it provides.
11   '[...] the obscenity of the female sex is that of every gaping thing; it is an appeal to being, as indeed are all holes; in herself, woman calls for an alien flesh to transform her into fullness through penetration and dilution. And conversely woman feels her condition as an appeal, precisely because she has holes'. *L'Etre et le néant: essai d'ontologie phénoménologique* (Paris: Galli-mard, 1943), 706.

subjective identity, and Western culture in its self-representation, the violent assimilation or eradication of the other appears to be the only available response.

Jewish identity, as contemporary theory suggests, constitutes a hole in the wholeness, a threat to the integrity of Western self-consciousness, self-control, self-mastery. Jewishness is that perpetual difference that will not be reduced to sameness.[12] The European attempt to assimilate Jewry from the eighteenth century onwards represents precisely a desire to dilute the effect of the foreign body in its midst. By penetrating or absorbing this force which appeals to the Subject to help bring it into being, that same Subject can pacify, control and contain the difference that the Other represents. There is a further, still specifically Sartrean, aspect to this cannibalistic attempt at incorporation but which may also be interpreted in the wider context of the non-Jewish community's fear of the Jew as Other. A note from *Les Carnets de la drôle de guerre* once more focuses on the hole in relation to women, but this time the emphasis is much more on its power to swallow up and assimilate (the term is Sartre's): 'le trou [...] ce symbole des refus pudiques et violés, bouche d'ombre qui engloutit et assimile'.[13] Perhaps the effort of eighteenth- to twentieth-century Europe to incorporate its Jewish communities, whether by assimilation or extermination, translates an unconscious desire to avoid being sucked into the black hole of the Jewish Other and assimilated by it.

Thus Sartre, in 1940s France, is attracted to the plight of the Jews, and will portray them as entirely determined by the surrounding situation because he identifies, unconsciously, with that situation. His own predicament as the product of his bourgeois environment, or so he would have us believe, is similarly a conditioning prison which

---

12   D. and J. Boyarin interpret Christianity, from the Pauline teachings onwards, as an early manifestation of a missionary drive towards sameness. In this context 'the place of difference increasingly becomes the Jewish place' (697).

13   'The hole, this symbol of modest and violated refusals, a dark mouth which swallows up and assimilates'. *Les Carnets de la drôle de guerre, novembre 1939–mars 1940* (Paris: Gallimard, 1983), 190. This volume has been translated by Quintin Hoare: *War Diaries: notebooks from a phoney war: November 1939–March 1940* (London: Verso, 1984).

renders him dependent on the hostile ideological determinism of the bourgeoisie which prevents him operating as a free agent. Yet he feels torn in his response to the plight of European Jewry. As well as a heroic desire to rescue the Jews from the anti-Semitic enemy, he feels threatened by the risk of becoming ensnared in Jewishness.[14] So when Sartre the philosopher hears the appeal of the victimised Jew he must, as a politically committed thinker, respond to this call. Like Pardaillon in Sartre-Poulou's fantasy, he launches himself into the fray as yet unaware of the complex ramifications that lie in wait on the battlefield where Western subjectivity is in conflict with the significant Other of that time, the Jew.

Sartre's *Réflexions* can be read as a gallant if foolhardy attempt to 'boucher le trou', to plug the hole, to penetrate the enigma of what it means to be a Jew. In the writing of this text, he comes up against questions of identification which are too painfully close to his own (though it will be another eight years before he begins, in 1954, to conceptualise his own difficulties by starting to write the text that eventually becomes *Les Mots*). Unable at this stage to resolve these difficulties, he administers a primitive form of justice which explains, in part, his disempowering portrait of the Jew at this stage. A brutal separation from the mother relegated the child-Sartre to vindicating the separate identity to which he was condemned. Although he longs, at some level, for creative intercourse with the maternal or feminine part of his subjectivity – and will spend much of his philosophical career in pursuit of an ethics, of the good, the right relationship with the Other – he must reject the caring, incomplete or porous and vulnerable self as life-threatening. Thus his earlier analysis condemns Jewish identity also to isolation and abandonment, unable to allow that a kind of strength may derive from the non-affirmation of transcendent selfhood, from the refusal of violence, from dispersion to the margins. An ethics that is a way of life is invisible to the Sartre that identifies historical existence as nationalism, ideological hegemony and territorial allegiance. For a better understanding of what

14   This might shed light on the ambiguous nature of Sartre's practical assistance to Jews in trouble during the war. See Pierre Birnbaum, 'Sorry Afterthoughts on *Anti-Semite and Jew*', *October*, 87 (1999), 89–106.

identity, and Jewishness, might mean, in the positive sense of the integration of the masculine and feminine identificatory positions, Sartre has to encounter the Jewish Other in the flesh.[15] This brings us back to the theme of creative violence and ethics in his work mentioned earlier. The encounter with Benny Lévy forces the later Sartre to go beyond the limited perceptions of an earlier self, in establishing the possibility of an integrated ethico-Jewish genealogy for himself and by extension, existentialist to the end, for humanity.[16]

Sartre, in *L'Espoir maintenant*, claims that the gap in his early philosophy was the absence of the Other: 'je cherchais la morale dans une conscience sans réciproque ou sans autre'.[17] He encounters a Jewish son and daughter, Benny Lévy and Arlette Elkaim, and learns more about Jewishness from relationships with living Jews. He concludes his life praising the revolutionary and messianic potential of Judaism as 'la finalité à laquelle tout juif tend plus ou moins consciemment, mais qui doit finalement réunir l'humanité, [...] cette fin au fond sociale aussi bien que religieuse'.[18] Benny Lévy functions as the mirror, a Jewish mirror, in which Sartre encounters the Jewish Other again and in which, this time, he reads the possibility of a new future humanity. Lévy's questioning is tough, uncompromising, a form of violation which shows no respect for reputation, convention, self-protection – almost a revenge on Sartre as object, exposed to self-scrutiny by the unworshipful gaze of the Jewish subject. It forces Sartre to look at himself and his past critically. This encounter with Jews – Claude Lanzmann, Lévy himself, Bianca Lamblin, Arlette Elkaim among others – raises Sartre out of his partial ignorance of

---

15   *Ent*, 38–9/*Int*, 69–71.

16   There has been considerable debate about whether the ideas expressed in the interviews are actually Sartre's or whether Lévy exerted an inappropriate power of suggestion over Sartre. Ronald Aronson's introduction argues convincingly that no one voice is victorious in this dialogue and that Sartre holds onto what matters most to him.

17   'I was looking for ethics in a consciousness that had no reciprocal, no other' (*Ent*, 39/*Int*, 71).

18   'the finality to which every Jew is more or less unconsciously inclined and which must ultimately reunite humanity, [...] this end, which is at bottom social as well as religious' (*Ent*, 77/*Int*, 106).

Jewish culture, bringing him a fuller understanding of the living value of a reciprocal consciousness in contrast to the sad solipsism of *Réflexions* and *Les Mots*.

Sartre interprets his encounter with the Jewish Other, this time round, as fruitful. His own destiny and that of humanity is now inextricably implicated in the destiny of Jewishness. At last, or so he would have us believe, he can envisage a more creative intercourse between the non-Jewish and Jewish components of Western culture. Of course, we are still in the realm of projection, of fantasy, but this time Jewishness as Messianic Judaism is a sought-after ideal, potential ethical inspiration for the non-Jewish world which, by the late twentieth century, has nothing else to fall back on.[19] At stake here is not whether Sartre 'really' adopts a Jewish perspective but the symbolic usefulness to him of Jewishness in his final vision of integration. Ever the actor, he appropriates Jewish identity for his own purposes yet again. The younger Sartre rejected the position of passivity, porous identity and incompleteness characteristic, in his view, of the 'typical' Jew, promoting rather the need to become a tough and transcendent agent of History. Now, made vulnerable by age, betrayed by History, radically dependent on others for his daily living, penetrated by the piercing darts of Lévy's pointed questions, multiply-holed in a metaphoric sense (his theories no longer hold water, as he suggests in his discussion of failure),[20] Sartre can perhaps empathise more readily with what it might mean to occupy the stereotypical Jewish position promoted by his earlier text.[21]

A partial explanation of how this transformation has come about is that Sartre's encounter with his Jewish Other leads him to a different understanding of the debt to the mother. In a section of *L'Espoir maintenant* entitled 'Fils de la mère' ('Children of the Mother') he defines the fundamental social bond as 'un certain rapport

19   *Ent*, 79/*Int*, 108.
20   *Ent*, 22–9/*Int*, 54–61.
21   While the younger Sartre interpreted identification with the Jew as a threat since it appeared to mean 'becoming' a Jew, Sartre at the end of his life is perhaps more able to understand it as 'occupying the place of' the Jew. I am indebted to Leak's analysis of identification for helping me to make this distinction (see Leak, 54).

qui existe entre les hommes et qui est le rapport de fraternité. Qui est le rapport d'être né de la même mère'.[22] One's identity as a Jew is, classically, defined as being born of a Jewish mother: all Jews, in a sense, are born of the same, Jewish, mother. Previously, in the unacknowledged subtext of *Réflexions*, Sartre rejected a viable Jewish identity precisely on the grounds that it seemed inevitably to lead either to conflict with the Gentile identity or to the status of the disempowered (m)other; assimilation (getting rid of Jewishness), he implied at this stage, is the solution to anti-Semitism. Now he comes at assimilation again from another angle: let us all, Gentiles and Jews alike, work towards our assimilation into a shared ethical identity to which we have access as children of the same mother.[23]

In his ultimate vision of a new option for humanism, our redemption is shown to be dependent on the mother, not the father: the ethical future of the West and the world derives from a maternal genealogy. This is no longer the feminine, or Jewishness, as abject, passive, object of the Subject's desire but as origin, agent, symbol of promise. It is messianic in outlook and revolutionary in its means.[24] The characterisations of masculine and feminine identity outlined above have merged in this projected healing of the rift between non-Jewish and Jewish identity. The vision of a parousia which would transcend the schism dividing the two original monotheisms displaces the naivety of the Socialist solution advocated in the conclusion of *Réflexions* onto a still revolutionary but primarily ethical trans-formation of culture, jointly begotten by Judaism and Christianity.

We return now to violence. By 'killing Christ', as the myth claims, the Jews invalidated the name and the power of the Christian God. They paid a heavy price for this, as much of world history till

---

22 'a certain fraternity that obtains amongst us. It's the relationship of being born of the same mother' (*Ent*, 57/*Int*, 86–7).
23 Sartre's discussion of the mother in the interviews points in various directions. On one level, she is a mother without eyes and without a face, purely a womb (*Ent*, 57/*Int*, 87–90). Yet she also confers fraternity, a fundamental human bond, on mankind. Sartre, by thus rejecting the possibility that fraternity might emerge from offspring of the father (*Ent*, 57/*Int*, 86), clearly valorises the ethical potential of the mother.
24 *Ent*, 79/*Int*, 108.

now indicates: that alleged act of violent rebellion has long been one of the ingredients of anti-Semitism. Jews were rarely thereafter, or not until the founding of Israel, allowed openly to rebel and to inscribe the integrity of their Jewish identity in the Symbolic Order of mainstream Western culture.[25] Sartre's disempowerment of Jewish identity in *Réflexions*, or the greater weight which he gives to inauthenticity as a likely choice of response on the part of Jews, may have expressed his own transferred fear of the consequences which rebellion against the norm, violence against the father, incurs on the perpetrator.

Perhaps he sought unconsciously to protect the Jews from bringing yet more punishment down upon their heads from an implacable father. This might explain why there is virtually no mention in his 1940s text of Jewish nationalism, of Zionism, of the Jewish Bund – of any active, organised, self-affirming Jewish solidarity – although these were all historically recognised phenomena as Sartre was writing *Réflexions*. While he openly attacks the anti-Semite in his text, and issues a clear imperative for a change of Western consciousness, he does not convincingly argue the possibility of Jews asserting or defending themselves. The power remains with the non-Jewish Subject to determine whether the Jewish situation will be tenable or untenable in the future. By remaining the underdog, by eschewing any militancy, by accepting all the blows, the Jew might be able to escape the worst of the wrath of the vengeful anti-Semite.[26] This is not unlike Poulou's retreat into the imaginary realm to escape the confrontation with, or rebellion against, Karl's power.

Sartre's final image of the restoration of a pre-schismatic oneness of Jew and non-Jew can be read as the belated empowerment of his own and of Jewish identity. Yet again, he projects his own unfinished business onto a surrogate Jewish identity. In his final attitude towards Jewish messianism and its inspirational value for Western ethics, Sartre's is a doubly emancipatory move. On a personal level, he frees

---

25   See Boyarin and Albert Memmi, *Portrait d'un juif* (Paris: Gallimard, 1962) on
      the non-violent path of Judaism.
26   Sartre remained a supporter of the Jewish and Israeli cause throughout his life.
      Even as Israel was increasingly sucked into nationalistic violence, he attempted
      to maintain a balanced loyalty to Jew and Arab.

himself from the grip of Karl/God the Father by reinstating the power of the mother, thus coming closer to fulfilling his aim as ethical philosopher. On a political level, he at last empowers Jews not only to be actively engaged in History but to take the ethical lead if necessary – but this time in an alliance with non-Jews which should defuse the provocative nature of the challenge which this might pose. Jewish identity, in a dramatic reversal of its portrayal in *Réflexions* as viscous and needing to be beefed up or eradicated, emerges towards the end of the interviews as triumphant, unifying, revolutionary, the one true way.

How has all this become possible? What has changed in Europe, the world, the Jewish situation, and in Sartre himself, to enable this shift? Certainly, external factors encouraged Sartre to arrive at a more mature identity for himself and, similarly, at a more compassionate appreciation of what Jewish identity might be. Full accounts of the Nazi genocide which only emerged in extensive detail after the publication of *Réflexions* forced him to relinquish the fantasy figure of the Jew in favour of a more historically real Jewish predicament.[27] Israel's political path through the second part of the century offered clear, if controversial, proof of Jewishness as will, agency and historical embeddedness. The changing attitude of the liberal democracies to assimilation, under the pressure of the critique of universalist Enlightenment values, increasingly opened the way for 'le droit à la différence'.[28] Above all, it is History, both in its external realisation and in Sartre's understanding of it, which has changed. The apparent failure of left-wing revolution, and disillusionment with his own too narrow, Hegelian-derived view of History as nation, agency, conflict, require him to change his mind about what constitutes History so that the reality of the Jewish past is now included.[29]

By the end of his life Sartre was relatively disabled; the political, historical and social world of the late twentieth century was, in his

---

27   The mention of Lublin alias Madianek in the text shows, however, that knowledge of the death camps was available as he wrote.

28   See Alain Finkielkraut's *Le Juif imaginaire* (Paris: Seuil, 1980) for clear condemnation of assimilation as suicide for the Jews.

29   *Ent*, 74–5/*Int*, 104.

words, 'horrible'. All that remained was hope.[30] More particularly, as
the intensity of the dialogue shows at this point, Sartre's hope for
humanity is that, beyond Marxism, beyond revolutionary violence and
beyond History even, an ethical end or rebirth awaits the world.[31] It is
here that Sartre privileges the Jew's metaphysical existence. He makes
very clear to Lévy that it is the fact that the Jew has a destiny that
interests him. He describes it enviously as a specific destiny characterised by the immediacy of his relationship with God.[32] He is also
attracted by the possibility of resurrection offered by Judaism (and one
cannot help recalling the morbidity of the child-hero of *Les Mots*,
condemned to a premature death at the hands of an alien ideology):
'les morts juifs [...] ressusciteront, reviendront sur terre'.[33]

The Jewish way offers Sartre a last chance to realise his own
destiny as a philosopher whose primordial concern has been to reconcile individual self-realisation with the constraints of the collec-
tivity, to make possible the ethical within history. This project has
driven his thought through a series of modulations, none conclusive
and all brought up short against the challenge of how to channel
violence creatively towards the humanisation of mankind.[34] The ethics
of Judaism, as he sees them, can obviate the need for violence since it
is not a projection into the future but, quite simply, the beginning of
the existence of men who live for each other.[35] The value to Sartre of
his encounter with the Jew is that he has been enabled to appreciate a
different history which, until recently in terms of world historical
developments, could not instigate violence, drew its will to endure
from the strength of the community, from a shared moral contract and
from its scattered and fragmented situation.[36] Sartre's final appreciation of Jewishness comes close to that envisaged in the con-

30   *Ent*, 80–1/*Int*, 109–10.
31   *Ent*, 76–7/*Int*, 105.
32   *Ent*, 75–6/*Int*, 104.
33   'the Jewish dead [...] will return to earth, will be reborn as living beings in this
      new world' (*Ent*, 77/*Int*, 105).
34   Francis Jeanson, 'De l'aliénation morale à l'exigence éthique', *Les Temps
      modernes* 531–33 (oct.–déc. 1990), 890–905.
35   *Ent*, 77/*Int*, 106.
36   *Ent*, 74/*Int*, 104.

temporary dialogue between Jewish and non-Jewish identity. In a recent contribution, Boyarin suggests that the political and ethical future for Judaism and for the wider world lies not in the pursuit of an already anachronistic and self-protective nationalism but in realising the strengths and values of a diasporic identity. Diasporic identity, according to this view, draws on Jewish experience in providing a non-violent, non-racist model for cultural identity insofar as cultures can only continue to exist as a product of mixing.[37] Diasporic identity touches hands with Sartre's integrative ethical vision: all members of the human community can safely be assimilated, in their difference, into its embrace.

37   Boyarin, 720–3.

TOBY GARFITT

Camus between Malraux and Grenier: Violence, Ethics and Art

It is hardly possible to consider French attitudes to violence in the twentieth century without taking account of the contribution of Albert Camus. His major essay *L'Homme révolté* is a study of the origins of organised violence in the form of modern totalitarianism, both fascist and Marxist. His plays *Caligula* and *Les Justes* explore violence on the individual and political levels respectively. In Part Four of *La Peste*, Tarrou denounces the violence of capital punishment at length. In fact all of Camus's work is concerned with violence, as he reflects on the relationship of the individual to history and society, in a post-Nietzschean world in which nihilism has replaced the older certainties, but in which the philosophy of Hegel is increasingly being used to justify forms of collective action that lead to violence. Unlike many of his contemporaries, Camus was not prepared to accept ready-made answers to the big questions. He had to feel his way forward gradually, often using the thought of others to shape his own. Two who helped him to develop his own ideas were André Malraux and Jean Grenier. By looking at the relationship between self and other in *L'Étranger* and in *L'Exil et le royaume*, particularly 'L'Hôte', I hope to show how Camus negotiated his way between the positions of Malraux and Grenier to make the transition from a post-Nietzschean ethical culture of individualism towards a more generous spirit of sacrifice.

Colin Davis sees Camus's *L'Étranger* as the classic example of a text which enacts the murderous (altericidal) relationship between self and other.[1] Against Girard's more positive reading of the murder as

---

1   Colin Davis, 'The Cost of Being Ethical', *Common Knowledge* 9.2, Spring 2003, 241–53. See also the same author's 'Altericide: Camus, Encounters,

'really a secret effort to re-establish contact with humanity',[2] Davis
uses Girard's own theory of mimetic desire to show that it can be seen
as doubly motivated, by emulation of Raymond's hostility towards the
Arab, and by rivalry with the latter (eliminating him in order to claim
his place on the beach). He then goes beyond Girard to claim a third
motivation, namely the desire to escape from meaninglessness and
submit to the order and structure represented by the penal system – an
order which obscures the intolerable knowledge that there is no higher
order, no truth, and that Meursault's act has failed even to achieve his
more limited goals of acceptance and belonging. For Davis, *L'Étranger* 'leads to an ethical and epistemological impasse'; but he builds on
Jill Beer's groundbreaking study of 'L'Hôte'[3] to show how the short
story rewrites the earlier novel, refusing the trap of mimetic desire and
sketching out a proto-Levinasian ethical space in which encounter
with the other is characterised by generosity and hospitality, but also
risk, pain, inevitable failure, rejection, and quite possibly death.[4] This
willing 'exploration of ignorance' is favourably contrasted with 'the
self-righteous claim to say the final word on who is the host and who
the guest, who the friend to be welcomed and who the enemy to be
expelled': a condemnation which applies as much to Girard (pos-
itioning himself as 'the prestigious mediator who possesses and offers
us the key to understanding') as it does to the Camus of *L'Étranger*.[5]

Camus himself was of course well aware of the 'impasse', a term
he used in his correspondence with his mentor Jean Grenier,[6] and also
of the danger of complacent categorisation. As early as 1939, with
reference to the overblown lyricism of *Noces*, he wrote to Grenier: 'je

Readings', *Forum for Modern Language Studies* 33.2, 1997, 129–41, and
Ethical Issues in Twentieth-Century French Fiction: Killing the Other (Basingstoke: Macmillan, 2000).

2   René Girard, 'Camus's Stranger Retried', in *Modern Critical Views: Albert
     Camus*, ed. Harold Bloom (New York: Chelsea House Publishers, 1989), 95.
3   Jill Beer, '*Le Regard*: Face to Face in Albert Camus's "L'Hôte"', *French
     Studies* 56.2, April 2002, 179–92.
4   Davis, 'The Cost of Being Ethical', 250–3.
5   Ibid., 253.
6   See *Correspondance Albert Camus – Jean Grenier 1932–1960*, ed. Marguerite
     Dobrenn (Paris: Gallimard, 1981) (hereafter cited as *Corr*), 89.

n'essaierai plus de conclure' (*Corr*, 34).[7] One result, as in the case of
La Peste, was that, as he put it, 'On commence par disserter sur le
parricide et on en revient à la morale des braves gens. Il n'y a pas de
quoi être fier' (*Corr*, 141).[8] Yet that self-restraint, manifested in
Rieux's 'je ne sais pas', was costly: 'Je suis revenu de bien loin pour
arriver à cet aveu d'ignorance' (*Corr*, 141).[9] And it was self-restraint
that kept Camus in the impasse for so long, when others, such as
Malraux, broke out of it through action.

　　Malraux was a constant reference for Camus as soon as he read
La Condition humaine in 1933. Grenier's volume of essays *Les Iles*
also appeared within a month of *La Condition humaine*, and it was
natural for his pupil to try to situate his own thought in relation to
these two seminal works. In an unpublished article dating from 1934,
Camus began to explore the possibility of reconciling two such different responses to nihilism, one looking to man-centred action, the
other to the Indian metaphysical tradition of contemplation which
found it impossible to ascribe true value to anything other than the
Absolute.[10] As late as 1947 he was still able to note in his *Carnets*: 'Le
monde d'aujourd'hui est un dialogue M[alraux] G[renier]'.[11] His own
decision in 1935 to join the Communist Party – a decision that was
perhaps surprisingly endorsed by Grenier – of course took him closer
to Malraux, but after he left the Party he recognized the wisdom of
Grenier's warnings about totalitarian systems,[12] especially as ex-
pounded in the volume published in 1938 as *Essai sur l'esprit*

7　'I will no longer try to reach conclusions'. The English versions of the
　　quotations from this correspondence are taken from Jan F. Rigaud's translation:
　　A. Camus and J. Grenier, *Correspondence, 1932–1960* (Lincoln: University of
　　Nebraska Press, 2003). All other translations are my own, except where
　　otherwise indicated.

8　'One begins with a discourse on parricide and comes back to the morality of
　　common men. That's nothing to be proud of'.

9　'I came a long way to reach this admission of ignorance'.

10　See Olivier Todd, *Albert Camus, une vie* (Paris: Gallimard, 1996), 69.

11　'The world of today is a dialogue between M[alraux] and G[renier]'. *Carnets
　　(II) janvier 1942–mars 1951* (Paris: Gallimard, 1964), 214.

12　See for instance the footnote in *L'Homme révolté*, in *Essais* (Paris: Gallimard,
　　Bibliothèque de la Pléiade, 1967 printing), 626; and *Corr*, 31.

d'orthodoxie, which included an open letter to Malraux challenging some of the presuppositions of his new novel *L'Espoir*.

In an earlier article on Malraux, Grenier had drawn attention to Sisyphus as the implied model for each successive generation of European reformers since Descartes.[13] In another text of the same period, he rejected the model of Prometheus 'qui incarne l'esprit moderne dans son inlassable élan vers un monde qu'il croit meilleur, à travers une série ininterrompue de catastrophes', in favour of Orpheus, 'qui, les yeux fixés sur l'ordre du ciel, y conforma l'ordre de la terre'.[14] Camus was evidently more taken by the reference to Sisyphus, and as he worked on the 'conséquences logiques d'une philosophie de la non-signification' (*Corr*, 96),[15] it was Sisyphus rather than Prometheus or Orpheus who came to represent the absurd human condition for him.

Le Mythe de Sisyphe stated the philosophical position without giving much indication of how one might proceed in practice. Camus was wary of action for action's sake. In his correspondence with Grenier he recognized the impasse which the intellectual acceptance of the absurd had got him into.[16] 'Remarque sur la révolte' then showed how it might nonetheless be possible, through the instinctive movement of revolt, to establish a value, that of 'l'homme', with its implication of solidarity. Only then would action be justified: and Camus was careful to point out that political action was only one of the 'deux manifestations essentielles de la révolte humaine', the other being artistic creation.[17]

---

13 Grenier, 'Le cas Malraux', *Les Cahiers du Plateau*, 3, Pentecôte 1935, 45–7.

14 Prometheus 'who incarnates the modern spirit in his tireless straining towards a world that he believes to be better, through an uninterrupted series of catastrophes'; Orpheus 'who, with his eyes fixed on the order of heaven, made that of the earth conform to it'. Grenier, *Inspirations méditerranéennes* (Paris: Gallimard, 1961 printing), 109–10.

15 'logical consequences of a philosophy of non-signification'.

16 See *Corr*, 89.

17 'two essential manifestations of human revolt'. Camus, 'Remarque sur la révolte', in *Essais*, 1696.

Maurice Blanchot later accused Camus, in *L'Homme révolté*, of misinterpreting the response of Sisyphus.[18] 'L'homme absurde dit oui', but for Blanchot it is an 'étrange oui',[19] merely a taking-on of the extreme suffering and fragility of the human condition, and not at all (or at least not yet) the first step on the way to an affirmation of value. The philosophical leap to the concept of revolt would then be un-justified. But of course Camus, unlike Blanchot and Grenier, was not operating in a purely philosophical context, and was all too well aware of the realities of war, resistance, the *épuration*, and Stalinism. Nevertheless, he was concerned not to rush into the kind of action associated with some of Malraux's characters, whose nihilistic basis seemed to him to lead directly to violence and indeed murder (though in many cases of course that does not happen). The human value that he asserted was not that of the conquering hero, but rather that of the oppressed, suffering, but still dignified communities that he had des-cribed in his remarkable pre-war journalistic accounts of the situation in Kabylia, published as 'Misère de la Kabylie'.[20]

Political action in the modern world seemed to Camus to lead inevitably to 'le crime logique': it was no longer a question of denying God, but of denying others, and 'c'est alors qu'on tue'.[21] The only solution he could see, after years of wrestling with the question, was for the activist to accept that killing others must require the sacrifice of his own life. He was of course not thinking of religiously-inspired suicide bombers (though the figure of Tchen in *La Condition humaine* must have been in his mind): this is not a self-sacrifice which guar-antees a place in paradise, but rather a supreme statement of the absurd contradiction of the human condition. 'Il tue et meurt pour

---

18   See Maurice Blanchot, 'Réflexions sur l'enfer', *NNRF* [*La Nouvelle Nouvelle Revue française*], 16 (April 1954), 677–86; 'Réflexions sur le nihilisme', *NNRF*, 17 (May 1954), 850–9; 'Tu peux tuer cet Homme', *NNRF*, 18 (June 1954), 1059–69.

19   'the absurd man says yes', 'a strange yes'. Blanchot, 'Réflexions sur le nihilisme', 855. I am grateful to Jill Beer for drawing my attention to the importance of Blanchot's criticisms.

20   See *Actuelles III: Chroniques algériennes*, in *Essais* ('Misère de la Kabylie' is pp.905–38).

21   'logical crime'; 'that is when one kills'. *Essais*, 413–4.

qu'il soit clair que le meurtre est impossible'.[22] The examples Camus
gives are Kaliayev, from his own play *Les Justes*, and Saint-Just. Just
as Sisyphus had to be deemed happy, so these two are said to be
characterised by 'bonheur tranquille' and 'sérénité'.[23]

This sense of calm and indeed happy acceptance of the consequences of murder is of course reminiscent of the end of *L'Étranger*, which is itself indebted to Stendhal's *Le Rouge et le Noir*. (*La
Mort heureuse* is rather a different case, with both the moral and the
social context deliberately removed.) But Julien Sorel had in fact not
committed a murder, and it is highly questionable whether Meursault's killing of the Arab should be seen as murder either, rather than
homicide. What both Julien and Meursault accept, indeed insist upon,
is paying the penalty for an outbreak of violence against another
human being.

This brings us back to Girard, for whom the key social response
to violence is to identify and ritually punish a scapegoat.[24] Davis parts
company with Girard in his article before he comes on to discuss
'L'Hôte', and even in his analysis of *L'Étranger* he is not interested in
the interpretations suggested by his own reading of Girard's *Mensonge romantique et vérité romanesque*, in particular the claim made
there that in great literature, the violence of the mimetic triangle
(defined by Davis thus: 'I desire what the other desires, I desire it
because the other desires it'[25]) is defused because 'desire *according to
self*' is ultimately seen as a viable and more authentic alternative to
'desire *according to the other*'.[26] Davis's emphasis is on the so-called
murder in *L'Étranger*, rather than on any self-knowledge that Meursault may acquire towards the end of the novel, or indeed on his
insistence on giving his life while knowing himself to be innocent. Is
there not a sense in which he is voluntarily taking on the role of
scapegoat which has been allotted to him by society? The religious

---

22   'He kills and then dies to make it clear that murder is impossible'.
23   'tranquil happiness' and 'serenity'. *Essais*, 686.
24   See Girard, *La Violence et le sacré* (Paris: Grasset, 1972), and *Le Bouc émis-
      saire* (Paris: Grasset, 1982).
25   Davis, 'The Cost of Being Ethical', 243.
26   Ibid., 244.

allusion is no doubt obscured by the Stendhalian intertext, but Camus was certainly impressed at this period by specifically Christian ideas of renunciation if not of sacrifice, as is shown by his use in a letter to Grenier in early 1943 of a quotation that purports to be from Newman: 'Admirer les choses de ce monde au moment où nous y renonçons'.[27]

Renunciation is the deliberate waiving of one's rights, to property, relationships, freedom or life itself: indeed all renunciation is a form of dying. The death of Meursault, to which the final page of *L'Étranger* looks forward, is a response both to that of his mother and to that of the Arab. While he is in some measure responsible for both of them, that responsibility arguably does not extend very far. His ultimate forceful appropriation of the role of the scapegoat involves a deliberate renunciation of his rights, including the right to judge his judges. As Camus noted in his *Carnets* at the same period as he was quoting Newman to Grenier, 'Quand on choisit le renoncement malgré la certitude du *Tout est permis*, il en reste tout de même quelque chose, c'est qu'on ne juge plus les autres'.[28] At the same time Meursault's death draws attention to the cycle of mimetic violence that Girard analyses, and the text of the novel lays open the processes at work, very much as Girard sees the New Testament as exposing what he calls the Satanic lie.[29] To that extent, the death of Meursault can be seen as more significant than the death of the Arab. This latter may represent either the violence of the absurd in general rather than any specific personal or social animosities (in which case it should not properly be given the ethically-loaded label of altericide), or the natural conclusion of the encounter with alterity, to which I shall return later, and which, while it may be altericide, is not necessarily murder. I am not denying the importance of the death of the Arab, but I am suggesting that we have tended to over-emphasise it at the expense of the other deaths.

27 'To admire the things of this world at the very moment when we renounce them' (*Corr*, 89). I have been unable to trace the original of the Newman quotation.

28 'When you choose renunciation despite the certainty that *All is permitted*, there is one thing that still remains: you no longer judge others'. *Carnets II*, 89.

29 See Girard, *Je vois Satan tomber comme l'éclair* (Paris: Grasset, 1999), e.g. 74, 80, 195–7.

In an earlier article, Davis had seen the Arab, like the woman in *La Chute*, as also being 'a figure of the reader, whose murder is staged at the centre of the text in order to deny her the possibility of stealing its secrets'.[30] Davis considers that Camus is high-handedly controlling the interpretation of his work. He is by no means alone in this: another recent critic has called the discourse of *L'Homme révolté* totalitarian.[31] I would like to suggest that the deaths that are most significant in *L'Étranger* and 'L'Hôte' are more subversive in their implications, and can open up a space that is both ethical and aesthetic, without going as far as Levinas in his demand for a radical 'ethics of hospitality' in which '[t]he guest may turn out to be a murderer or rapist (and so might the host)'.[32] In this I acknowledge a major debt to both Colin Davis and Jill Beer, whose pioneering analyses have established the possibility of a whole new approach to Camus.

Meursault represents the human condition, both as the unwitting perpetrator of violence and as the condemned prisoner. In his simultaneous affirmation of life and espousal of death he shows up the mimetic cycle and reclaims the dignity of the victim. In *L'Étranger* there is still a colouring of Nietzschean heroism which prevents full identification with the fragile, the downtrodden and the oppressed. By the time of 'L'Hôte', on the other hand, Camus has moved further in that direction. As in the earlier novel, the text is bracketed by two deaths, in this case the killing of the Arab's cousin and the execution of the Arab himself. The threats issued against Daru will not necessarily lead to his death, although that outcome is possible. The death that corresponds most closely to Meursault's is therefore arguably that of the Arab, who is significantly referred to some of the time as the prisoner.[33] He is the one who, like Meursault, is the victim of society's

30   Davis, 'Altericide', 137.
31   John McCann, 'Revolt and the Limits of Freedom' (paper given at the 'Camus and Revolt' conference, Coleraine, September 2002).
32   Davis, 'The Cost of Being Ethical', 251. Davis acknowledges his debt to Mireille Rosello, *Postcolonial Hospitality. The Immigrant as Guest* (Stanford, CA: Stanford University Press, 2001).
33   See for instance *L'Exil et le royaume* (Paris: Livre de poche, 1971 printing), 92 (two occurrences).

need for a scapegoat, and he is the one who voluntarily assumes that role when the opportunity to escape is presented to him.

This interpretation is not entirely new. English Showalter and Michel Grimaud have both already suggested that Camus puts a twist in the tale and to some extent makes the Arab the hero.[34] For Grimaud, 'he becomes a new embodiment of the Noble Savage in his ability to adapt to another, assumedly better culture. The Arab will accept death in the name of the same kind of ideal Daru exemplifies: the brotherhood of two men from different backgrounds living different situations but coming to comparably high moral decisions'.[35] Grimaud speaks of 'poetic justice' and of a 'universalist ethic',[36] but suggests that just as lack of communication is a key theme in *L'Exil et le royaume*, so both Camus and we as readers have failed to communicate adequately the voice of 'those who are made to be invisible exiles in their own kingdom'.[37] Personal morality is all very well, he seems to be saying, but it doesn't get us very far. Although he uses the word 'sacrifice',[38] he is not envisaging the kind of social and ethical context implied by the Levitical system of either sacrifice or atonement by means of a scapegoat.[39]

Grimaud's rehabilitation of the Arab comes at the expense of Daru, who, although the narrator shares his point of view, is 'tacitly but strongly criticised'.[40] I would like to suggest a middle way. Daru is an unusual name. Its form, reminiscent of a past participle (compare Bardamu in Céline's *Voyage au bout de la nuit*), may suggest passivity, the sense of being a victim of circumstances, and as a schoolteacher Daru is certainly part of a system that he cannot control.

34   English Showalter Jr, '*The Guest*: The Reluctant Host, Fate's Hostage', in his *Exiles and Strangers* (Columbus: Ohio State University Press, 1981); Michel Grimaud, 'Humanism and the "White Man's Burden": Camus, Daru, Meursault, and the Arabs', in Adele King (ed.), *Camus's L'Étranger: Fifty Years On* (Basingstoke: Macmillan, 1992), 170–82.

35   Grimaud, 'Humanism and the "White Man's Burden"', 177–8.

36   Ibid., 178, 179.

37   Ibid., 180.

38   Ibid.

39   See Leviticus 16.

40   Grimaud, 177.

But just as importantly, it is a name with a strong Stendhalian resonance. The Daru family, closely related to Stendhal's, plays an important part in the *Vie de Henri Brulard*, and particularly in chapter 29. The key moment in that chapter, and arguably in the whole book, is when 'M. Daru le père' takes the narrator on one side and tells him that his son will give him a job in the War Office. The job itself was tedious, but it gave the young Henri Beyle the independence to start writing, and Pierre Daru would soon take him to Italy in connection with Napoleon's military plans, thus launching Stendhal's lifelong love-affair with Italy. The paragraph mentioning the War Office job is preceded by this striking comment: 'Je vais naître, comme dit Tristram Shandy; et le lecteur va sortir des enfantillages'.[41] In other words, Daru in the *Vie de Henri Brulard* acts as the midwife bringing the writer to birth. In Camus's story, Daru is also a kind of midwife, though not in the way that either his mission as a teacher or his personal liberal humanism at first envisaged. His drawing of the rivers of France evokes not patriotism but hatred, and then despite himself he enables the Arab to choose not to escape but to embrace the role of scapegoat, and in his death to bring about the birth of a new kind of humanity, in a community of suffering. This also of course marks the birth of the work of art in Girard's terms, with the renunciation of the mimetic triangle.[42]

Daru in 'L'Hôte' can equally be seen as a figure of the author, though not superior in that respect to the Arab. He is a mediator, but not a prestigious one. His function is not to impose a particular interpretation but rather to be drawn into sharing the pain (torture, death) of his temporary guest: that's what it means to 'be one of us'.[43]

'L'Hôte' can thus be read in Girardian terms as offering an ethical development of the idea of a basic human value implied at the end of *Le Mythe de Sisyphe* and sketched out more fully in the 'Remarque sur la révolte', without the terrible starkness of a fully

---

41   'I am going to be born, as Tristram Shandy says, and the reader will escape from these puerilities'. Stendhal, *Vie de Henri Brulard*, ed. C. Stryienski (Paris: Émile-Paul Frères, 1923), 264.

42   See Girard, *Mensonge romantique et vérité romanesque* (Paris: Grasset, 1961).

43   The Arab twice says to Daru: 'Viens avec nous': see *L'Exil et le royaume*, 94.

Levinasian position in which the other, while accepted, remains totally other. The shift of emphasis from the educated white settler Daru to the unnamed member of the colonised and oppressed majority takes account of Blanchot's argument that Sisyphus really operates at a much more basic level than Camus's later rebel-figure. At the same time the renunciation of mimetic violence is in line with a long Biblical tradition that goes back to the Deuteronomic rules setting up 'cities of refuge' for those responsible for manslaughter that was not murder.[44] Camus is not suggesting that it is possible to avoid blood-shed totally. In the Sisyphean space which Blanchot evokes so power-fully, death is almost inevitable:

> Quand, dans l'immense vide du désert, nous rencontrons le compagnon équivoque qui tout à coup surgit à nos côtés, tout nous conseille, si nous ne voulons pas périr dans l'illusion fascinante de l'absence, si nous voulons nous dérober au mirage qui nous fait soudain rencontrer le désert sous la figure d'un compagnon, de lui faire subir cette interrogation extrême, nécessairement violente, qui a la mort pour horizon.[45]

But this kind of altericide is not necessarily murder (and the deaths in Camus's stories are not always murder either); and as Blanchot says, the painful moment of encounter is also that which permits the birth of the word, of communication.[46] This is not a triumphalist word, im-posing a system or a judgement, but a fragile and vulnerable one, easily ignored, misrepresented, or stifled. Although the stories of *L'Exil et le royaume* follow a trajectory which leads in each case to silence, they are none the less offered as an invitation to dialogue, just as Camus himself, despite his growing perplexity about the Algerian situation, was willing to engage in dialogue up to a late stage.

---

44   Deuteronomy 21: 1–9.
45   'When, in the immense emptiness of the desert, we encounter the equivocal companion who materialises at our side, everything counsels us, if we do not wish to perish in the fascinating illusion of absence, if we wish to escape the mirage that makes us suddenly encounter the desert in the guise of a com-panion, to subject him to that extreme form of interrogation which is nec-essarily violent and has death as its horizon'. Blanchot, 'Tu peux tuer cet Homme', 1061–2.
46   Ibid., 1062–3.

But as in 'Jonas, ou l'artiste au travail', the artist cannot really expect to be listened to. Camus had learned from Grenier the value of understatement. In the preface he wrote for the 1959 re-edition of *Les Iles*, he commented:

> Rien n'est vraiment dit dans ce livre. Tout y est suggéré avec une force et une délicatesse incomparables. [...] [Grenier] nous parle seulement d'expériences simples et familières dans une langue sans apprêt apparent. Puis, il nous laisse traduire, chacun à notre convenance.[47]

And more than that, if the artist accepts his responsibility, he will himself become a victim, as Camus noted in his *Carnets* towards the end of 1945: 'Si je choisis à la fois contre Dieu et contre l'histoire, je suis le témoin de la liberté pure dont la destinée dans l'histoire est d'être mis à mort'.[48] That fate of course befell Orpheus, and Camus's Sisyphus is perhaps beginning to resemble Grenier's Orpheus. As Camus had written to Grenier a couple of years earlier, when they were discussing the 'impasse' of absurd thought: 'je suis infiniment plus près de ce que vous dites que vous ne l'imaginez'.[49]

Since Camus's untimely death in 1960, his work has all too often been appropriated by those with ideological axes to grind. The famous quarrel with Sartre over *L'Homme révolté* did not help, nor did the erroneous perception that Camus represents American-style liberalism, or alternatively that his novels are colonialist, anti-Arab texts. Algerian writers like Mohammed Dib were fortunately willing to own him as one of theirs, a true 'écrivain algérien',[50] which indicates that

---

47   'Nothing is really said in this book. All is suggested with incomparable force and delicacy. [...] [Grenier] speaks to us only of simple and familiar experiences in a language without affectation. Then he allows us to translate, each at his own convenience'. 'Préface', in Jean Grenier, *Les Iles* (Paris: Gallimard, 1959), 15. Translation by Steve Light in Jean Grenier, *Islands: Lyrical Essays* (Copenhagen and Los Angeles: Green Integer, 2005).

48   'If I choose both against God and against history, I represent pure freedom, whose destiny in history is to be put to death.' *Carnets II*, 155–6.

49   'I am infinitely closer to what you say than you suppose'. *Corr*, 95.

50   Speaking in 1995 at the Centre Culturel Algérien, at an event in honour of Rachid Mimouni: see *Bulletin d'information [de la Société des Études Camusiennes]*, 67, juillet 2003, 49.

Camus's offer of dialogue has been accepted in some possibly un-expected quarters. His ethical itinerary towards a position not a million miles away from the Judaeo-Christian tradition has much to offer the modern world: he remains *actuel*, just as he recognised the continuing *actualité* of Grenier's *Essai sur l'esprit d'orthodoxie*,[51] or that of Roger Martin du Gard, of whom Camus said, as one might say of him, 'Il aidait à vivre'.[52]

51   See *Essais*, 626n.
52   'He helped us to live'. See Jacqueline Lévi-Valensi, 'Préface', in François Chavanes, *Albert Camus: "Il faut vivre maintenant"* (Paris: Cerf, 1990), 6; and *Essais*, 1155.

MAIRÉAD HANRAHAN

Genet and the Cultural Imperialism of Chartres Cathedral[1]

The complex relations between culture, violence and identity are at the heart of Jean Genet's writing in a way paralleled by few other authors. A violent relation to the reader can be considered one of the hallmarks of his writing, ever since the scandalous opening to his first novel in which he described a well-known murderer in religious terms:

> Weidmann vous apparut dans une édition de cinq heures, la tête emmaillotée de bandelettes blanches, religieuse et encore aviateur blessé, tombé dans les seigles, un jour de septembre pareil à celui où fut connu le nom de Notre-Dame-des-Fleurs.[2]

More than in the disconcerting equivalence between a murderer and a nun, the violence lies in the pronoun 'vous' (you). From the outset, Genet's writing introduces a disruption between the narrator and the reader he addresses, marking a hostile difference whose importance the author himself emphasised in a later interview, remembering that he had had to insist on keeping the 'vous' over the 'nous' with which the type-setter wanted to replace it: 'J'ai tenu à ce qu'on conserve "*vous apparut*", parce que je marquais déjà la différence entre vous à qui je parle et le moi qui vous parle'.[3] In this interview, one of the few

---

1   I am grateful to the Irish Research Council for the Humanities and Social Sciences for a Senior Fellowship during which this project was completed.

2   'Weidmann appeared to you in a five o'clock edition, his head swaddled in white bandages, a nun and yet a wounded pilot fallen into the rye one September day like the day when the name of Our Lady of the Flowers became known'. *Notre-Dame-des-Fleurs*, in *Œuvres complètes* (Paris: Gallimard, 1951–), I, 9. All translations from the French are mine.

3   'I insisted on keeping "appeared to you", because I was already emphasising the difference between you to whom I speak and me who speaks to you'.

to probe Genet on his relationship with language, the violence of the act that writing represented for the author is moreover made explicit in the terms he chooses to describe it: 'Il fallait que je m'adresse, dans sa langue justement, au tortionnaire [...], il fallait les agresser dans leur langue'.[4] Writing, then, is a way of attacking his torturers, a *response* to an initial violence; it represents a – violent – assertion of identity in the face of an assault. Genet's description of *Soledad Brother* (the book by the black prisoner George Jackson for which he wrote the preface) as a murder is thus of obvious relevance for his own writing: 'Le livre de George Jackson est un meurtre [...], tout le mal fait à Jackson par l'Amérique blanche, il devait l'exorciser, le laisser stagner en lui, le contenir, et le libérer par un acte de violence extrême: le livre'.[5] Indeed, in one of the few moments where he is willing to theorise about himself, he himself suggests that his 'pulsions de meurtre ont été déviées au profit de pulsions poétiques'.[6] Writing, in Genet's own words, is a deviation, a sublimation of a murderous impulse.

As a reaction to a prior violence, writing invites interpretation in the first instance as an act of vengeance. In the same interview, remembering the intense feeling of exclusion a childhood scene caused him, Genet continues:

> J'étais immédiatement tellement étranger, oh! le mot n'est pas fort, haïr la France, c'est rien, il faudrait plus que haïr, plus que vomir la France, enfin je... et... le fait que l'armée française, ce qu'il y avait de plus prestigieux au monde il y a trente ans, ait capitulé devant les troupes d'un caporal autrichien, eh bien ça m'a ravi. J'étais vengé, mais je sais bien que ce n'est pas moi qui ai mis en œuvre ma vengeance, je ne suis pas l'ouvrier de ma vengeance. [...] Ensuite,

'Entretien avec B. Poirot-Delpech', *L'Ennemi déclaré*, édition établie et annotée par Albert Dichy (Paris: Gallimard, 1991), 231.

4   'I had to address the torturer in his language, precisely, [...] I had to attack them in their language'. Ibid., 229–30.

5   'George Jackson's book is a murder [...], Jackson had to exorcise the evil done to him by white America, let it stagnate in him, contain it, and liberate it by an act of extreme violence: the book'. 'Le Rouge et le Noir', *L'Ennemi déclaré*, 101–3.

6   'murderous impulses were diverted in favour of poetic impulses'. 'Entretien avec Hubert Fichte', *L'Ennemi déclaré*, 160.

comme j'étais sur-satisfait par ce qui s'était accompli, par l'ampleur du châtiment qui avait été donné à la France: [...].[7]

'Enfin je... et... le fait que...': as well as expressing the depth of his emotion, the (extremely atypical) aposiopoesis that shifts the sentence from a personal recollection to the memory of the pleasure Hitler's invasion of France gave him twenty years later indicates an association between the German 'châtiment', punishment, of France and acts of his own agency. This would suggest that for Genet writing is a form of retaliation, which of course means literally a way of repaying an injury *in kind.* Just as the *lex talionis* decrees 'an eye for an eye, a tooth for a tooth', Genet explicitly attributes his writing to the fact that he was assaulted in French. French represents for him not only the language he knows best but specifically 'celle dans laquelle j'ai été condamné. Les tribunaux m'ont condamné en parlant français'.[8]

For Genet (and this remains true right up to *Un Captif amoureux*, his posthumously published last book), writing is thus a hostile act, an attempt to return a hurt. This violence is, however, as much that of self-defence as of vengeance. In what was perhaps Genet's single most controversial text, 'Violence et brutalité', the preface he wrote to a collective book by members of the Red Army Faction whose prepublication on the front page of *Le Monde* caused uproar, he distinguished between violence and brutality, arguing that whereas brutality is repressive violence, 'violence et vie sont à peu près synonymes'.[9] For Genet, in other words, violence is 'vital' in every sense of the word: full of life, but also essential for life, essential to

---

7   'I was instantly so foreign, oh! the word is not too strong, hating France was nothing, I would have to do more than hate, more than vomit up France, well I... and... the fact that the French army, the most prestigious in the world thirty years ago, should have capitulated before the troops of an Austrian corporal, well that delighted me. I was avenged, but I know well that it wasn't I who implemented my revenge, I am not the craftsman of my revenge. [...] Later, when I was thrilled at what had happened, at the extent of the punishment given to France: [...]'. Ibid., 149.

8   'the one in which I was condemned. The courts condemned me in French'. Ibid., 165.

9   'violence and life are roughly synonyms'. 'Violence et brutalité', *L'Ennemi déclaré*, 199.

the existence of something. As he says in another interview, 'c'est dans le fait même de se révolter qu'il y a affirmation d'une existence'.[10] Many years previously, he had asserted in *Miracle de la rose*: 'je n'aime pas les opprimés. J'aime ceux que j'aime, qui sont toujours beaux et quelquefois opprimés mais debout dans la révolte'.[11] Thus from Genet's perspective, in the case of movements such as the American Black Panthers or the Palestinians, violence is not only a justifiable but an admirable affirmation of an identity under attack.

For Genet, then, culture affords a means of asserting a singularity in the face of aggression, of resisting domination. But Genet's texts also offer a reflection on culture, and in particular French culture, *as a form of domination itself.* Not surprisingly, this is perhaps most evident in *Un Captif amoureux*, where Genet is keenly aware of the danger that his text might in effect serve to lessen rather than to increase the visibility of the Palestinian resistance to which his aim is to bear witness. A key moment deals with two young Frenchmen, both named Guy, who had crossed Europe to fight with the *fedduyin*. Today the passage reads like a textbook lesson in postcolonialist criticism. While acknowledging the extent of the sacrifice the Frenchmen were prepared to make (both men died), Genet highlights the fact that their participation did not derive from any real understanding of the Palestinians they were defending (for example, he mocks them for their clichéd representations of Arabs: 'Pendant tout le voyage [...] ils avaient gardé la barbe et la moustache, juvéniles mais déjà fournies, car ils avaient cru venir chez un peuple barbu'[12]). Rather, it represented an extension of French politics:

> Autour de ces trois Français et deux Françaises, les Palestiniens regardaient sans rien dire, ignorant qu'en cette chambre d'Amman ils assistaient à une

10   'it is in the very fact of revolting that one affirms one's existence'. 'Entretien avec Rüdiger Wischenbart et Layla Shahid Barrada', *L'Ennemi déclaré*, 291.
11   'I do not love the oppressed. I love those I love, who are always beautiful and sometimes oppressed but upright in revolt'. *Miracle de la rose*, in *Œuvres complètes*, II, 430.
12   'Throughout the journey [...] they had kept their youthful but already abundant beards and moustaches, for they thought they were coming to a bearded people'. *Un Captif amoureux* (Paris: Gallimard, 1986), 194.

bataille française en territoire d'outre-mer, ou que l'endroit reproduisait une salle de bistrot parisien [...] tant leur exigence était forte de vexer Pompidou.[13]

Even in Jordan, in other words, the two men are addressing other Frenchmen, rather than engaging with their Arab hosts. Genet moreover signals their implicit – and patronising – assumption that they have nothing to gain from an encounter with another culture:

> Guy II m'embrocha par cette phrase prononcée plutôt à la cantonade:
>
> – Pour faire la révolution chez les sous-développés, tu t'es sapé: chemise en soie blanche, écharpe en cachemire.
> Nous échangeâmes encore quelques phrases. Sauf les Palestiniens, tous furent d'avis que je me moquais des révolutionnaires quand je dis qu'au Caire j'avais fait une escale de vingt-quatre heures afin d'aller, au lever du soleil, revoir, roses au-dessus des brouillards du Nil, les Pyramides.
> – Vous êtes passés par Istanbul. Personne n'a été voir Sainte-Sophie?[14]

For these Frenchmen, there is in effect no encounter with another culture: they never even entertain the notion that the category of 'sous-développés' might *also* include some of civilisation's greatest monuments.

One could of course protest here that the men's attitude may be more a product of their class than of their nationality. While Genet regularly invokes a Marxist viewpoint when discussing North-South relations, paradoxically he practically never differentiates between social classes within France. Indeed, one of the interesting aspects of

---

13 'Around these three Frenchmen and two Frenchwomen, the Palestinians looked on without saying anything, not knowing that in that Amman bedroom they were present at a French battle on overseas territory, or that the place was recreating a Parisian bistro [...] so strong was their need to annoy Pompidou'. Ibid., 191–4.

14 'Guy II skewered me with this sentence said for all to hear: "To make revolution with the underdeveloped, you did dress up: a white silk shirt, a cashmere scarf." We exchanged some further sentences. Except for the Palestinians, they all thought that I was mocking the revolutionaries when I said that I had stopped off in Cairo for twenty-four hours to go and see the Pyramids again, rising pink over the mists of the Nile. "You came through Istanbul. Did nobody go to see Santa Sofia?"'. Ibid., 193.

this passage is that it shows how the Frenchmen's homogenising
statements bring out an equally homogenising attitude in Genet:

> – On est tous des frères.
> Je reconnus l'universel don français: on (nous) leur apportions tout, l'art du
> bétonnage, la politesse, la libération de la femme, le rock, l'art de la fugue, la
> fraternité, et dans l'universel don français je me reconnaissais, tenant une place
> infime peut-être, mais mafflue.[15]

The fact that Genet expressly recognises himself in 'l'universel don
français' suggests that he is perfectly aware that he is himself prac-
tising the homogenisation with which he reproaches them. But there
may be another reason for his unenthusiastic inclusion of himself
among the French, as evidenced by the shift from 'on' to 'nous'. This
may derive from a reluctance to elide the difference which he
recognises the *Palestinians* perceive between himself and themselves,
however much closer he may feel to them than to his compatriots.
Elsewhere in the book the narrator reports a conversation in which M.
Mustapha, the father of one of the *feddayin*, addresses him in terms
reminiscent of the opening of *Notre-Dame-des-Fleurs*: 'Pouvait-il [the
Palestinian people] savoir dans les XIVe, XVe, XVIe siècles, toujours
vos siècles puisque vous avez colonisé le Temps après l'Espace, et
puisque vous me dites écrire un livre qui s'adresse aux chrétiens
[...]'.[16] For Mustapha, Genet is one of 'them', that is, one of 'you',
because he is French, or at least Christian, and because – like the two
Guys – he addresses Christians. Both these points are problematised at
other moments in the text: for example, the narrator himself talks of
'*votre* calendrier grégorien'[17] and while he does state that '[i]l est
évident que ces notes s'adressent aux Européens',[18] he also wonders:

15   '"We are all brothers." I recognised the universal French gift: they (we) brought
     them everything, how to make concrete, politeness, women's liberation, rock
     music, the art of fugue, fraternity, and in the universal French gift I recognised
     myself, occupying a perhaps tiny, but plump-cheeked, place'. Ibid., 192.
16   'Could they know in the fourteenth, fifteen, sixteenth centuries, always *your*
     centuries since you colonised Time after Space, and since you tell me you are
     writing a book addressed to the Christians [...]'. Ibid., 376; Genet's italics.
17   '*your* Gregorian calendar'. Ibid., 162; my emphasis.
18   'it is obvious these notes are addressed to Europeans'. Ibid., 201.

'Puisque ce livre ne sera jamais traduit en arabe, jamais lu par les Français ni aucun Européen, puisque cependant sachant cela je l'écris, à qui s'adresse-t-il?'[19] Far from an unequivocal endorsement of Mustapha's opinion, Genet's reproduction of his comment can thus at most be read as an acknowledgement that, *insofar as he is French*, he too is a coloniser. At a broader level, it should also be remembered that Genet's hostility towards his country of origin regularly manifested itself through his dissociating himself from the French. In his first interview, for example, he claimed: 'J'aime manger quand je retourne d'Angleterre. Les deux seules choses qui font que j'appartiens à la nation française sont la langue et la nourriture'.[20] A similar provocative attitude can be discerned in the text he published in *Le Nouvel Observateur* days after the death of George Jackson, where he exceptionally admits to having 'compatriots', although the 'patrie' they would share is founded on literary rather than national allegiances:

> Il faut remettre en question l'appartenance d'un homme au pays où, tout compte fait, fortuitement il est né. George Jackson était l'un des nôtres. [...] Je reprends cette idée: de qui donc George Jackson était-il le compatriote, sinon de nous tous qui avons lu, aimé et admiré son livre, des peuples, – mais des peuples entiers, des pays immenses d'hommes – pour lesquels, du fond de la prison de Soledad, il l'a écrit?[21]

Genet's (rare) use of the first person plural pronoun here – 'l'un des nôtres', 'compatriote [...] de nous tous' – has the effect of including the (French) readers of *Le Nouvel Observateur* in the same nation as

19 'As this book will never be translated into Arabic, never read by the French or any European, as notwithstanding knowing that I am writing it, to whom is it addressed?'. Ibid., 339.

20 'I like eating when I come back from England. The only two things by which I belong to the French nation are the language and the food'. 'Entretien avec Madeleine Gobeil', *L'Ennemi déclaré*, 16.

21 'We need to question a man's belonging to the country in which as a matter of chance, all things considered, he is born. George Jackson was one of us. [...] I return to this idea: George Jackson was the compatriot then of whom if not of all of us who read, loved and admired his book, of the peoples – the entire peoples, huge countries of men – for whom, from the depths of Soledad prison, he wrote it?'. 'L'Amérique a peur', *L'Ennemi déclaré*, 109.

Jackson. Moreover, Genet asserts their approval for a more radical and violent politics than many readers of the magazine probably felt comfortable with, while leaving them no opportunity to mark the sort of difference that he himself insists on.

Genet's attitude towards those he perceives as dominant is thus very different from his attitude towards the dominated. On the one hand, his texts never grant a hearing to figures of domination, on the contrary placing them always in the second person, in the position of addressee, while on the other hand, as we saw with Mustapha, he shows solidarity with – and respect for – the colonised not by agreeing with their point of view but by giving expression to it, including transmitting their perception of him as coloniser.[22]

To return to 'l'universel don français', then, it seems that in *Un Captif amoureux* French culture stands accused of imperialism above all because of its pretention to universality, more than because of particular instances of cultural domination or subordination.[23] Years previously, Genet had very clearly expressed the opinion that if national cultures are always imperialist, France had managed to

22   Similarly, Genet's choice of clothes can be read not as an arrogant gesture but as the opening up of a sartorial difference ultimately less repressive and patronising, because less homogenising, than the Guys' prescription of a revolutionary uniform.

23   In contrast, Genet details specific instances of what he considers to be Israel's cultural dominance over the Palestinians. For example, he describes the response to a Palestinian slogan painted in huge capitals on the Opera in Paris: '[…] à ce PALESTINE VAINCRA, j'eus l'occasion, vingt fois ou plus, aux environs de l'Opéra ou ailleurs, de lire sur les murs gris de Paris, les bombages rapides, discrets, presque timides, de la réplique israélienne: *Israël vivra*. […] La force, immensément plus grande, de cette réponse – et non réplique –, où mieux, à l'affirmation limitée du *vaincra*, l'affirmation presque éternelle du *vivra*. Dans le simple domaine rhétorique Israël, dans la demi-nuit parisienne, par ses bombages furtifs, allait, je l'ai dit, immensément loin' ('to this PALESTINE WILL CONQUER, on the grey walls of Paris around the Opera or elsewhere I twenty or more times had the opportunity of reading the swift, discreet, almost timid graffiti of the Israeli retort: *Israel will live*. The immensely greater power of this response – not a retort – where, better than the limited affirmation of *will conquer*, the nearly eternal affirmation of *will live*. In the field of rhetoric alone, Israel with its furtive graffiti went, as I said, immensely far in the Parisian twilight'). (*Un Captif amoureux*, 91).

colonise culture *per se*: 'Nous savions que nous étions, nous, Français, les maîtres du monde, pas seulement du monde matériel mais de la culture aussi'.[24] For Genet, what distinguishes France from other colonialist nations is that its economic domination goes hand in hand with cultural suprematism, as he later articulates in greater detail to Tahar Ben Jelloun:

> Tous les pays capitalistes, néo-colonialistes ou non, protègent leur main-d'œuvre nationale. Aucun de ces Etats, la France exceptée, ne s'est coiffé d'une auréole le désignant modèle de civilisation. L'Africain qui vient en France pour travailler, pour étudier, pour se promener, on pourrait croire qu'il en partira émerveillé... Nous autres, civilisations, savons maintenant que la civilisation c'est aussi ce projet de lois mis au point contre les hommes les plus pauvres du monde.[25]

Genet thus narrows further to France the association with culture which Valéry had previously attributed to Europe in 'La Crise de l'esprit': 'L'idée de culture, d'intelligence, d'œuvres magistrales est pour nous dans une relation très ancienne – tellement ancienne que nous remontons rarement jusqu'à elle – avec l'idée d'Europe'.[26] But his reworking of the famous opening sentence to Valéry's text indicates a much more hostile attitude towards the position of the earlier writer. 'Nous autres, civilisations, nous savons maintenant que nous sommes mortelles':[27] Valéry's incipit reflects his nostalgia for the era of European cultural hegemony he believed was drawing to a close after World War I. In contrast, Genet's trenchant reformulation

---

24   'We knew that we, the French, were the masters of the world, not only of the material world but of culture also'. 'Entretien avec Madeleine Gobeil', 20.

25   'All capitalist countries, neo-colonialist or not, protect their national labour-force. None of these states, with the exception of France, has put on a halo designating it as a model of civilisation. It is as though one believed that the African who comes to France to work, study, travel, goes away filled with wonder [...] We other civilisations know now that civilisation is also the drafting of laws targeting the poorest men in the world'. 'Entretien avec Tahar Ben Jelloun', *L'Ennemi déclaré*, 209.

26   'The idea of culture, of intelligence, of brilliant works has a very old relationship – so old we rarely go back that far – with the idea of Europe'. Paul Valéry, *Variété* [I] (Paris: Gallimard, 1924), 23–4.

27   'We other civilisations know now that we are mortal'. Ibid., 11.

Mairéad Hanrahan

spells out that the inequality Valéry regretted was a means for the rich
to oppress the poor. Moreover, as we shall now see in the text alluded
to in my title, Genet strongly contests Valéry's notion that 'l'inégalité
si longtemps observée au bénéfice de l'Europe devait *par ses propres
effets* se changer progressivement en inégalité de sens contraire'.[28] In
his analysis, writing fifty years later, French cultural domination, far
from declining in influence, continued unabated, if not unabashed.
Cultural and economic domination remained in effect as firmly
intertwined as ever, although an overtly colonialist discourse had
become unacceptable with the era of decolonisation. The only change
was at the level of discourse: the economic exploitation that goes in
tandem with the obliteration of cultural difference implicit in
'l'universel don français' now hinged on the paradoxical construction
of the other as radically *different*.

    'Cathédrale de Chartres: Vue cavalière' was the first of a series
of short articles published in *L'Humanité* over the summer of 1977
under the title 'Lire le pays' (Reading the country), in which a
hundred and ten authors – including Roland Barthes, Milan Kundera,
Gabriel García Marquez, Françoise Sagan, Georges Simenon, and
Michel Tournier – evoked some place of personal, historical or
geographical significance. As Albert Dichy says in the notes to the
text, the rootless Genet must indeed have been amused at being asked
to inaugurate a series of reflections on 'le pays', a word which in
French can mean region, or homeplace, as well as country. In this
slyly malicious text, Genet chose as his topic one of the greatest
French monuments, Chartres Cathedral, but far from treating it as a
superb example of French culture, he uses it to undermine the very
notion of a 'patrie', of France as the homeland of a uniquely French
identity, and to expose and attack the hegemonic aspirations of French
culture.

    From the outset, the text undermines the notion of a national
identity that would be expressed through its culture. Its form
immediately signals a lack of unity, offering a series of fragments

---

28   'The inequality that for so long was observed to favour Europe had *by its own
      effects* to change progressively into an inequality in the opposite direction'.
      Ibid., 28; Valéry's italics.

whose relation to each other is often not developed. It begins moreover with the deliberate inscription of a difference:

> Deux pôles: Chartres et Nara, pôles d'un axe autour duquel tourne la Terre. Nous tombons sur Chartres presque à l'aveuglette. Chartres la Beauceronne. Les deux sanctuaires sont immédiatement évoqués afin d'ouvrir plus loin une phrase sur le 'droit à la différence'.[29]

Instead of representing Chartres as a unique masterpiece, Genet situates it in relation to the Japanese holy city which is far removed from the French town both spatially and culturally,[30] yet similar in having a founding role of religious and cultural significance. But the last sentence quoted introduces another difference of interest to Genet. The 'droit à la différence' was the slogan of a government campaign in 1977 to revalorise manual work, and introduces precisely the question of the relation – that is the difference – between the cultural and the economic spheres. The main point of the article is that French culture is built on economic exploitation, although Genet is considerably more exercised by the exploitation of the Third World than by that of the French working classes. He insists that the 'joyau national: pis, culturel'[31] that is Chartres Cathedral was not a French creation:

> Les constructeurs de cathédrales étaient des étrangers venus des chantiers de Burgos, de Cologne, de Bruges: maîtres d'œuvre, imagiers, tailleurs de pierre, fondeurs du verre de vitrail, alchimistes des émaux…
> – Nous allons tout à l'heure nous planter devant *L'Arbre de Jessé* – ces étrangers considérables auront donc construit une église qui sera française. Les

---

29 'Two poles: Chartres and Nara, poles of an axis around which the Earth turns. We fall on Chartres nearly blindly. Chartres in the region of Beauce. / Both sanctuaries are immediately evoked in order to open onto a sentence on the "right to difference" further on'. 'Cathédrale de Chartres: Vue cavalière', *L'Ennemi déclaré*, 191.

30 For example, in *Un Captif amoureux* it is during a journey to Japan that Genet feels lifting from him 'la noire et certainement épaisse morale judéo-chrétienne' ('the black and certainly thick Judæo-Christian morality') (65).

31 'national: worse, cultural jewel'. 'Cathédrale de Chartres', 192.

musulmans y furent peut-être pour une part, petite ou grande, Tolède n'étant qu'à quelques semaines de galop.[32]

The sentence 'Nous allons tout à l'heure nous planter devant *L'Arbre de Jessé*' merits particular attention. 'We are going to plant ourselves before an already planted tree': especially in the light of the use of the future anterior ('auront construit') in the following sentence, Genet is clearly suggesting that 'we' – a pronoun that leaves no space for the difference between the French guide who is presumably speaking and those (foreign or French, those who are not 'du pays') s/he is addressing – have used the church to construct a genealogical tree retrospectively. The famous stained-glass window is a French plantation, in the colonial sense of the word; the French have expropriated the creation of the 'étrangers', Christians and Muslims, who are now in the position of tourists being guided around a foreign monument that their ancestors created. The expropriation becomes more explicit when Genet later briefly returns to the window, and likens it to the Vénus de Milo, another cultural icon only 'French' by appropriation:

> À qui appartient *L'Arbre de Jessé*? Pas de doute aux Beaucerons qui l'ont trouvé là au pied du berceau et qui ne l'ont jamais vu.
> Comme les Turcs possèdent la Vénus de Milo.[33]

Note the ironic syntax: 'Pas de doute aux Beaucerons' can be heard both as 'doubtless to the Beaucerons' and as '*not* to the Beaucerons'. The effect is above all to cast doubt on the certainty of those for whom culture is a question of possession rather than of 'affinity':

---

32   'Cathedral builders were foreigners come from the construction sites of Burgos, Cologne, Bruges: project managers, figurine carvers, stone-cutters, stained-glass window workers, enamel alchemists [...] / – Later we shall plant ourselves in front of The Tree of Jesse – these remarkable foreigners thus built a church that would be French. Muslims perhaps played some part, small or great, in it, Toledo being only a few weeks' ride away'. Ibid., 191.

33   'To whom does *The Tree of Jesse* belong? Doubtless to the Beaucerons who found it there at the foot of their cradles and who have never seen it. / Like the Turks possess the Vénus de Milo'. Ibid., 193.

Reprenons le mot démodé d'affinité. [...] Les amoureux de Chartres et de Nara sont autant au Maroc, en Afrique du Sud, en Allemagne, en Grèce, au Japon, en Hollande, si l'on veut dans toutes les nations du monde, qu'en France ou qu'en Beauce.[34]

As this last quotation shows, Genet's reflection on the 'patrie' problematises the relationship between nation and region. In particular, he attacks another current platitude concerning the 'droit à la différence', the notion that each French person has a regional as well as a national identity. He signals explicitly that one is not a simple subset of the other: 'Une nation n'est pas une patrie. [...] Que la France des régions soit un œuf de Pâques en chocolat plein de petits œufs en chocolat, chaque œuf ne sera pas une patrie'.[35] And the reason why a nation is not merely the sum of its parts is because any cultural identity, national or regional, is associated with a process of aggrandisement: 'Chaque région fait déjà des siennes. Ainsi les méridionales qui, tous les matins, astiquent et font reluire *leur* soleil'.[36] The process of appropriation is emphasised not only in that the sun 'belongs' to the Southerners, but also in that the idiomatic expression 'faire des siennes', meaning 'do silly things', literally signifies *make its own*. Far from situating itself differentially, then, as Genet does in relation to Chartres, the region tends to construct an exclusive identity. Genet goes on to play on the signifier 'sol', signifying ground or soil (that is, the upper, or as the French say, superior, part of the earth), but with echoes both of a Southern (Spanish) sun, 'sol', and of money, as in 'sous':

34   'Let us use the old-fashioned word affinity. [...] Those who love Chartres and Nara are as much in Morocco, in South Africa, in Germany, in Greece, in Japan, in Holland, in fact in all the nations of the world, as in France or in Beauce'. Ibid., 192.

35   'A nation is not a homeland. [...] Were the France of regions to be a chocolate Easter egg full of little chocolate eggs, each egg would not be a homeland'. Ibid., 192.

36   'Each region does silly things. Hence the Southern ones who, each morning, polish and shine *their* sun'. Ibid., 194.

Vertus du sol. Bonheur d'être chez soi, sur son sol.
Convoitise du sous-sol: appropriation des sols pour l'exploitation des sous-sols par l'étranger cupide.[37]

Note the ambiguity of the genitive in 'convoitise du sous-sol': while the parallel between its grammatical structure and that of 'vertus du sol' leads us initially to assume that the greed is on the side of the 'sous-sol', the end of the quotation leaves little doubt that it is rather those in the superior position, the 'haves', that are greedy to extend their possessions by exploiting the (subterranean resources of the) 'have-nots'. For Genet, who famously lived in hotels throughout his life, having is always the desire to have more. Thus the regions in a nation no more coexist peacefully than the nations in the world:

Avant-hier le monde. Aujourd'hui la région. Demain l'Europe.
Il semble que nous percevions la respiration d'un être qu'on croyait moins vivant: la sphère idéale se gonfle, tend et se tend vers un gouvernement unique. Elle aspire. Et tout se rétracte, se fragmente, se craquelle en minuscules patries. Elle expire.[38]

---

37   'Virtues of the soil. The happiness of being at home, on one's own soil. / Greed of the basement: appropriation of the soil by the grasping foreigner in order to exploit the undersoil'. *Ibid.*, 194. The play on *sol* and *sous-sol* in relation to regional difference suggests that 'La Crise de l'esprit' may be a significant intertext for 'Cathédrale de Chartres' also, as these signifiers occur precisely in the passage where Valéry describes the 'système d'inégalités' that operated in favour of Europe: 'Considérez un planisphère. Sur ce planisphère, l'ensemble des terres habitables. Cet ensemble se divise en régions, et dans chacune de ces régions, une certaine densité de peuple, une certaine qualité des hommes. A chacune de ces régions correspond aussi une richesse naturelle, – un sol plus ou moins fécond, un sous-sol plus ou moins précieux, un territoire plus ou moins irrigué, plus ou moins facile à équiper pour les transports, etc. / Toutes ces caractéristiques permettent de classer à toute époque les régions dont nous parlons, de telle sorte qu'à toute époque, *l'état de la terre vivante peut être défini par un système d'inégalités entre les régions habitées de sa surface*'. 'La Crise de l'esprit', 24 (Valéry's italics).
38   'The day before yesterday, the world. Today, the region. Tomorrow, Europe. / It seems we perceive the breathing of a being we believed less alive: the ideal sphere swells, tends and extends toward a single government. It breathes in. And everything retracts, fragments, cracks into tiny homelands. It expires'. *Ibid.*, 195.

Clearly at issue here is the relation between the part and the whole. As in English, the word 'sphère' inscribes both a totality (such as the Earth itself, the world) and a part (such as a sphere of influence). Genet here exploits both senses of the verb 'aspire', breathes in, but also has aspirations. Tensions arise precisely insofar as the part has aspirations to be a whole, to be *the* whole. 'La sphère tend et se tend vers un gouvernement unique': in striving for an all-encompassing unity, the sphere 'se tend', gives rise to tensions which ultimately lead to its breaking apart. But note that the sphere cracks into tiny 'patries', rather than its anagram 'parties', parts. In other words, the whole is a conglomeration of parts *all of which want to be wholes*, of parts with expansionist aspirations.

Genet, however, is not particularly interested in the conflict produced by competing regional identities. His concern is the analogous conflict produced at (inter)national level by countries' universalising policies. The fear for those who share Valéry's nostalgia for France's dominant position is that her dominance is logically at risk from the aspirations of other countries similar to the aspirations which led to her dominant position in the first place. Thus the 'droit à la différence': for Genet, this recent policy is only the most recent avatar of the same urge to maximise one's sphere of domination that has characterised French history since the Crusades:

> Pendant des années nous avons pressenti que tous les hommes étaient semblables. Nous feignons de croire aujourd'hui au 'droit à la différence' pour les peuples du 'là-bas'.
> Hier, sous des différences crevant l'œil nous avons découvert le semblable presque insaisissable: aujourd'hui par décret admiratif, nous dissolvons le semblable afin que soit surtout évidente la différence.[39]

The 'décret admiratif' shares the same aims of promoting French power as the 'décret admi[nist]ratif' it ironically displaces. Genet

---

39   'For years we had the premonition that all men were similar. We pretend to believe today in the "right to difference" for peoples "over there". / Yesterday, under blindingly obvious differences we discovered the almost imperceptible similarity: today by admiring decree, we dissolve the similarity so that the difference above all will be evident'. Ibid., 195.

explicitly reads the new-found right-wing interest in preserving difference, whether regional, national or economic, as an attempt to mask the hierarchy produced by a system of domination as a union of equals. It is a sop to the 'peuples du "là-bas"', those at the bottom of the hierarchy, to deflect them from claiming the same advantages as those at the top.

The revalorisation of manual work, then, is a hypocritical ploy to maintain the distinction between it and other, 'higher' forms of work, in particular cultural expression. Genet is at pains to stress the historicity of this distinction, suggesting that a quarryman become sculptor came gradually to look down on the work he used to do, increasingly distanced from it through different 'modes de levage'.[40] He uses another image of height to evoke the way this distinction became naturalised, representing the recent drive to promote French culture throughout the world via the international exhibitions first organised on the initiative of André Malraux, the French Minister of Culture, as the '*lévitation* des œuvres d'art contemporaines et antiques mises sur orbite autour du globe'[41]: their height seems a phenomenon unexplained by material causes. In reality, of course, their height is explained very simply by a material cause: they are in the air because 'prenant l'avion, [ils] volent d'un pays à l'autre'.[42] But, as the author of the *Journal du voleur* is only too well aware, 'voler' means to steal as well as to fly. The globalisation of culture is not neutral: it does not merely reflect an already existing injustice but exacerbates it, given that the countries best-placed to benefit from the commodification that such globalisation entails – notably France – are precisely those who have amassed the most cultural riches in the first place. In other words, culture is yet another weapon with which to attack the Third World, as the military vocabulary in the following quotation implies:

> Et Chartres là-dedans? Et *L'Arbre de Jessé?* Et Nara au Japon? Et les envois culturels, missiles de luxe à l'impact frileux: vraiment c'est peu de chose quand

---

40   'modes of lifting'. Ibid., 192.
41   '*levitation* of contemporary and ancient works of art sent into orbit around the globe'. Ibid., 193; my italics.
42   'taking the plane, [they] fly from one country to another'. Ibid., 193.

nous savons que, malgré 'ça', un Arabe à Paris n'aura vraiment la paix que dans son douar misérable, sa véritable patrie.[43]

By including them in the one sentence, Genet suggests that the French policies of dispatching its culture throughout the world on the one hand, while on the other hand maintaining that Arab immigrants would be better off in the poverty they sought to escape by emigrating, are merely different aspects of the same imperialist strategy.

But if, in Genet's analysis, culture is used as a weapon to extend France's sphere of influence, let me reiterate in conclusion that he too uses culture aggressively. 'Cathédrale de Chartres' indeed offers a 'vue cavalière': a bird's eye view, but also a cavalier view. In particular, I would argue, Genet aims to be cavalier by taking a bird's eye view. He aims to needle his French readers where he believes it will hurt most – in their aspirations to universality – by situating Chartres in relation to Nara, by reminding them that, however successful they may have been in dominating 'une grande partie du monde',[44] their domination must remain partial, that no 'patrie' can ever be more than a 'partie'. Thus, even in this text directly criticising the aggressive use of culture (albeit at the expense of the colonised), his own practice of culture is a hostile one. While manifestly extremely generous at a personal level to those for whom he felt an 'affinity' (to borrow his own word which, as distinct from an identification, does not suggest a reductive assimilation), Genet's writing is adversarial in nature, rooted in a violent impulse addressed to the oppressor from whom at the same time he so forcefully asserts his difference.

43   'And Chartres in all of this? And *The Tree of Jesse*? And Nara in Japan? And cultural dispatches, luxury missiles with a shivering impact: really it is not much when we know that, in spite of "that", an Arab in Paris will really only have peace in his wretched camp, his true homeland'. Ibid., 196.
44   'a large part of the world'. Ibid., 196.

DERVILA COOKE

Violence and the Prison of the Past in Recent Works by Patrick Modiano: *Des inconnues, La Petite Bijou,* 'Éphéméride', and *Accident nocturne*

This essay is concerned with the question of violence, including im-aginings around violence and violent memories, in Modiano's recent work. Modiano's readers are sometimes faced with extremely violent actions, and with narrators who sporadically voice feelings of real anger, and occasionally even carry out violent actions themselves. Moreover, the seething violence of the Holocaust lies just beneath the surface of many of the texts. This discussion will stress that the recent texts show a persistent concern with – and a deep wounding by – the legacy of the war years from the parent generation in France, as well as lingering trauma of a personal nature.

For Modiano, the collective past of the Occupation and Deport-ation years is so much part of his personal psychological make-up that it is often difficult to distinguish between the private and public spheres in his writing. Typically with this writer, allusions (however subtle) to the almost unspeakable brutality of the Holocaust are often mixed with fierce emotion surrounding more personal experiences. The most important of these were his parents' neglect of him as a child and the traumatic loss of his younger brother Rudy, whose death when Patrick was just twelve years old tore cruelly at the already loose fabric of the Modiano family. Pain surrounding the loss of this real brother often blends with indirect pain concerning the deaths of 'brothers' and 'sisters' in the Holocaust (his Jewish kin). Equally, Modiano's sense of neglect at the hands of his parents, who shunted him off to boarding school and avoided discussing their sometimes questionable activities in Occupation Paris, frequently merges with a feeling of neglect by a parent *generation*, whose members distanced themselves from the Occupation past by refusing to talk about the

Vichy era until the late 1960s.[1] We shall see how violent events in the
recent texts link in with feelings of anger at imprisonment in a past
that generates feelings of oppression by memory (and often by lack of
adequate first-hand memory) as well as feelings of problematic
identity. These imprisoning pasts (for there are several) also engender
strong feelings of irrational guilt for being alive when so many others
died or risked death, namely Rudy, the murdered Jews, and even
Modiano's father, who was Jewish and who narrowly escaped deportation.

It may be impossible for Modiano ever fully to put behind him
the past of the war years, the Jewish tragedy, and his own personal
family trauma, given the haunting nature of these issues. In *Livret de
famille* (1977), the epigraph from René Char reads, 'Vivre, c'est
s'obstiner à achever un souvenir'.[2] The French word 'achever', meaning both to complete and to kill, neatly encapsulates Modiano's
ambivalent approach to memory. He wishes to get to the bottom of a
memory that he cannot access (the memory of the war years and his
repressed memories of the trauma of losing Rudy), while also seeking
to be rid of the pain of that past, and in the case of the war years, the
oppressive duty to remember them. As that particular haunting past
precedes his birth, it is dependent on what people and records can
reveal. And while it is a defining element in his identity, it is also
fragmentary, and in part deliberately withheld by others, just as so
much of the truth about collaboration and deportation was long
withheld or misrepresented. On a personal level, Modiano seems to
have worked through in fiction some of the pain experienced in his
family life. However, a considerable amount of that pain still remains,
in particular a clear rage against neglectful or hostile mother-figures, a

---

[1]   This opening up of Occupation memory in the French national psyche was itself
     partly facilitated by Modiano's own *La Place de l'étoile* (Paris: Gallimard,
     1968), which featured an hysterical and deliberately caricatural Jew made
     delusional through the effect of the stereotypical identities imposed on him.

[2]   'Life is about obstinately trying to complete (or to finish off) a memory.'
     Modiano, *Livret de famille* (Paris: Gallimard, 1977, [7]). (All translations are
     mine.) The ambiguity of the term 'achever' was first pointed out in Colin W.
     Nettelbeck and Penelope A. Hueston, *Patrick Modiano: pièces d'identité:
     écrire l'entretemps* (Paris: Minard, Lettres modernes, 1986), 81.

lingering love-hate attachment to father-figures, and residual pain at the loss of a beloved companion (Rudy).

Modiano's father Albert was both physically absent from his son's life and psychologically distant, since he remained, in the main, tantalisingly silent about his activities in the war years. During the Occupation, in order to survive as a Jew in hiding, he participated in the black market, and even appears to have had links with the Gestapo through those activities.[3] Through his self-compromising actions and especially through his marked silence about his wartime experiences, Albert unwittingly fostered a strong attachment in his son to the only hazily understood war years, as well as a problematic relationship with Jewish identity. Modiano appears to feel at once very involved in the recent Jewish past and cut off from it. This is partly due to Albert's refusal to talk about the past and partly to the fact that Patrick, who was born in 1945, narrowly escaped a period of extreme violence on a national and international level. Father-figures are most overtly present in Modiano's early work, where they form extremely problematic role models for their son-representatives, eliciting strong emotions that range from outright hatred to protective tenderness. In the recent works, figures based on Albert are still very present (especially in both 'Éphéméride' and in *Accident nocturne*), but these works contain far less specifically father-directed anger and bitterness than the early texts. Fiction-writing seems to have been cathartic for this author with respect to Albert's dubious wartime past and slip-shod parenting, and the father's death in the late 1970s may also have softened his son's feelings towards him. Furthermore, some of the violence of emotion against parents seems to have been deflected onto mother-figures, as we shall see.

As Albert has been dead for almost thirty years, and as Modiano's mother, Luisa Colpeyn, is still alive at the time of writing, but

---

[3]   On Modiano's father Albert, see Thierry Laurent, *L'Œuvre de Patrick Modiano: une autofiction* (Lyon: Presses universitaires de Lyon, 1997), 79–102; the early chapters of Morris, *Patrick Modiano* (Oxford: Berg, 1996); and Nathalie Rachlin, 'The Modiano Syndrome: 1968–1997', in Martine Guyot-Bender and William VanderWolk (eds), *Paradigms of Memory: The Occupation and Other Hi/Stories in the Novels of Patrick Modiano* (New York: Peter Lang, 1998), 121–36.

very elderly, perhaps close to death, it is not surprising that mother-figures have recently come to the fore. Another part of the explanation is, I contend, Modiano's preoccupation with Jewishness in the immediate wake of his writing of *Dora Bruder*, published in 1997, despite (or indeed because of) the fact that he lacks the matrilinear descent technically required for Jewishness. In *La Petite Bijou* (2001), which focuses on a difficult mother-offspring relationship, there is an association between the mother character and Holocaust-related metaphors, which I see in part as a desire to create a matrilinear Jewish link in fiction.[4] This mother-offspring relationship is rendered even more problematic by the pain caused by Luisa's part-time parenting, and her occasional hostility towards her son.[5] In *Accident nocturne*, the narrator commits an act of violence against a negatively charged mother-figure – an elderly woman, who shares several of the characteristics attributed to Luisa Colpeyn and whom he knees in the stomach (in self-defence as she is clawing at his face). It is, however, fairest to say that, even in the recent works, the mother-figures are always tinged with characteristics also associated with the father (for example with black-market activities or through their association with places beginning with A (for Albert) in *La Petite Bijou*, and, in the case of *Accident nocturne*, through a mannish gait or demeanour). As such, it is more accurate to speak of a recent merging between Albert and Luisa representatives rather than of any clear-cut supplanting by mother-figures.

The early texts are far more explicitly violent than the recent works, and the violence they contain has, in most cases, to do with emotions concerning Albert-like figures. Modiano's début novel, *La Place de l'étoile* (1968), is marked by obsession with the Holocaust and by his early identity crisis as a technically non-Jewish Jew. There, murder and torture figure strongly, and the narrator, Schlemilovitch, commits, or envisages, suicide on at least nine occasions, in delusional

<hr />

4   See also Dervila Cooke, *Present Pasts: Patrick Modiano's (Auto)Biographical Fictions* (Amsterdam/Atlanta: Rodopi, 2005), 145 and 149–53.

5   At least as far back as *Quartier perdu* and *Vestiaire de l'enfance* (1984 and 1989 respectively), neglectful and hostile mothers have generated forceful emotion in the narrators.

fantasies. These seem in the main to stem from reasons of self-hatred, as Schlemilovitch has internalised an anti-Semitic mindset. Violence also manifests itself in willingness to murder, as when the narrator kills a certain Gérard in a particularly revolting fashion with a Gillette razor blade, in order to avenge his father. Violence is also strongly present in the form of torture in *La Ronde de nuit* (1969). In *Les Boulevards de ceinture* (1972) a narrator again commits a murder for the sake of his father, although he repents of his action almost immediately afterwards. In *Villa Triste* (1975) torture and suicide feature in connection with René Meinthe, a persecuted, marginalised figure. Yet a desire to annihilate the father also features, not least through Schlemilovitch's many imagined suicides. These are both a kind of self-abnegation and a type of murder, as Patrick in a sense 'becomes' Albert (whom he 'kills' through the imagined suicides) through identification with a Jewish character confused by anti-Semitic identities imposed upon him from without.

In the later texts, violence is less overt, and less grotesque, but it is still strongly present. Murders still abound, due in part to Modiano's predilection for the detective genre, and the thought of suicide recurs frequently, albeit in a less exhibitionist fashion than in the previous works. Parent-related violence remains an issue, and in some cases (especially in *Des inconnues* and *La Petite Bijou*, the texts most strongly marked by the real-life Jewish deportee Dora Bruder), violence of emotion with regard to particular parents has collective resonances for the whole parent generation. As concerns Rudy, his death continues to echo through all the instances of loss of a loved one. And the Holocaust continues to be evoked, albeit in discreet references that contrast strongly with the earlier more brutal prose. Let us now turn to the recent texts in more detail in order to examine the subtle yet forceful presence of violence there.[6]

Des inconnues (1999) directly follows *Dora Bruder* (1997), Modiano's memorial to the young deportee of the title and to all of the

---

[6]   The editions of these works to which page-numbers in the text refer are as follows: *Des inconnues* (Paris: Gallimard, 1999); *La Petite Bijou* (Paris: Gallimard, 2001); 'Éphéméride', supplement with *Le Monde*, 30 June 2001; *Accident Nocturne* (Paris: Gallimard, 2003).

French Jewish victims of the Holocaust. In *Dora Bruder*, the brutal facts of Jewish persecution are stated simply and clearly, although Modiano stops short of imagining the extreme physical and emotional violence of the camps, focusing on the lead-up to deportation. It is significant that *Des inconnues* is narrated exclusively by female narrators, like the directly subsequent *La Petite Bijou*, in a new step for Modiano, at least as concerns his texts for adults.[7] It would appear that Modiano wished, in these texts, to remain connected with Dora in fiction by using a female narrative voice, and thus to come as close as possible to the psyche of lost young girls beset by feelings of panic, of imprisonment, and the desire to flee.

The collection of three short stories that constitutes *Des inconnues* is in many respects a very muted work. However it does contain an attempted rape and a murder in self-defence in its central text, along with thoughts of suicide on the part of the first narrator, and a preoccupation with the horse slaughterhouses of the rue Brancion in Paris in its third section, all very violent features. Violence and thoughts of violent happenings erupt through the work's poetics of understatement, like the sad, indistinct music with which the second narrator identifies, the 'musique triste, voilée' (83) (literally, sad, 'veiled' music), that appears to need silence so that it can be heard a little.

A sense of imprisonment features particularly strongly in this text, mediated through images of spatial confinement within a city, a country or a dormitory. The first narrator 'escapes' a traumatic past life to an unspecified southern country, but feels imprisoned there too, living like a robot when not caught up in thoughts of the past that constitute more of a burden than a release. The third narrator feels trapped in Paris, and the second narrator feels imprisoned in her school dormitory (reflecting Modiano's own painful experience in boarding schools, to which he was often abandoned by his parents). All of these details reflect the prison of the past – personal and collective – in which Modiano languishes. Yet, on the other hand, there is also a strong *attachment* to the past, especially to father-figures. The

---

[7]   *Catherine Certitude*, a children's book narrated by the eponymous Catherine, was published in 1988.

second narrator is fond of a poem her father used to recite: Verlaine's 'Chanson d'automne', especially the line, 'Je me souviens des jours anciens'.[8] This narrator commits a murder with, significantly, the revolver left to her by her father. Through this murder, an act of self-defence against a would-be rapist, Modiano seems to be gesturing to his paternal Jewish heritage, and to the anger and pain bequeathed to him because of it. Moreover, the bedside reading of the negatively portrayed 'fils de famille' – a bourgeois youth who resembles the would-be rapist in his arrogance and wealth – is *Comme le temps passe* by the anti-Semitic and collaborationist writer Robert Brasillach. In the first story, another real-life collaborationist writer, Jacques Chardonne, is attacked at his book-signing by Guy Vincent. As such, while the second narrator commits her murder in self-defence (and asserts that she does not like weapons), the act can be seen as an attempt at revenge against the violence carried out against the Jewish victims.

For Modiano, oppressive memory seems impossible to annihilate. A boarding school run by a religious order with the death-defying name of 'Lazaristes' features in the first story, prefiguring the death-cheating nickname, 'Trompe-la-Mort', of the mother linked to wartime activities who returns from a supposed death to haunt the narrator in *La Petite Bijou*. Yet, in another sense, as always with Modiano, it is *lack* of memory/knowledge that causes the most obsession and confusion. Guy Vincent, who shares many of Albert Modiano's characteristics (Vincent's 'real' name is Alberto), is an older man with whom the narrator is in love. This father figure keeps her in the dark concerning his activities, and only briefly mentions his wartime youth, during which he was sent to Switzerland as a refugee. As Switzerland is the country of amnesia for Modiano,[9] this may be a metaphor for the silence surrounding Albert's experience as a Jew living with a new identity in Occupation Paris. Just as the first narrator is locked out from Vincent's underground FLN dealings in Switzerland during the

---

[8]   'I remember the old days'. Verlaine's poem expresses nostalgia for an unspecified past.

[9]   See Franck Salaün, 'La Suisse du cœur' in Jules Bedner (ed.), *Patrick Modiano* (Amsterdam and Atlanta: Rodopi, 1993), 15–42.

Algerian War, Modiano is blocked off from adequate information about his father's experiences.

While the first story of *Des inconnues* suggests Jewish connections on the part of Vincent, none of the girls is said to be Jewish and there is little *overt* reference to Jewishness in the three stories overall. It is possible that only readers aware of Modiano's allusive technique will pick up on other references to the Holocaust, for example in the final story, where Modiano uses the constant accompaniment of footsteps of horses being led to the slaughterhouse to mirror the rising existential panic felt by the narrator. This appears to be an echo of the panic and despair with which Modiano empathised in *Dora Bruder*, when he described Dora running away from home in late 1941, only to be deported to Auschwitz a few months later. The suggested link between horse-slaughterhouses and death camps is made more explicit in the subsequent text, *La Petite Bijou*, where the reference is taken up near the start of the text (31) and again towards the end (149), in the description of the condemned circus horse with its yellow harness, the colour of the Jewish stars of David   and the colour of the mother's coat.

Disappearance features strongly in *Des inconnues*. The vanishing of Guy Vincent sets the tone, and in the third story, the narrator's boyfriend René disappears inexplicably, along with the couple's dog. This vanishing occurs first in actual fact, and then later more symbolically through a photograph of the couple with their dog that fails to materialise, much to the distress of the narrator. The episode is of defining importance for her (127); indeed she sees the disappearance of the photograph as a death sentence – 'un arrêt de mort' (125). Readers unaware of Modiano's cultural baggage may be perplexed at the intensity of the narrator's emotion when this photograph is withheld from her (there is a suggestion that it may in fact have been developed but that the salesman pretends that it has been lost). However, seasoned Modiano readers will recognise the reference to loss of proof of the past as an indication of the fragility of memory and its aptness to disappear, or to be deliberately obliterated, especially memory of the Holocaust. The notion of a lost dog – and the presence in the preceding story of a dog named Bobby Bagnard ('bagnard' is a term for a prisoner in a penal colony) – is another echo of the Holocaust, evoking the reference in *La Place de l'étoile* to the slaughter of six million dogs. As so often with Modiano, the dog also reflects the loss in childhood of Rudy, his only faithful companion at that time, and who, as Guy Neumann has pointed out, often appears in the texts in canine form.[10]

La Petite Bijou (2001) is likewise characterised by confusion relating to memory, but emerges as a much more overtly anguished text than its immediate predecessor. Here, murder remains a fantasy for Thérèse, the narrator, but she does make a real attempt at suicide. References to the Holocaust are also more prominent than in *Des inconnues*; indeed *La Petite Bijou* is pervaded by that horrific event. While it is never directly named, nightmarish hallucinations, crowded trains, stars, the colour yellow, echoes of Georges Perec's *W ou le souvenir d'enfance*, feelings of imprisonment, and the desire to flee all reinforce the references.[11] Memory is more overtly problematic in this text than in *Des inconnues*, and questions of memory and lack of memory are at the root of the violent feelings Thérèse has towards her mother. She dreams of murdering her (61, 116) in order to gain revenge for memories of neglect as a child, and also, it seems, due to the anger she feels at never having been properly told about (in a sense, not being able to 'remember') her activities during the war, when the mother was nicknamed 'La Boche' ('the Kraut') because of her seemingly drug-related connections with the Germans. This parent, who lives at the 'cours Albert 1er', staircase A, is, though female, is in part invested with Albert Modiano's ambiguous past. Yet it should be noted that Modiano's own mother who was Flemish – and thus Germanic – was a minor actress like 'la Boche', and did some translation work in Paris for the German cinema company 'Continental' during the war. While this activity cannot, strictly speaking, be deemed collaborationist, it does constitute a link with the murderous Occupying forces.

---

[10]   See Guy Neumann, '"Aux carrefours de la vie": le chien dans les romans de Modiano', *Australian Journal of French Studies*, 36, 2 (May–August 1999), 246–64 for a fascinating discussion of dogs in Modiano's texts.

[11]   On the Perec links, see Cooke, 147–8.

While Thérèse's lack of knowledge of the wartime period of her mother's life certainly angers her, stronger fury is reserved for the likes of the Valadier couple, who at times represent the criminal elements of the parent generation, with their 'visages lisses d'assassins qui demeureraient longtemps impunis faute de preuves' (107).[12] Although the vague black-market activities in which the Valadier couple seem to be involved do not explicitly encompass murder, such powerful wording by Modiano suggests he is extending his anger to those who collaborated in, or indeed initiated, the more damning human crimes of the war years. In this context, the dog to be avenged (the black poodle that the narrator's mother abandons in the woods) is clearly, on one level at least, one of the six million led to the 'dog pounds' in *La Place de l'étoile*, and forgotten by so many, abandoned in the forest of the collective unconscious.

While there is much anger in this text, there is also considerable self-hatred. Thérèse feels like a criminal, echoing other Modiano works, where vague feelings of guilt are frequently mentioned. These guilt-feelings are a complex issue. They seem, in part, to arise from the sense of having escaped annihilation in the Holocaust (had Modiano been born a generation earlier he might well have perished), while always being linked with more personal guilt-feelings concerning his own survival when Rudy died in childhood. Matters are further complicated by Albert Modiano's possible links with the Gestapo, however indirect these may have been. Since Thérèse identifies with her shady parent – here with her mother (partly due to same-sex role-model identification) –, her negative feelings towards this 'double' serve to reinforce her self-loathing.

Part of Thérèse's anger at her mother stems from anger at having to take up the burden of the past when others are content to let it be forgotten. Symbolically, she is the only person willing to pay the debts of this 'dead' parent.[13] Yet 'La Boche', alias 'Trompe-la-Mort', cannot ever really die. And it is arguable that Modiano does not want her

---

[12]   'smooth faces of murderers who would long remain unpunished for lack of evidence'.

[13]   These are presented as financial debts in the form of outstanding rent, but also evoke other unfinished business from the national past.

to. The memory of the shameful elements of France's Occupation past and of the deaths of the Holocaust victims needs to be kept alive. There is, nonetheless, a strong pull in this text towards forgetting the unpalatable past. The appeal of forgetting stems mainly from the fear of stasis in obsession, as though by voluntary self-imprisonment in the past Modiano risks a sort of death by becoming sucked into the frightening 'Café du Néant', which appears in one of Thérèse's hallucinations as a place full of mummified figures (95–6). Indeed, the ending of the book seems to reject an unhealthy obsession with the pain of the past, as Thérèse wakes to a tentatively hopeful fresh start after her suicide attempt. Yet the very existence of so many reminders of that unsavoury collective past (sometimes in capitals in the texts, as with the words LA BOCHE, and the star in ÉTOILE) demonstrates Modiano's concern that it not be forgotten, despite the violence of the emotions it arouses in him.

It should be stressed that the most important instance in *La Petite Bijou* of oscillation between the contrary desires to forget and remember concerns the mother character. Her scar and her yellow coat associate her with some of the Holocaust-related imagery, as though Modiano now wishes to remember the Holocaust through a mother figure, for the reasons of matrilinear linking stated above. Conversely, the fact that Thérèse wishes to kill her may, in part, reflect a desire by Modiano to banish his problematic Jewish connections. However, the text as a whole counteracts this urge, constantly reminding the alert reader of the author's Jewish links. In any case, Modiano has admitted that any question of being free of the past in *La Petite Bijou* is a delusion.[14]

Modiano's brief text 'Éphéméride' was published shortly after *La Petite Bijou*, as a supplement with *Le Monde*, on 30 June 2001. It was subsequently republished (sadly without its original photographs) as a small pamphlet by Mercure de France in 2002, with some typological changes and some additions, mainly concerning expanded

---

[14]   Antoine de Gaudemar, 'Modiano, souvenir écrin', *Libération*, 26 April 2001, pp.i–iii (p.ii). See also 'Le Club Grand Livre du Mois reçoit Patrick Modiano. Interview du 20/04/2001' available at http://www.grandlivredumois.com (accessed 28 June 2004).

memories of the narrator's parents. The tone is of a collection of autobiographical snippets.[15] Autobiography and personal memory are here deliberately mixed with murder story elements, as the text starts with an account of a killing. This crime, which appears to have little real connection with Modiano's life, was committed by a certain 'P.', perhaps another gesture to the author's feelings of survivor guilt. Another of the violent events mentioned in the text is the SS atrocity in France of the 'massacre of Oradour', a particularly horrific mass killing in Oradour-sur-Glane in 1944 by Nazi forces (including some French Alsatian soldiers).[16] Other more subtle references to violence are scattered through the text. The narrator mentions, for example, the noise of the lawnmower in the Carrousel gardens in his childhood days (6). This 'tondeuse' evokes, as in *Chien de printemps*, not only an innocent gardening tool but also the post-war purges. It conjures up the head-shavers (also called 'tondeuses') of the post-war 'Épuration', used to humiliate women who had slept with or helped the Germans, in some cases even if this was against their will.[17] One can even see the military barracks situated in the East of France, to which the narrator's father wishes to send him, as an echo of other more sinister camps in Eastern Europe (4).

As in the other two texts, feelings of imprisonment are strong. After the account of the murder case, the narrator reflects at some length on his feelings of having been 'locked away' in the lycée Henri IV on the place du Panthéon. Again, feelings of imprisonment are directly related to a parent, here to an Albert Modiano-like figure. Albert not only 'locked his son away' in a series of boarding-schools but also, as Modiano sees it, locked him into the past, through his Jewishness, his ambiguous black-market involvement, and his reluctance to speak of events his son so dearly wished to understand. Other imprisoning forces are the above-mentioned feelings of guilt and shame, however irrational or unmerited, that Modiano seems to

[15]   However, it seems to have been commissioned as a short story. See Josyane Savigneau, 'Une conversation avec Modiano', *Le Monde*, 30 June 2001, 32.
[16]   On Oradour, see Jacques Delarue, *Trafics et Crimes sous l'Occupation* (Paris: Fayard, 1968), 407–39.
[17]   See Cooke, 251 and Modiano, *Chien de printemps* (Paris: Seuil, 1993), 83.

feel in relation to the Occupation past, the Jewish tragedy, and to having survived when Rudy died. (One of the texts mentioned as youthful reading material for the narrator contains a direct reference to a prison: *La Colonie pénitentiaire* – Kafka's *In der Strafkolonie* (6).) Indeed, here as so often with Modiano, the personal seems inextricably linked with the collective, so that the reference to Cain the criminal brother not only evokes Modiano's survivor guilt concerning Rudy, but may also refer to the murderous actions of some collaborationist French 'brothers'.

Again, violence is hidden in this text without really being hidden. In this it resembles the mark of the branding iron on Milady's shoulder, with which the narrator says he was obsessed as a child (6). This is the mark which Milady de Winter of Dumas's *Three Musketeers* novels bore, and which could be concealed under clothing yet never obliterated. An English spy responsible for much violent death in the novels, she was branded with the 'fleur de lys', the royal lily of the French ruling classes, a symbol with which brigands and prostitutes were traditionally marked. Modiano may here be hinting at the self-prostitution of collaborationist France.[18]

In the final lines, the narrator speaks of having left 'someone' behind in a former life (a vague 'quelqu'un'). This statement may refer to the loss of Rudy but can also be interpreted as encompassing others who have died, including Albert Modiano and of course the wartime dead, whose lives Modiano has often metaphorically shared through reflection on the war years and through imaginative identification with victims such as Dora Bruder. In this sense, the reference to being branded with a red-hot iron also links the text to the Holocaust references in *La Petite Bijou*, where Thérèse feels 'marquée AU FER ROUGE' (in capitals in the text) by her mother's failure to treat her as a human being (82). In *La Petite Bijou*, the motif of branding is connected to the starfish tattoo on the shoulder of 'la grande Thérèse', and thence, via the imagery of the stars, to the Star of David ignominiously imposed on the Jews by the Nazis and their

---

[18]   The link between collaboration and prostitution is strongly established early on in Modiano's work, for example in *La Ronde de nuit*, with its cast of Gestapo whores.

French helpers, and indeed to the numbers tattooed on deported prisoners.

The title 'Ephéméride' stresses fleetingness, literally referring to the type of calendar with fragile pages that are torn off from day to day. The photographs (mainly by Robert Doisneau) with which the first edition of the text was illustrated serve to emphasise the notion of flimsiness, as well as the passage of time, since what they represent is so clearly in the past. These photographs also bolster the auto-biographical credentials of the text, seeming to represent events from Modiano's childhood and youth. However, they do so only indirectly, featuring anonymous strangers who seem to be carrying out some of the actions described or alluded to in the text. A lonely student dawdles in melancholy fashion by the Seine (his foreignness reflecting Modiano's feelings of not quite belonging in France); a group of children evoking the young Patrick and Rudy play in the Tuileries gardens; a car with passengers waits in the Bois de Boulogne near Modiano's birthplace; a man like one of Albert Modiano's cronies, or Albert himself, sits in a café near the Porte d'Orléans; and the shadow of the Bastille column turns the street below into a sun-dial marking the passage of time. The very fact that these photographs are both of Modiano's life *yet not of it* in any direct understanding emphasises the feelings of indirect memory that haunt the writer.

Accident nocturne, Modiano's latest text at the time of writing, is ostensibly a much more optimistic text than either *Des inconnues* or *La Petite Bijou*, and initially at least, less 'haunted' than any of the texts examined so far.[19] Certainly, the narrator, who, like that of 'Éphéméride' has reverted to a male voice, takes pains to portray himself as a fairly normal type of fellow: 'un type assez banal' (72). And it is true that the scene that figures in the final pages is a rel-atively calm, hopeful one, which sees the narrator ascending a lift with Jacqueline, a woman who, on some levels at least, reminds him of a protective female figure from his past, and with whom there may be the beginnings of a romantic relationship. However, this scene does

---

[19]   I would like to acknowledge the useful discussion at the Modiano conference at the University of Canterbury, Kent (March 2004). It confirmed my views on the unfinished trauma in this text, while also clarifying some issues.

not conclude the timescale of the events narrated. The latest in time of the events in fact occur early on (57–8). At that point, on a date in the very recent past (more than thirty years after his encounter with Jacqueline in the car-accident), the narrator appears to hallucinate the sound of her name in Orly airport and to experience a strong feeling of loss when he is told that all the passengers for 'her' flight have long since boarded. Furthermore, the following pages (57–77) demonstrate that he is still haunted by other episodes in his past, especially by the occasion when his father, in a bout of extreme hostility, delivered him to the police station as if he were a hooligan (65; 76–7).[20] Until three years previously, he was also haunted by his father's involvement in the Gestapo-linked black-market office called the 'bureau Otto' and by the old woman ('la vieille') whom he knees in the stomach.[21] While critics tend to overlook this question of chronology, it is highly significant, since although the general movement of the text as one turns the pages is towards escape from the past, the narrator does not seem to be able to leave some elements of that past behind.[22]

For reasons of space, this discussion of *Accident nocturne* will focus on the extremely violent act of kneeing an old woman in the stomach (64–6). This is a rare, and significant, instance of physical violence in the text, and is portrayed as a 'real' rather than a fantasy event. However, as always with Modiano, it is difficult to distinguish between imagined and 'real' fact, since the narrator displays the Modianesque tendency to dream and hallucinate (the very title of the text may link it to the nocturnal activity of dreaming). The emotion behind this act seems to be mainly personal in nature (in the sense of relating to Modiano's own family), given that 'la vieille' shares many of Luisa Colpeyn's characteristics (at least those attributed to her in the fictions).[23] Yet there is also a level on which 'la vieille' also represents the wartime and collaborationist past, as she is explicitly

[20]   An identical episode is described in detail in *Dora Bruder*, 70–4.
[21]   On the 'bureau Otto', see Delarue, 16–142, 'Les dessous du marché noir'.
[22]   His age can be established from the reference on page 76.
[23]   The narrator attributes most of the blame to his parents for the fact that, as far back as he can remember, he has, metaphorically, always walked with only one shoe (21).

likened to Leni Riefenstahl (63). Riefenstahl was initially a dancer and an actress (like Luisa Colpeyn), and then a celebrated filmmaker. More importantly, she was condemned as a Nazi sympathiser, spending four years in prison after the Nuremberg trials.[24] In the narrator's account, the Riefenstahl look-alike, who is of similar age to Modiano's mother, has a military aura, and gazes at him sternly, as if to make him feel ashamed about something, or to remind him of some crime he might have committed. Again, Modiano seems to be gesturing to feelings of being haunted by the war and by his country's shameful Nazi-linked activities. Typically, his narrator feels an irrational guilt, as though he were taking on the burden of shame for the French (and indeed the German) national psyche, mixed, as always, with personal survivor guilt concerning Rudy.

'La vieille', who claims to be his mother, evokes not only Leni Riefenstahl but also the 'Boche'/ 'Trompe-la-Mort' of *La Petite Bijou*.[25] In *Accident nocturne*, as in *La Petite Bijou*, Modiano is once more portraying a state of haunting by the past of a parent generation, and, as in *La Petite Bijou*, he is using a figure with maternal connotations to do so, partly because Luisa is the only parental representative left. However, it is important to note that the narrator claims that he has not been haunted by 'la vieille' for the past three years. If this is applied to Modiano's own life, it could refer to the writing and publication of *La Petite Bijou*, which, as we have noted, is shot through with Holocaust references. Given that there are very few references to the Holocaust in *Accident nocturne* (although rage

---

[24] Riefenstahl died in September 2003 (the year of publication of *Accident nocturne*) at the age of 101. She is most famous for her formally magnificent documentaries, having been hired by Hitler to produce the famous *Triumph des Willens* (1935), glorifying the Nazi Party rally of 1934, and then, in 1938, a film record of the 1935 Olympic games.

[25] The follow-on from *La Petite Bijou* is clear. Both narrators are lost young people who have repressed painful memories, especially of childhood, are looking for stability, have a little- or never-known mother and an unknown or absent father, and possess small boxes containing barely a few documents pertaining to their identity, and to the little that is known of their past. Both lived at one point in Fossombrone-la-Forêt, and both encounter medical intervention that seems to help them at least some way towards healing.

against a mother figure on a personal level is, if anything, stronger), it seems fair to assume that *La Petite Bijou* may have had some cathartic effect in Modiano, diminishing his haunting by Dora Bruder and the other Jewish deportees.

While the narrator does appear to be successful in banishing the ghost of 'la vieille', he continues to be obsessed with Jacqueline. This highly complex figure is predominantly an object of desire and a reassuring mother-substitute, but is also an imagined companion in distress (in this she is also a Rudy-substitute). Like the narrator, she carries traces of a wound. She is repeatedly mentioned in connection with the narrator's feelings of imprisonment, figuring as a co-prisoner, and as a co-'criminal'. Yet she was, after all, the secretary of the frightening Solière, and the narrator initially presumes her to be his wife (this is one of the aspects that link her to Luisa Colpeyn, since Solière is one of the Albert Modiano representatives in the text).[26] She is also linked to the militaristic 'vieille' through her name of Beau-*sergent*. These apparent contradictions may be a manner in which Modiano can express a remembered Oedipal attraction and longing for a maternal presence, in connection with a mother bound up with the prison of the Occupation past in which he finds himself. The negative aspects with which Jacqueline is associated suggest the problems surrounding any overly positive representation of a mother figure in Modiano's work, given Luisa Colpeyn's relative neglect of him in childhood, and perhaps also due to her German-linked Occupation activities.

There is, nonetheless, a strong desire for peace, harmony and healing in *Accident nocturne*.[27] Generally positive feelings surround

[26]   On the publication of this text, reviewers made much of the fact that the figure of the father seems to be moving further and further away towards the suburbs. In a recent interview (Christine Ferrand, 'Modiano apaisé', *LivresHebdo*, 524, 5 September 2003, 3–7 (p.6)), Modiano agreed with this analysis (he often avoids contradicting interviewers), but many elements suggest that this may be wishful thinking. This narrator is still haunted by dreams of his father at the age of fifty-seven, and Albert Modiano pervades the text in the guise of Solière/Morawski and Bouvière.

[27]   The narrator's accident takes place while he is on his way towards the place de la *Concorde*, and he longs for a harmony he feels once existed (117). There is a

the fortuitous, if physically 'violent', encounter in the car-accident with Jacqueline, who, through her resemblance to the young girl who took care of him as a boy, triggers a set of memories that return what he knows of his childhood to him. Yet despite the wish for healing, considerable fear and darkness remain, along with a suggestion that the narrator, like Modiano himself, will be faced with the eternal recurrence of the past described by Bouvière (66). More than thirty years of efforts to live his life in a fashion as calm and ordered as a French park – no doubt a reference to Modiano's writing style, with its classically French syntax – can be obliterated in a flash, as with the nightmarish encounter with 'la vieille'. While his feelings of guilt have abated somewhat with the banishing of 'la vieille', the narrator's dream of his father delivering him to the police suggests that they may still continue in some form. And when he returns to the rue de la Coutellerie in order to verify his impressions of it, he experiences a feeling of being caught in a time-warp (79). At the time of writing, he ruefully states: 'J'arrive à l'âge où la vie se referme peu à peu sur elle même' (32), as though to emphasise the impossibility of escaping the past.[28]

All of this suggests that the desire by Modiano to be completely rid of his obsession with the past, while strong, may be doomed to failure. However, it would appear that, at least for the moment, Modiano has moved away from the type of panicked oppression by the Holocaust imagery that surfaced in *La Petite Bijou*. The violence in *Accident nocturne* seems to stem largely from anger at personal experiences with Luisa Colpeyn, although, as shown, it is difficult to extricate this from wider resonances with the wartime past. Since the violence that concerns Modiano is held both in the memory of his nation and his family, this affects both his own personal identity and his sense of French cultural identity, dislocating *both* of these matrices. However, it seems that, for the moment, Modiano's grieving for the wartime past is progressively less hysterical, although there is still a desire for commemoration, and even for some imagined revenge in

powerful wish for healing, with many references to doctors, nurses and paramedical matters.

[28]   'I'm at the age when life is gradually closing in on itself'.

fiction. He continues to take the violence of the unpalatable collective past and to diffuse (and perhaps defuse) it in fiction, thereby responding to the demand in the national psyche for emotionally complex yet allusive reflection of the violent past to which France is still, to some extent, in thrall.

ALAN MORRIS

Roman noir, années noires: The French Néo-Polar and the Occupation's Legacy of Violence

> A force de s'intéresser au polar, il est difficilement évitable de s'intéresser enfin aux documents historio-graphiques.
> Jean-Patrick Manchette.[1]
>
> Il y a des moments où l'histoire, on la fabrique.
> Didier Daeninckx.[2]

Writing on 12 April 2001, the film critic Robert Roten asserted that 'violence has been a part of cinema since "The Great Train Robbery" of 1903', and proceeded to note that it had played an increasing role in that medium since 1960.[3] Few film-goers of long standing would contest these observations, especially where the *noir* genre is concerned. Roman Polanski's *Chinatown* (1974), Quentin Tarantino's *Reservoir Dogs* (1992) and *Pulp Fiction* (1994) are just some indicative examples of the well-known movies in which brutality features strongly, and is presented more graphically than was the case in earlier decades. Although the public might be less aware of it, a similar development has taken place in the *roman noir*, the form with

---

1   'When you are interested in the *roman noir*, it is ultimately hard to avoid taking an interest in historiographical material'. Jean-Patrick Manchette, *Chroniques* (Paris: Payot & Rivages, 1996; repr. 2003), 224. All translations into English are my own. Unless otherwise stated, the place of publication of all books cited is Paris. I gratefully record my indebtedness to David Gascoigne, whose perceptive suggestions have proved invaluable.

2   'There are times when history is fabricated'. Didier Daeninckx, *Éthique en toc* (Baleine, 2000; repr. E.J.L., 2002), 15.

3   Robert Roten, 'Laramie Movie Scope: An Essay on Violence in Cinema', <http://www.lariat.org/AtTheMovies/essays/violenceinfilm.html> [accessed on 28 June 2006] (paragraphs 1 and 2 of 15).

which *film noir* is widely acknowledged to exist in symbiosis.[4] Over the last thirty years or so, the extreme and explicit violence that is central to the genre has undergone a notable step-change.

Against the background of this broader international trend, the present essay will spotlight the situation in France, and seek to examine French *noir*'s depiction of a specific kind of barbarity, that associated with the 'Dark Years' of 1940–1945. In particular, attention will be focused on two leading contemporary *polardiers*, Thierry Jonquet and Didier Daeninckx. Consideration of these major figures, and the ways in which they portray the war, will suggest some wider conclusions on how the heritage of violence from the Occupation is evoked by *polar* writers, especially since 1968, why it continues to fascinate them, and how this reflects on issues of French culture and identity.[5]

The first of the two authors chosen for study, Thierry Jonquet, has written two novels which hinge on reference back to the *années noires* (or 'dark years') of the early 1940s. His initial re-creation of the period came in 1982, when he published *Du passé faisons table rase*,[6] a story of deception and murder centring on the career of politician René Castel. The character is well named. Now Secretary-General of an unspecified political party, he is clearly its bastion, its *castel*, but he is also *rené*, reborn, because his wartime collaboration has been expunged from the records – for the greater good of *le Parti*.

---

4   See e.g. Margaret Atack, *May 68 in French Fiction and Film* (Oxford: Oxford University Press, 1999), 126–7.

5   Since this essay was first conceived, Claire Gorrara has published *The 'Roman Noir' in Post-War French Culture* (Oxford: Oxford University Press, 2003). As its title suggests, this work provides a broader-based account of French noir's cultural significance. It also provides further detail on some of the issues raised below, particularly those relating to two of the texts mentioned, Didier Daeninckx's *Meurtres pour mémoire* and Léo Malet's *120, rue de la Gare*, both of which have individual chapters devoted to them.

6   Thierry Jonquet, *Du passé faisons table rase* (Albin Michel, 1982; repr. Arles: Actes Sud, 1998). The title of this work (translation: 'Let us sweep away the past') is a quotation from the *Internationale*, anthem of international socialism. Used ironically, as will shortly become clear, it exemplifies the *polar*'s liking for humorous cultural allusions.

As Jonquet conducts his masterful exposé of Castel and his organisation, the picture of the Occupation that he paints is an intensely negative one. There is, it is true, recognition of the honour, courage and personal sacrifices of Resisters, such as Jean Coulvin, a survivor of Buchenwald, Maurice Leguilvec, the valiant leader of a local resistance group, and Jean Perduis, a victim of the Gestapo's torturers. However, these positive aspects are more than offset by the sheer weight of darker elements. The text recalls the many letters sent by French citizens to the Germans denouncing friends and neighbours, and the massive round-up of Jews in Paris in July 1942. The Nazi death camps loom menacingly throughout, not just Buchenwald, with its crematory furnaces and its Communist prisoners 'pendus, […] un croc de boucher planté dans la gorge',[7] but also Sachsenhausen and its 'prisonniers squelettiques'.[8] Furthermore, much is made of the rough justice, or travesty of justice, of the post-Liberation period: 'C'était l'époque des femmes tondues et des procès sommaires, dissimulant parfois de sombres règlements de compte',[9] a time whose general problem is perfectly summarised by Delouvert: 'Quarante mille résistants, quarante millions de pétainistes; si les résistants jugent les pétainistes, on n'en sortira jamais'.[10] Above all, at the heart of the narrative, the spotlight falls on the abominable actions of Castel himself.

Starting with a job at a French airfield requisitioned by the Luftwaffe, repairing 'des Focke-Wulf, qui tentaient d'anéantir la

7   'hanging, […] with meat hooks stuck in their throats'. Ibid., 119.
8   'skeleton-like prisoners'. Ibid., 222.
9   'It was a time of women with shaved heads and of summary trials, which sometimes masked the sordid settling of scores'. Ibid., 103. Cf. also 159, 163.
10   'Forty thousand Resisters, forty million Pétainists; if the Resisters put the Pétainists on trial, we'll never see the end of it'. Ibid., 119. The reference to forty million Pétainists here may indicate Jonquet's knowledge of the work of historian Henri Amouroux, the second book in whose *La Grande Histoire des Français sous l'Occupation*, 10 vols (Laffont, 1976–1993) is entitled *Quarante millions de Pétainistes: Juin 1940–Juin 1941*, and was published in 1977, five years before *Du passé faisons table rase*. This apparent reliance on existing documentary material is an issue which will be taken up later.

résistance des pilotes de la RAF',[11] Castel is shown to slide down the slippery slope to ever-greater infamy. His next move is to go to work in Germany, as a paid volunteer in a Messerschmitt factory, and although he chooses to abscond while on leave in France, his conduct hardly changes for the better. He quickly meets up with a certain Jubienet, and helps him in his unscrupulous private enterprise: 'marché noir en tous genres, victuailles, faux tickets de rations et, pour se couvrir, de temps en temps, ravitaillement des maquis'.[12] Even after the Liberation, Castel continues to trade profitably on the black market, and it matters not one iota that 'des milliers et milliers de gens en ont fait autant',[13] because by this stage the future Secretary-General of the Party has already compromised himself far more profoundly. Before hostilities end, he is caught by the Germans and denounces Jean Perduis as a *résistant* to the Gestapo, a betrayal that leads to Perduis's horrendous torture, to the dismantling of part of his network, and to the arrest and deportation of a Jewish family, only one member of which will survive. These brief details in themselves suffice to convey the impact of *Du passé faisons table rase*. Potent as they are, however, Jonquet increases still further their power to disturb by adding one final twist, allowing his readers easily to discern that his fiction is based on a real-life (and, at the time of writing, contemporary) political controversy: the scandal which blew up around the wartime activities of Georges Marchais, Secretary-General of the French Communist Party.[14]

---

11   'Focke-Wulfs, which were trying to crush the RAF pilots' resistance'. *Du passé faisons table rase*, 72.
12   'black market dealings of all sorts, food, fake ration cards and, to cover his back, from time to time, supplying groups of maquisards'. Ibid., 213.
13   'thousands and thousands of people did the same'. Ibid., 112.
14   On the similarities between René Castel's past and that of Georges Marchais, see e.g. Jacques Duquesne and others, 'Marchais: les énigmes', *Le Point*, 23 February–1 March 1981, 38–43. That Jonquet intends his readers to spot the party to which he is alluding is evident from his decision to name a character Robert Dia – via the French expression *à hue et à dia* (= [to pull] in opposite directions), the name evokes Robert Hue, Georges Marchais's eventual successor at the head of the Parti Communiste Français.

Jonquet's second major novel to deal with the war years is *Les Orpailleurs*, published in 1993.[15] Starting in modern-day Paris, where the police are searching for a savage serial killer who distinctively cuts off his female victims' right hands, the narrative eventually goes back in time, via a doom-laden ring which the dead women have worn, to the more distant origins of the crimes – the death camps of World War II and the so-called 'Final Solution'. As might be expected, the anti-Semitic policy of the French authorities during the Occupation and their role in the Holocaust are underlined. After one wartime house visit to arrest the Jewish occupants, it is troublingly reported that 'les flics avaient tout piqué',[16] while the description of another swoop is more explicitly damning: 'En 1944, au mois de mai, les auxiliaires français de la Gestapo sont venus rafler toute la famille. Direction Drancy, puis Auschwitz'.[17] Indeed, this selfsame shameful complicity is presented as a mainspring of one of the main characters, the investigating magistrate Nadia Lintz, who confesses to the guilty secret behind her own family's riches: 'Mon père […] a tout volé… Oh, lui-même, il n'a jamais frappé personne! Il travaillait en collaboration avec la milice, la Gestapo, et leur versait une commission'.[18] The closing sentence of the book, 'Nadia pleurait, seule sur la rampe, la rampe de Birkenau',[19] emphatically epitomises her own sense of involvement in the genocide. It also serves to place particular weight on the final word, *Birkenau*, and thereby provide a telling

---

15   Thierry Jonquet, *Les Orpailleurs* (Gallimard, 1993; repr. Folio policier, 1998). Although this text is rightly said to be Jonquet's second to focus on the war years, the intervening *Comédia* (Payot, 1988), a cold-war spy novel, does mention the Nazi concentration camps as part of its broad historico-cultural sweep. Moreover, his later novel *Moloch* (Gallimard, 1998; repr. Folio policier, 2001) will reutilise the main characters from *Les Orpailleurs*, and consequently reiterate, briefly, many of the disturbing details mentioned in the paragraphs below.

16   'the cops had nicked everything'. *Les Orpailleurs*, 394.

17   'In 1944, in May, the Gestapo's French auxiliaries came to round up the whole family. For dispatch to Drancy, then Auschwitz'. Ibid., 372–3.

18   'My father […] stole everything […] Oh, he never hit anyone himself! He worked in conjunction with the militia and the Gestapo, and paid them commission'. Ibid., 373.

19   'Nadia was crying, alone on the ramp, the ramp at Birkenau'. Ibid., 400.

conclusion, underscoring the key to the present-day murders – the Polish death camps – and indicating the link between the geographical return to Auschwitz and the investigative temporal journey back to its gas chambers.

It is, significantly, precisely from this conflation of past and present that *Les Orpailleurs* draws its intriguing title, a title whose import is made clear as the end of the work approaches: 'Vous voyez ces champs, ces vergers?' Sosnowski asks, contemplating the now much-changed site of the wartime genocide and its inhabitants:

> C'est rassurant, n'est-ce pas? Et bien chassez cette image de votre tête, mon vieux! Vous vous trouvez dans le plus grand cimetière du monde! Il n'y a pas une seule motte de terre, pas une seule, vous entendez, qui ne renferme des cendres humaines! Des millions, des millions de cadavres... brûlés, enterrés sous cette herbe si tendre! [...] Et ces gens-là vivent ici, dans ce... ce charnier! Heureux! Tranquilles! [...] Ah, ils l'ont retournée, cette foutue terre! Et ils n'ont pas trouvé que des os! [...] Dieu sait sur combien de kilos d'or ils ont pu mettre la main! Vous savez, les dents... et puis les bijoux, les diamants, enfouis dans la glaise. Ils chargeaient la terre dans des sacs et la tamisaient dans les éviers de leurs cuisines.
> – Exactement comme des orpailleurs! murmura Rovère, consterné.
> – Dégueulasse, hein? Ces salauds ont trouvé un Eldorado à leur mesure. [...] C'est un secret tellement honteux... personne n'en parle![20]

20   'You see these fields, these orchards? They're reassuring, aren't they? Well get this image out of your head, my friend! You're in the biggest cemetery in the world! There's not one clod of earth, not a single one, do you hear, which doesn't contain human ashes! Millions, millions of bodies... burned, buried beneath this fresh young grass! [...] And those people live here, in this... this charnel house! Happily! Peacefully! [...] Oh how they've turned this bloody earth over! And they've not just found bones! [...] God knows how many kilos of gold they've managed to get their hands on! You know, teeth... and then jewels, diamonds, buried in the ground. By loading the soil into sacks and sifting it in their kitchen sinks.
– Just like gold panners! murmured Rovère, filled with consternation.
– It's sick, isn't it? The bastards have found an El Dorado in their own image. [...] It's such a shameful secret... nobody mentions it!' Ibid., 388–9.
Disturbingly, Jonquet has revealed that these details are based on facts – see Jonquet, 'Voilà comment ça s'est passé...', *Les Temps Modernes*, 595 (August–October 1997), 146–56 (p.154).

This perceived taboo was, of course, more than sufficient cause for Jonquet – true noir writer that he is – to take a tremendous interest in the topic and to construct a fiction around it, imagining what might happen if a ring were discovered, and later recognised as that of a loved one long since lost in the Holocaust.

Like Thierry Jonquet, Didier Daeninckx also regularly seeks his inspiration in real life, and especially in recent French history. Pithily described as 'le Michelet de la *Série noire*',[21] he has the same aim and outlook as one of his characters in *Nazis dans le métro*: 'Il tente de retrouver le fil d'une mémoire que beaucoup trop d'entre nous ont perdu'.[22] From the Paris Commune to World War I, from the Front Populaire to the Algerian War, Daeninckx's gaze travels backwards and forwards over the past, and one of the key staging posts on this journey is the period of the Occupation, as demonstrated by two of his best-known novels, both published in the 1980s: *Meurtres pour mémoire* and *La Mort n'oublie personne*.[23]

Taken together, these two texts exhibit a number of notable similarities. Firstly, they both explore the interaction of past and present, official history and personal memory, by intertwining the 1980s, the 1960s and the 1940s; secondly, they both foreground father-son relationships, with the respective sons dying violently because of the actions of their fathers; and thirdly, and of more direct relevance in the present context, they both, like Jonquet's *Du passé faisons table rase* and *Les Orpailleurs*, depict the war as the seat of

21   'the Michelet of the *Série noire*' (an unidentified critic in *Le Matin*, quoted in Charles Forsdick, '"Direction les oubliettes de l'histoire": witnessing the past in the contemporary French *polar*', *French Cultural Studies*, 12 (2001), 333–50 (p.341).

22   'He tries to rediscover the recollective thread that far too many of us have lost' (Didier Daeninckx, *Nazis dans le métro* (Baleine, 1996; repr. E.J.L., 1998), 91). Like Jonquet's *Du passé faisons table rase*, Daeninckx's title involves a humorous cultural allusion, this time to Raymond Queneau's famously irreverent novel, *Zazie dans le métro* (Gallimard, 1959).

23   Didier Daeninckx, *Meurtres pour mémoire* (Gallimard, 1983; repr. Folio policier, 1998) and *La Mort n'oublie personne* (Denoël, 1989; repr. Gallimard, Folio policier, 1999).

problems so severe and so enduring that they can only be addressed by the recourse to murder decades later.

Meurtres pour mémoire and *La Mort n'oublie personne* are not, however, the only works by Daeninckx to recall the early 1940s. Since their publication, the author has regularly returned to the period, recalling provocative facts in his own inimitable style. Often, admittedly, his references are brief, but they never fail to make a point. Nor do they fail to complement earlier comments, so that when his writings are considered in their entirety, the picture that emerges is a consistent one.

One of the vital elements of this picture is, quite naturally, the Resistance, and it is clear that Daeninckx, like Jonquet, sees much that is positive here. In *La Mort n'oublie personne*, he clearly recognises the qualities of the very best freedom fighters, as personified by Jean Ricouart. Jean is 'un gars courageux, pas un résistant en peau de lapin',[24] a man who is atrociously tortured by means of 'un casque composé d'une dizaine de morceaux de fer, une sorte de heaume ajouré hérissé de boulons',[25] and eventually deported to Germany. Yet he is a man who, after the war, manifests a laudable dignity and humility in comments such as: 'Je n'ai rien fait d'exceptionnel... Ni plus ni moins que les copains'.[26] Elsewhere in the novel, and in subsequent texts as well, the experiences of other Resisters promote afresh this selfsame view – that of a Resistance characterised, at its leading edge, by courage in the face of danger and uncomplaining self-sacrifice.[27]

24   'a courageous bloke, not a mouse in Resister's clothing' (*La Mort n'oublie personne*, 45).

25   'a headpiece composed of about ten bits of iron, a sort of openwork helmet with bolts sticking out of it'. Ibid., 112.

26   'I didn't do anything exceptional... Nothing more and nothing less than my comrades did'. Ibid., 95.

27   See ibid., 45–7, and *Éthique en toc*, 21, 27–9, 34, 51, 70, 109, 111. Cf. Daeninckx, *Les Figurants*, with illustrations by Mako (Lagrasse: Verdier, 1995; repr. E.J.L., 1998), 48–9, 87–8; 'L'Arithmomane', in Daeninckx, *Autres lieux* (Lagrasse: Verdier, 1993; repr. E.J.L., 1995), 64–72 (p.69); 'La Page cornée', in Daeninckx, *Main courante* (Lagrasse: Verdier, 1994; repr. E.J.L., 1997), 47–55 (p.55); 'F.X.E.E.U.A.R.F.R.', in Daeninckx, *Zapping* (Denoël, 1992; repr.

So far, so conventional, it might be said, but this is to ignore the broader canvas. More often than not, Daeninckx goes beyond this rather stereotypical depiction by rummaging through the cupboards of the Occupation so as to expose (yet again like Jonquet) the skeletons to be found inside, a task he undertakes so successfully that his standpoint ultimately emerges as heretical.

An eloquent indication of this (and a fine example of his overlapping agendas) is his recognition of the role played by Resisters of North African extraction in the struggle to free France. Thus in 'La Mort en dédicace', attention is drawn to a plaque declaring: '*Ici est tombé / le 23 août 1944 / Ali Brahim / à l'âge de 32 ans / Mort pour la France*',[28] while in *La Mort n'oublie personne*, Jean Ricouart escapes capture thanks to the intervention of a Moroccan comrade, whose deed remains tellingly uncommemorated:

> On pense qu'il a été fusillé le 21 juin [...]. Son corps n'a jamais été retrouvé et comme il n'y avait sûrement pas assez de place au cimetière de Cauchel, on a évité de lui creuser un trou. L'étoile et le croissant au milieu des croix, ça aurait déparé![29]

Just as unorthodox as this focus on the origins of those who opposed the Nazi occupiers is Daeninckx's conviction that the fight for freedom was not always as pure or as popular as many would like to believe, and once more it is *La Mort n'oublie personne* that

Gallimard, Folio, 1994), 133–44 (p.136); 'Le Psyshowpathe', in *Zapping*, 93–100 (p.93).

28   'Here, on 23 August 1944, fell Ali Brahim, aged 32. He died for France'. 'La Mort en dédicace', in Daeninckx, *La Mort en dédicace* (Lagrasse: Verdier, 2001), 65–91 (p.78). This plaque actually exists, and can be found, as Daeninckx says, in the town hall square in Aubervilliers. Significantly, the author has chosen it in preference to the arguably more visible plaque (affixed to the wall of the *mairie* itself) that honours a certain Lucien Leveau.

29   'It is thought he was shot by a firing squad on 21 June [...]. His body was never found and as there was no doubt not enough room in the cemetery at Cauchel, the gravediggers were left in peace. A star and crescent in the middle of the crosses just wouldn't have looked right!' *La Mort n'oublie personne*, 47. A similar insistence on the international nature of the Resistance is found in 'F.X.E.E.U.A.R.F.R.', where Daeninckx depicts a freedom fighter who is Italian.

underlines this point. The narrative revolves around the Resistance's killing of three men in the period immediately after D-Day (6 June 1944), two of them summarily executed for collaboration of varying degrees, and the third the victim of a settling of personal scores (as an accomplice to which Jean will be tried and imprisoned in 1948); it recalls the tendency among many to exaggerate, or even to fabricate, Resistance activity once the war was over, as encapsulated by the phrase 'moins on en a à son actif et plus on en raconte';[30] and it suggests that, during the 'dark years', the French people often had other, less altruistic things on their minds than the liberation of France: 'Est-ce qu'il faudra exécuter tous ceux qui ont trafiqué avec les nazis, qui ont dénoncé les voisins juifs, qui ont envoyé une lettre à la Kommandantur… On est partis pour liquider la moitié du pays…'.[31]

Hand in hand with this insistence on the unedifying actions of both the Resistance and the country at large during the Occupation come regular mentions of the extent and the diversity of the nation's involvement with the Occupier. Indeed, on the basis of what Daeninckx says here and throughout his work, it is possible to draw up a catalogue of virtually all of those aspects of the collaboration that had for so long proved a thorn in France's side.

To begin with the various forms of (para)military co-operation with the Nazis, readers are reminded of the 'Légion des volontaires français contre le bolchevisme', the French Gestapo, the Milice, the Parti Populaire Français, the Parti National Breton and 'la centaine d'hommes qui constituaient la Bretonische Waffenverbände SS, une légion SS bretonne sous uniforme nazi baptisée *bezen* Perrot, c'est-à-dire milice Perrot'.[32] Equally visible is the author's abiding interest in

---

30 'the less people have done, the more they talk it up'. *La Mort n'oublie personne*, 45. Cf. *Meurtres pour mémoire*, 212, where two former collaborators are shown to have hastily changed sides and reaped the benefits.

31 'Will all of those who had dealings with the Nazis, or denounced their Jewish neighbours, or sent a letter to the Kommandantur have to be executed… We'll end up eliminating half the country…'. *La Mort n'oublie personne*, 104. See also ibid., 71–3, 88, 158, and Daeninckx, *12, rue Meckert* (Gallimard, 2001), 26.

32 'the hundred or so men who made up the Bretonische Waffenverbände SS, an SS unit composed of Bretons in Nazi uniform called the *bezen* Perrot, that is to

the 'Malgré nous',[33] who, if not quite in the same category as those who willingly partnered the Germans, were nevertheless not entirely immune from controversy, as is shown by this extract from 'Le Fantôme de l'Arc-en-ciel', which follows the death of a certain Roger Kagen:

> Comme cent trente-deux mille Alsaciens, il avait été enrôlé de force dans la Wehrmacht, en 1942. Comme des milliers d'entre eux, on l'avait affecté à un régiment SS. Quelques dizaines s'étaient trouvés dans la division Das Reich et le destin de Roger Kagen s'était scellé à Oradour-sur-Glane, le 10 juin 1944, devant une église en flammes.
>
> Depuis son retour clandestin, quarante ans plus tôt, il avait vécu en reclus dans sa maison de la rue de l'Arc-en-Ciel, au cœur de Strasbourg; seule la mort de sa compagne l'avait obligé à retourner dans le monde des vivants.[34]

What these lines clearly show is both the ease of slipping from the status of victim (a man forcibly conscripted) to that of war criminal (a participant in the massacre of civilians at Oradour), and the postwar

say the Perrot militia'. 'La Complainte oubliée', in *La Mort en dédicace*, 7–63 (p.52). For Daeninckx's treatment of all of the infamous organisations listed here, see e.g. *La Mort n'oublie personne*, 60–1, 89, 110–4, 156; *Nazis dans le métro*, 63–5; *Éthique en toc*, 25, 51, 64, 107–9, 121; 'Le Penochet', in *Zapping*, 220–8 (pp.225–6); 'La Complainte oubliée', 51–3, 58–61; and *Je tue il...* (Gallimard, 2003), 94.

33   The phenomenon to which this phrase relates is 'the forcible conscription of Alsatians into the German Army. The reluctant soldiers were known as *malgré-nous* – despite ourselves'. Paul Webster, *Pétain's Crime* (London: Macmillan, 1990; repr. London: Pan, 2001), 251.

34   'Like a hundred and thirty-two thousand Alsatians, he had been forcibly conscripted into the Wehrmacht, in 1942. Like thousands of them, he had been put into an SS regiment. A few dozen had ended up in the Das Reich division and the fate of Roger Kagen had been sealed at Oradour-sur-Glane, on 10 June 1944, in front of a blazing church. Since his secret return, forty years earlier, he had lived in seclusion in his house in the rue de l'Arc-en-Ciel, in the heart of Strasbourg; only the death of his wife had forced him to re-enter the world of the living'. 'Le Fantôme de l'Arc-en-ciel', in *Main courante*, 68–80 (p.79). Daeninckx also mentions the SS Das Reich division and its involvement in the Oradour massacre in 'F.X.E.E.U.A.R.F.R.', 134–8. For his interest in the 'Malgré nous' more generally, see e.g. 'Non Lieu', in *Autres lieux*, 31–51 (p.46).

Alan Morris

reaction to this development, whereby Kagen's position hardly differs
from that of the volunteer (para)military collaborators, who on the
whole similarly felt obliged to keep a low profile.

On a far broader level, the above extract is noteworthy in two
additional respects. Taken at face value, it exemplifies Daeninckx's
general procedure as far as the collaboration is concerned: he draws
attention to a troubling historical fact (here, the ambiguous position of
the 'Malgré nous') and uses a related *affaire* (the horror at Oradour) to
make his retrospection more striking and memorable. Yet simultane-
ously, on the figurative level, the passage functions metaphorically,
with Roger, like the inglorious past to which he is tied, being brought
into the wider public domain by Daeninckx as part of the narrative
process.

Also presented to a larger audience, across his whole body of
work, is the phenomenon of collaboration in high places. Prominent
among the novelist's targets in this area are those intellectuals who
compromised themselves during the war, the many names named
attaching both to relatively familiar faces – most regularly Robert
Brasillach, Louis-Ferdinand Céline, Pierre Drieu La Rochelle and
Lucien Rebatet – and to lesser-known historical figures like Alexis
Carrel and Henri Béraud.[35] Not mentioned as frequently as collaborationist writers and thinkers, but just as much part of Daeninckx's
hall of infamy, is a host of other professional people: industrialists,
like Marius Berliet, whom *L'Humanité* is said to have called 'un
collaborateur fanatique qui subventionna le Parti Populaire Français et
la Milice, et livra ses ouvriers aux nazis';[36] famous show-business
celebrities, such as the pioneering Lumière brothers, who allegedly
'avaient des faiblesses pour MM. Hitler et Mussolini, [et...] émar-
geaient au Parti populaire français';[37] and the black sheep of the legal

35   See e.g. *Nazis dans le métro*, 27, 85, 87; *Éthique en toc*, 63, 102; 'La Com-
      plainte oubliée', 42–4, 56; 'Le Penochet', 224–5.
36   'a fanatical collaborator who helped finance the Parti Populaire Français and the
      Milice, and handed his workers over to the Nazis'. *Éthique en toc*, 25.
37   'had a weakness for Messrs Hitler and Mussolini, [and...] were heavily
      involved with the Parti populaire français'. Daeninckx, *La Route du Rom*
      (Baleine, 2003), 71. Cf. *Éthique en toc*, 34, 73, 95. See also *Meurtres pour
      mémoire*, 183, and *Les Figurants*, 68.

system, such as Laulnay, 'une ordure qui siégeait à la cour spéciale de Douai pendant la guerre',[38] and Naudrin *père*, who 'après avoir prêté serment à Pétain et livré quelques dizaines de résistants aux Allemands, [...] a présidé le tribunal de Châteauroux, à la Libération, et s'est refait une virginité en envoyant quelques collaborateurs devant le peloton d'exécution'.[39] Last but not least comes what is arguably the most influential group of collaborators of all – the politicians; and it is still the early *Meurtres pour mémoire* that best illustrates Daeninckx's attack on this body of luminaries. His accusatory stance is apparent in the way he recalls there Pierre Laval's role in the deporting of children, or in the now well-broadcast fact that, rather like Jonquet with Castel and Marchais, he modelled his character André Veillut on the controversial figure of Maurice Papon.[40]

To complete this demonstration of Daeninckx's unconventional approach to the Occupation, one further aspect of his fiction needs to be elucidated: his repeated exposure of the persecution of minorities, and the part played by the French in this persecution. In one of his most recent texts, *La Route du Rom*, he highlights the plight of gypsies in wartime France, asserting that, in 1941, 'des dizaines de camps ont été créés à travers tout le territoire, [...] avec l'aval des autorités

---

38 'a real bastard who was a member of the special court in Douai during the war'. *La Mort n'oublie personne*, 171. Cf. ibid., 45, 166–7.

39 'after swearing an oath of allegiance to Pétain and handing over dozens of Resisters to the Germans, [...] presided over the tribunal at Châteauroux, at the Liberation, and wiped his own slate clean by dispatching a few collaborators to the firing-squad'. *12, rue Meckert*, 178.

40 The ex-minister would be convicted for his role in the Holocaust in 1998, then released from jail after a series of appeals in September 2002. For more on Daeninckx's view of Papon and the latter's central role in *Meurtres pour mémoire*, see Daeninckx, *Écrire en contre: entretiens avec Robert Deleuse, Christiane Cadet, Philippe Videlier, suivis de 'L'écriture des abattoirs'* (Vénissieux: Parole d'aube, 1997), 120–1. The same technique of the knowing nod towards an historical figure can be seen, albeit in a slightly different form, in the name chosen for Veillut's accomplice – Lécussan. During the war, the infamous Joseph Lécussan was head of the Commissariat aux Questions juives in Toulouse and a brutal regional leader in the Milice. He was executed for his crimes in 1946.

locales nommées par Pétain'.[41] In one of these, at Barenton, 'cinquante-cinq "nomades" [...] ont été parqués [...], sous la surveillance de cinq gendarmes français. Il n'y a jamais eu d'Allemands sur place'.[42] As the story progresses, the hidden consequences of this victimisation are made clear: confiscation of goods and property, slave labour, enforced sterilisation and, ultimately, the same fate as Manuel Cuevas. 'Il a disparu en compagnie d'un demi-million de Roms. Parti en fumée [...]. On n'a rien retrouvé de lui, même pas une poignée de cendres'.[43]

Poignant as these words may be, *La Route du Rom* does not restrict its sympathy to 'travellers'. In order to expose the full compass of Vichy's 'machine à exclure',[44] Daeninckx associates the gypsies' suffering with that of other so-called undesirables at that time, such as homosexuals. But principally, he draws a parallel with the Jews, and this is significant, for the fight against anti-Semitism is one of the constants both of his life and of his writing, where the ground-breaking, highly successful *Meurtres pour mémoire* can be seen to have set the tone for the career to come. Reminding the French of their nation's part in the 'Final Solution', it piles explosive statement on explosive statement. Statements such as the following:

> Le 20 août 1941, la cité de la Muette fut officiellement transformée en Camp de Concentration destiné au regroupement des Juifs français avant leur transfert en Allemagne et en Pologne occupée.
> Roger Thiriaud citait le chiffre de 76 000 personnes, femmes, enfants, vieillards rassemblés, en trois ans, à quelques kilomètres de la place de la Concorde, et déportées vers Auschwitz. Il estimait le nombre des rescapés à moins de deux mille.

41 'dozens of camps were created across the length and breadth of the country, [...] with the approval of local authorities appointed by Pétain'. *La Route du Rom*, 157.
42 'fifty-five "nomads" [...] were penned up [...], under the watchful eye of five French gendarmes. There were never any Germans on site'. Ibid., 122.
43 'He disappeared along with half a million Romanies. Went up in smoke [...]. No trace of him was found, not even a handful of ashes'. Ibid., 176.
44 'exclusion machine'. Ibid., 160.

Chaque semaine, trois mille personnes passaient par Drancy, gardées par quatre soldats allemands, secondés dans leur tâche par plusieurs dizaines de supplétifs français.[45]

Since these words were written, Daeninckx has warmed to his theme, and has continued to deplore Vichy's treatment of the Jews.[46] And he has done something more besides. He has updated his attack by extending his condemnation to neo-Fascists and Holocaust deniers, decrying anyone he considers as such so vociferously and so un-compromisingly that he has featured in a number of very public arguments and court cases, and earned himself a dismissive but highly telling nickname: 'Didier Dénonce'.[47]

Such, then, is an outline of Jonquet and Daeninckx's interest in the early 1940s, an interest which is by no means unique among contemporary *polardiers*,[48] and which has therefore significantly informed the development of the genre in France over the past few decades. But why should this be? How can the link between recent French noir and the war years be explained? There are a variety of possible answers to these questions.

45   'On 20 August 1941, the la Muette flats were officially transformed into a Concentration Camp where French Jews could be assembled before they were transferred to Germany or occupied Poland. Roger Thiriaud put at 76,000 the number of people, women, children and the elderly who, over three years, were detained en masse a few kilometres from the place de la Concorde, and deported to Auschwitz. He estimated that the figure for survivors was under two thousand. Every week, three thousand people passed through Drancy, guarded by four German soldiers, assisted in their task by several dozen French auxiliaries'. *Meurtres pour mémoire*, 178. See also ibid., 64, 210–2.

46   See e.g. *Nazis dans le métro*, 61; 'Le Psyshowpathe', 95; and *La Route du Rom*, 117, 157, 164, 175.

47   Patrick Besson has even written a satirical novel with this title, targeting Daeninckx: Besson, *Didier dénonce* (Gérard de Villiers, 1997). Daeninckx, for his part, has insultingly renamed Besson Bescon and linked him in his fiction to the fascistic Right. See 'Le Penochet', 225, and cf. Daeninckx, *Un Château en Bohême* (Denoël, 1994; repr. Gallimard, Folio policier, 1999), 40.

48   See e.g. Jean Mazarin, *Collabo-song* (Fleuve noir, 1981), Gérard Delteil, *KZ, retour vers l'enfer* (Carrère, 1987) or Roger Martin, *L'Affaire Peiper* (Dagorno, 1994). Besson's *Didier dénonce* additionally looks back to the period.

To take one of the most obvious ones first, noir, like other genres, relies on staple ingredients, and World War II offers perfect examples of these. For instance, the period has an ideal atmosphere, thanks to the blackness of the curfew and the constant sense of menace and desolation. It also has the required moral ambiguity, being a time when, confusingly, collaboration was the policy of the legal French government, Resisters were condemned as terrorists, criminals were released from jail to become the Gestapo's local policemen and, as Jonquet readily records,[49] Jews could survive the death camps by 'trafficking' with the personal effects of their gassed fellow inmates. Finally, and above all, the six years from 1939 to 1945 offer the requisite violence, and in abundance. They were in fact – and this is the crux of the matter – a *paradigm* for violent conduct. Genocide, mass murder of civilians, sadism, torture, and all of this often state-sponsored and legitimised, and on a scale never seen before or since. No self-respecting *polardier* could ask for more.

That much of this devastation took place in Europe is perhaps a second reason why writers like Jonquet and Daeninckx find World War II so attractive: it enables them to give a *local* dimension to their work. To explain why this should be so important, it will be nec-essary, briefly, to refer to the history of the *roman noir* and to clarify the relationship between its French and US versions.[50] In America, the genre came to prominence between the two World Wars, with pioneers such as Dashiell Hammett and Raymond Chandler laying the foundations of their future worldwide reputations. In France, however, the breakthrough came later, in 1943 to be precise, with the pub-lication of Léo Malet's *120, rue de la Gare*,[51] a work which, because it tapped into the culture of France itself (there are allusions to Sade, among others), as well as into the hard-boiled format of the USA (Malet's hero is a 'privé utilisant autant ses capacités physiques

---

49   *Les Orpailleurs*, 396.
50   On this development, see *Le Polar*, ed. by Jacques Baudou and Jean-Jacques Schleret (Larousse/HER, 2001), 13–44; Robert Deleuse, 'Petite histoire du roman noir français', *Les Temps Modernes*, 595 (August–October 1997), 53–87; and Jean-Paul Schweighaeuser, 'Du roman de voyou au roman engagé', ibid., 100–21.
51   Léo Malet, *120, rue de la Gare* (S.E.P.E., 1943).

qu'intellectuelles'[52]), is broadly acknowledged as the first example of French noir fiction. Building on this initiative, Marcel Duhamel created in 1945 the famous *Série Noire*, although, revealingly, it served at first to illustrate Anglo-Saxon dominance of the genre. French writers only appeared in the series from 1948 onwards, and even then they did so using English pseudonyms.[53] Another key moment came in the 1950s, when writers such as Albert Simonin and Auguste Le Breton introduced the argot of the French underworld into their novels.[54] But the external influence remained, so much so that as recently as 1997, Patrick Raynal, the general editor of the *Série Noire*, would admit that the series had still not completely broken away from America.[55] Thus, from its origins, the French *roman noir* has been engaged in a struggle with its dominant American precursor, and this is why Jonquet and Daeninckx's preference for a European focus is worthy of note – it consolidates and extends the break with an external tradition.

There is also another point that is relevant here. In the same way that noir in general and US noir in particular can be said to have been born of World War I,[56] the genesis of its French form, as has just been shown, is inextricably linked to World War II. In other words, there is at least one respect in which genre and Occupation are natural bedfellows. However, this 'partnership' was not able to flourish fully after the war, for although *polardiers* could and did mention the 'dark years', it was not always possible for them to broach every aspect of the period with impunity. As novelist André Héléna complained, following his much-criticised retrospection in 1949: 'Il ne fallait surtout

---

52   'private eye who uses his physical abilities as often as his intellect'. Alfu, *Léo Malet* (Amiens: Encrage, 1998), 59.
53   The honour of being the first Frenchman to have a book published in the Série Noire fell to Serge Arcouët, under the pseudonym Terry Stewart. Jean Meckert followed in 1950, calling himself John (later to become Jean) Amila.
54   A flavour of this development can be gained from the title of Simonin's break-through novel, *Touchez pas au grisbi!* (Gallimard, 1953), which might be translated as *Keep your mitts off the dosh!*.
55   See Patrick Raynal, 'Le Roman noir et l'avenir de la fiction', *Les Temps Modernes*, 595 (August–October 1997), 88–99 (p.89).
56   Daeninckx, for one, has expressed this view – see *Écrire en contre*, 41–2.

pas dire de mal des Allemands. Il n'y avait plus de SS, la Gestapo était un mythe, et citer la Milice française relevait de la diffamation.'[57] Such, then, was the nature of the problem posed. The Occupation was recognised as a mine of stories which the authorities would rather forget, a fact which enhanced their appeal to noir writers, who are nothing if not anti-Establishment. As a topic it was, however, fenced off by a sort of cordon sanitaire after the Liberation, its sensitive issues accessible to the unorthodox only at the risk of a stinging riposte. In these circumstances, it is unlikely that even a novelist as popular and as productive as Daeninckx would have been so successful had he been writing decades earlier, and this brings us to the main factor in Jonquet and Daeninckx's treatment of World War II – the importance of the post-1968 context.

Despite its invigorating shot of French argot in the 1950s, by the mid-1960s the *polar* in France was in decline, having, according to Robert Deleuse, 'plongé dans l'endormissement, préférant le rythme de croisière [...] aux secousses telluriques'.[58] But then came May 1968, and out of its momentous events came Jean-Patrick Manchette. Politically *engagé* on the far Left, as were many of those involved in the *événements*, Manchette brought a breath of fresh air to the French *roman noir*, redefining it as 'le roman d'intervention sociale très violent',[59] and quickly becoming the figurehead of a new version of the genre that he himself christened *le néo-polar*.[60]

Although the *néo-polar*'s full impact would not be seen until the 1970s had turned into the 1980s,[61] Manchette strikingly led the way,

57   'It was absolutely imperative not to say anything bad about the Germans. There was no SS any more, the Gestapo was a myth, and mentioning the French Militia was held to be defamatory' (quoted in Deleuse, 'Petite histoire du roman noir français', 63).

58   'gone into a deep sleep, preferring to go onto autopilot [...] rather than do anything earth shattering'. Deleuse, 'Petite histoire du roman noir français', 69.

59   'the very violent novel of social intervention'. Manchette, *Chroniques*, 12.

60   Manchette actually viewed this phrase negatively, and used it to designate a poor imitation of the original, masterful American *roman noir*; but it was soon taken up positively by commentators in the media and applied to the new 'school' they discerned, with Manchette as its leading light.

61   As is often the case with labels and categorisations, there is no unanimity regarding who or what comes under the banner of the *néo-polar*. Here (and

and within his 'new' hard-boiled universe, it is clear that the Occupation had a role to play. Not a dominant one, but a role all the same. In his 1976 novel *Que d'os!*, for instance, there is mention of the deportation of Jews via Drancy, the collaboration of the French police force is evoked, and among the key characters is an ex-Nazi and a former member of the Breton National Party who ends up 'un peu milicien, un peu Gestapo française'.[62] Similarly, two of the figures in *Fatale* are DiBona, who betrayed parachutists to the Germans in 1943, and Lorque, who helped to build the Atlantic Wall.[63] As is now widely accepted, one of the ways in which Manchette revived French noir was by updating its cast list, by increasing the contemporary relevance of its dramatis personae.[64] This being the case, is his portrayal of figures compromised during the war years to be seen in the light of this process of renewal?

An argument in favour of this view is the fact that the *néo-polar*'s emergence coincides exactly with that of the *mode rétro*, the 'fashion' for reassessing the Occupation that grew up after the demise of de Gaulle.[65] There are, of course, some significant differences between the two phenomena, such as the far greater political com-

throughout this essay, as its title suggests), I am using the expression in its broadest sense, and including Daeninckx, Jonquet and those who came to the fore with them, as for example do Baudou and Schleret (*Le Polar*, 42). Others, however, prefer a more limited and exclusive application of the term – see e.g. Gorrara, *The 'Roman Noir' in Post-War French Culture*, 15–7, 72, 77–9.

62   'part militiaman, part French Gestapo'. Manchette, *Que d'os!* (Gallimard, 1976; repr. Folio policier, 2000), 74.

63   Jean-Patrick Manchette, *Fatale* (Gallimard, 1977). See also Manchette, *Morgue pleine* (Gallimard, 1973; repr. Folio policier, 1999), 102–3, and *Le Petit Bleu de la côte ouest* (Gallimard, 1976; repr. Folio policier, 1998), 64. Once again, note the use of humorous, culturally allusive titles here – *Que d'os!* evokes President MacMahon's legendary 'Que d'eau!', while *Morgue pleine* derives from a much-quoted line in Victor Hugo's poem, 'L'Expiation' (*Les Châtiments*): 'Waterloo! Waterloo! Waterloo! morne plaine!'.

64   See e.g. François Cote, 'Le néo-polar français et les policiers', *Esprit*, 135 (1988), 46–50 (p.47).

65   For fuller details here, see Alan Morris, *Collaboration and Resistance Reviewed: Writers and the 'Mode Rétro' in Post-Gaullist France* (New York and Oxford: Berg, 1992). This work also discusses more fully the 'cordon sanitaire' imposed around the war years after the Liberation.

mitment of the new *polardiers*,[66] but these discrepancies cannot obscure the areas of overlap. For example, like its partner trend, what might be called neo-noir is driven by members of the young, 'innocent' generation, who have no direct adult experience of World War II (Manchette was born in 1942, Daeninckx in 1949, Jonquet in 1954), and who, for one reason or another, had not really gained a good insight into the period 1939–1945 from their elders. Although this basic ignorance has been intimated by Daeninckx,[67] it is Jonquet who is more palpably marked by it, for he has confessed that he suspected his grandfather (who was a policeman during the latter part of the 'dark years') of having a role in the 'Final Solution', but never dared verify this theory by asking his father.[68] Furthermore, he has evoked the same underlying problem, albeit with a different slant, in his fiction, in the form of this inter-generational rebuke from *Du passé faisons table rase*: 'Tais-toi, tu ne sais pas de quoi tu parles, tu ne peux pas juger, si quelqu'un a le droit de protester, c'est nous, nous qui avons vécu cette époque'.[69] This attempt to deny those born after

---

66   In his youth, Jonquet was an activist in the Trotskyite Ligue Communiste Révolutionnaire and, indeed, originally published *Du passé faisons table rase* under the politically charged pseudonym of Ramon Mercader (the man who killed Trotsky). Daeninckx admits to having always been attracted by Communism and/or anarchism (see *Écrire en contre*, 108), while Manchette began as a Marxist-Leninist and moved on to Situationism. Not all practitioners of the *néo-polar* (in the widest sense of the term) are on the Left, however. The pseudonymous A.D.G. was a renowned right-winger and a National Front activist to boot (see *Le Polar*, ed. by Baudou and Schleret, 127). These varied affiliations notwithstanding, the writers' extremist backgrounds might help to explain their common interest in violence.

67   See especially the children's trilogy he produced (with illustrations by Pef): *Il faut désobéir* (Voisins-le-Bretonneux: Rue du monde, 2002), *Un violon dans la nuit* (Voisins-le-Bretonneux: Rue du monde, 2003) and *Viva la liberté* (Voisins-le-Bretonneux: Rue du monde, 2004). In each of these works the young heroine is told horrific facts about the war that have been kept secret for sixty years. See also *La Mort n'oublie personne*, 168 and 'Le Psyshowpathe', 94.

68   'Voilà comment ça s'est passé…', 153–4.

69   'Shut up, you don't know what you're talking about, you can't judge, if anyone has the right to protest, it's us, we lived through the period'. *Du passé faisons table rase*, 268.

the war the right to pass judgement on the *années noires* was yet another component of the 'cordon sanitaire' outlined above.

A natural consequence of any lack of communication between the generations is an awareness, on the part of the inheritors, of a deficient legacy. It is thus perhaps not surprising that, again like the *mode rétro*, the *néo-polar* can be seen to encapsulate an interest in the *heritage* of the Occupation, and a belief that the period is a source of significant features in present-day French society and culture. One obvious demonstration of this is Daeninckx's ongoing struggle against neo-Fascists and Holocaust deniers, as translated most forcibly by *Nazis dans le métro* and *Éthique en toc* (where the investigator-hero even remarks: 'Le passé commence à éclairer l'étrangeté du présent').[70] Another is Jonquet's *Les Orpailleurs*, where the latter-day serial killings and 'thefts' (by the 'gold panners') from victims of the death camps replicate those of the Nazis decades earlier,[71] this reviewing of old horrors being symbolised by the fateful ring, eye-shaped and ruby-red. A third, and arguably the most notable, sign that the early 1940s are important because of the problematic heritage they bequeath is the key role given to parent-child relationships by the two writers in question: to the previously evoked appearances of Bernard and Roger Thiriaud (*Meurtres pour mémoire*), Jean and Lucien Ricouart (*La Mort n'oublie personne*), and Nadia Lintz and her father (*Les Orpailleurs*), can be added those of Gérard and André Béraut (*Éthique en toc*) and 'the woman on the lookout' and her son ('La Guetteuse').[72] In all instances, parental action relating to the war impacts on the child, as is particularly apparent in Nadia's 'quête éperdue d'un pardon pour des fautes qu'elle n'avait pas commises'.[73]

---

70 'The past is starting to shed light on the strangeness of the present'. *Éthique en toc*, 121. See also e.g. 'Leurre de vérité' (in *Zapping*, 204–19) and 'Le Penochet'.

71 Cf. *Les Orpailleurs*, 185, 281, 369, 381–2. Note also the comments above on the significance of the ending of this novel.

72 In Daeninckx, *Autres lieux*, 73–82.

73 'frantic quest to be forgiven for mistakes she had not committed'. *Moloch*, 130.

One final way in which neo-noir resembles *la mode rétro* is through its embodiment of a heretical quest for 'truth',[74] and if inverted commas have been used here, it is to indicate the ambivalence that lies at the heart of Jonquet and Daeninckx's project, the ambivalence inherent in the polar genre as they conceive it, for as novelists active in one period and looking back to another, they seem to be doing two different, and not always compatible things.

On the one hand, they appear to be exploiting the *roman noir*'s status as a source of entertainment, constructed around a *search* for the solution to a crime or a mystery. Traditionally, this involves the bringing to light of hidden information, and many of Jonquet and Daeninckx's fictions can be seen to be doing precisely this, thanks to their documentary 'feel', and the sense that the authors are exposing issues that have been played down, obfuscated, or simply ignored in more orthodox representations of the 'dark years'. This sanitised reading of the past by the Establishment might be termed a less evident, more insidious form of the violence stemming from the Occupation. This is not to suggest, however, that they have a great deal new to say about what went on under Vichy. They do not, as Daeninckx's re-presentation of familiar figures like Céline and Brasillach demonstrates. But they do manage to do something valuable nonetheless. Again like their *confrères* of the *mode rétro*, they tend to take information that is already in the public domain, often in history books, and use a more attractive medium to present it to a wider audience.[75] The *polar* is, after all, a pre-eminently popular and accessible genre.

On the other hand, the two novelists are making full use of the genre's capacity for subversion. Channelling their attack through the fictional and imaginative elements of their narratives, they are able to put the historical facts they recall into a contemporary context, and thereby show that, for them, the Occupation continues to exert its

74 This explains why well-known *affaires* – like those involving Marchais and Papon – regularly provide impetus to both trends.
75 As indicated above, Amouroux's *La Grande Histoire des Français sous l'Occupation* runs to ten volumes – hardly appealing to the young or to impatient readers.

sinister influence, infecting whole areas of French life in general, and the body politic in particular. Much more than the Célines and the Brasillachs – who had already been officially dealt with as part of a Collaboration that was acknowledged to exist, but deemed so limited in numbers that it could not undermine the notion of a glorious 'France résistante' – it is those who compromised themselves during the war and then rewrote their personal histories to secure positions of power (Marchais, Papon and their like) whom Jonquet and Daeninckx actively take to task. Convinced that they have the right to judge, they seek to reintroduce into their own time a requirement of humaneness and moral probity for their elected representatives, and to put an end, at long last, to the accommodations, backsliding and non-accountability that marked the early 1940s. What is more, allied to these fictionalised crusades against individuals is the wider crusade to provoke a collective *prise de conscience*, centred on the extent of France's wartime complicity with fascism and its persecution of minorities, such as Jews and gypsies, but additionally targeting the similar, ongoing 'terrorism' of the conservative 'moral majority'. In short, Jonquet and Daeninckx are far removed from the likes of Georges Simenon and his politically insipid Maigret novels; they are campaigning writers with long agendas.

In this way, then, Jonquet and Daeninckx employ a double thrust to conduct their assaults, serving up a challenging concoction in which the fictional (the attempt to solve a crime that is a convention of the genre) sits happily alongside the factual (the provision of real-world insights in the manner of a historian or an investigative journalist). This second feature of their work is plainly the more defining, for as Claire Gorrara has authoritatively observed:

> The *polar* is more than a novel; it is a cultural narrative of our times. It is a literary form that sets out to cast a jaundiced eye over the past and present and to [... contribute] to the construction of our social and cultural identities.[76]

---

76   *The 'Roman Noir' in Post-War French Culture*, 126. Gorrara has also pointed out the link between the detective and the historian/investigative journalist – see e.g. ibid., 78.

As may by now be clear, the depiction of the *années noires* – and their legacy of violence – is an essential and highly significant part of this project.

MARGARET-ANNE HUTTON

From the Dark Years to 17 October 1961: Personal and National Identity in Works by Didier Daeninckx, Leïla Sebbar and Nancy Huston

International conflict, as the recent Iraq War has demonstrated, pre-cipitates divisiveness, not only in the obvious sense of one nation's being pitted against another, but because it poses a fundamental challenge to the concept of national identity and to individuals' loyalty to the nation state. If those conflicts degenerate into civil wars, whose divisive effects pit those of the same national identity against one another, the potential for identity trauma at a national and a personal level is all the greater. Thus France's national identity was deeply traumatised, indeed threatened, by the Vichy years and by the Al-gerian War, both of which set French against French; in the case of the former, collaborationists against resistants, and in the latter, not only pro-Independence against anti-Independence French citizens, but also those of Algerian origin whose Frenchness was suddenly brought into question. These two crises have been refracted not only through the mediation of the experiences of those directly involved, but also through post-conflict generations who still feel impelled to develop their own response to the conflicts enacted by their forbears.

The trial of Maurice Papon, accused and found guilty in April 1998 of crimes against humanity for his involvement in the de-portation of Jews between 1942 and 1944, kept the Vichy régime firmly in the public eye, fuelling what has been described as the French nation's on-going 'obsession' with the Dark Years.[1] In the course of that same trial, historian Jean-Luc Einaudi's exposition of Papon's *curriculum vitae*, particularly his role as Prefect of the Paris

---

1   See E. Conan and H. Rousso, *Vichy, un passé qui ne passe pas* (Paris: Gallimard, 1996).

police during the brutal suppression of a demonstration held by French Algerians in Paris on 17 October 1961,[2] contributed to what has been regarded as the 'return of the repressed' of the Algerian War.[3] Like the Vichy regime in earlier years, the events of 17 October 1961 have gradually made their way into the cultural arena.[4] The following discussion is based on three texts, Didier Daeninckx's *Meurtres pour mémoire* (1984), Nancy Huston's *L'Empreinte de l'ange* (1998) and Leïla Sebbar's *La Seine était rouge* (1999),[5] all of which, with markedly different emphases, represent the physical violence of both the demonstration of October 1961 and France's Vichy past, as well as the less tangible violence of the nation's exclusionary construction of French identity. Beyond this, these are texts which engage with key issues of contemporary epistemological debate: the role and status of the witness in what has been described as the 'memory culture' of the late twentieth-century, and the related question of the search for identity by a post-conflict second generation.

Published well before the inception of the Papon trial in 1997, Daeninckx's *Meurtres pour mémoire* (1984) opens with a number of young Algerians making their way to the demonstration of 17 October 1961, and Frenchman Roger Thiraud, caught up in events on his way home to his pregnant wife. As the brutal repression by the CRS begins, Thiraud is assassinated by an unidentified figure. The text then fast-forwards some twenty years to Thiraud's son, Bernard, shot on

2   For a full account see J.-L. Einaudi, *La Bataille de Paris. 17 octobre 1961* (Paris: Seuil, 1991).

3   A. Donadey, adopting Rousso's terminology from the latter's *Le Syndrome de Vichy* (Paris: Seuil, 1990), suggests that the Algerian conflict passed from the phase of 'repression' in French public life to that of the 'return of the repressed' as of approximately 1992. See her *Recasting Postcolonialism. Women Writing Between Worlds* (Portsmouth, NH: Heinemann, 2001), 10.

4   See A. Donadey, 'Anamnesis and national reconciliation: re-membering October 17, 1961', in Susan Ireland and Patrice J. Proulx (eds), *Immigrant Narratives in Contemporary France* (Westport, CT and London: Greenwood Press, 2001), 47–56 for an overview of fictional works which represent the October demonstration.

5   All references are to the following editions: *Meurtres pour mémoire* (Paris: Gallimard, 1984); *La Seine était rouge* (Paris: Thierry Magnier, 1999); *L'Empreinte de l'ange* (Paris: Babel, 1998).

the streets of Toulouse after visiting the *préfecture* archives. Thereafter the plot is driven by police inspector Cadin's search for
Bernard's killer, an investigation which leads to the discovery that the
guilty party is one André Veillut – a fictionalised Maurice Papon –
who both ordered the assassination of Thiraud senior and killed
Bernard himself.

Beyond its scarcely veiled condemnation of Papon's crimes,
Meurtres pour mémoire can be read as a warning of the hazards
confronting both witnesses of conflict and members of a post-conflict
second generation seeking to make sense of, and situate themselves in
relation to, the past: the impact of trauma on the former, and the
danger of acting out faced by the latter.[6] Traumatised by her witnessing of Roger Thiraud's murder from her apartment window, Mme
Thiraud remains incarcerated in her home and in the past. It is only
when Inspector Cadin, temporarily cast in the symbolic role of
therapist-interlocutor, opens the shutters which have symbolically and
literally occluded the traumatic scene for some twenty years, that a
cure is effected, when Mme Thiraud articulates her memories for the
first time. As all three texts under consideration here reveal, trauma is
all too easily transmitted to the second generation. Mme Thiraud has
passed her depression on to her son Bernard (51). Unable to face
bringing up the child she was carrying when her husband died, Mme
Thiraud handed him over to his paternal grandparents, initiating what
can be interpreted as a process of symptomatic repetition which
continues into Bernard's adult years. Early in the text the reader's
attention is drawn to medieval historian Roger Thiraud's growing
interest in the history of childhood (16). We later learn that Bernard
was writing a doctoral thesis on childhood in the Middle Ages (69),
and that he sought to finish his father's monograph on Drancy in

6   For discussions of trauma and the eye-witness, see C. Caruth, *Trauma. Ex-
     plorations in Memory* (Baltimore, MD: Johns Hopkins University Press, 1995);
     S. Felman and D. Laub, *Testimony. Crises of Witnessing in Literature, Psy-
     choanalysis and History* (New York: Routledge, 1992), and L. Langer,
     Holocaust Testimonies. The Ruins of Memory (New Haven, CT: Yale Uni-
     versity Press, 1991). For a discussion of acting out and working through, see D.
     LaCapra, *History, Theory, Trauma. Representing the Holocaust* (Ithaca, NY:
     Cornell University Press, 1994).

memory of his father (136). Bernard Thiraud, it seems clear, models his identity on that of his father, repeating (and seeking to complete) the latter's life. He is, one might suggest, caught up in a process of acting out, an unwitting repetition which leads to his meeting with a similar fate to that of his father. Moreover, the hazards of acting out do not stop with Bernard. Whilst Inspector Cadin's literal retracing of Bernard's steps and growing personal involvement with the latter's partner, Claudine, constitute part of the generic code of the '*roman noir*', they also represent a further process of repetition: Cadin, who has been described by critics as both witness and historian,[7] only narrowly escapes being shot, like Thiraud senior and junior before him.

Just as the inspector's repetition of Bernard's trajectory can be read both in terms of the conventions of the *policier* genre and as part of a wider epistemological reading relating to the identity of secondary witnesses, so too are other aspects of Daeninckx's text open to dual interpretation. Roger Thiraud's covert afternoon visits to an unspecified location – 'Il entra furtivement dans la salle noire' (17); 'ce lieu de perdition' (18)[8] – set up a minor mystery for the reader. The solution – Roger has a penchant for fantasy films, not pornography – is revealed almost immediately, and this discovery later contributes towards Mme Thiraud's recovery (she had feared that her husband was having an affair). This is, however, not the only reference to the fantastic in the text. Hampered in his investigation by state censorship and public servants seeking to protect those in power, Cadin is informed that governments 'n'ont aucun intérêt *à voir*

---

7   See Geldof, K., 'Une écriture de la résistance: Histoire et fait divers dans l'œuvre de Didier Daeninckx', in P. Pelckmans and B. Tritsmans (eds), *Écrire l'insignifiant. Dix études sur le fait divers dans le roman contemporain* (Amsterdam, Rodopi: 2000), 135–53; Forsdick, C., '"Direction les oubliettes de l'histoire": witnessing the past in the contemporary French *polar*', *French Cultural Studies* 12 (2001), 333–50; Gorrara, C., 'Tracking down the past: the detective as historian in texts by Patrick Modiano and Didier Daeninckx', in A. Mullen and E. O'Beirne (eds), *Crime Scenes: Detective Narratives in European Culture since 1945* (Amsterdam: Rodopi, 2000), 281–90.

8   'He slipped unobtrusively into the dark room' ; 'that den of iniquity'.

resurgir certains fantômes' (82, my emphasis).[9] When the inspector learns about the missing bodies of French Algerians who participated in the October 1961 demonstration, he is warned not to probe any further: 'Ne vous amusez pas à les [the bodies] faire remonter à la surface; *ils feront comme Dracula, ils revivront avec votre propre sang'* (97–8, my emphasis).[10] Finally, on first meeting with Mme Thiraud, Cadin's description of her dysfunctional condition is articulated using a similar lexicon: 'J'avais l'impression de parler à un mur, à un *mort vivant'* (116, my emphasis).[11] In all of these cases the fantastic can be read as a figure for repressed or deliberately concealed material: in the former case, material which, because it remains hidden, potentially threatens the lives of both primary and secondary witnesses whose identities remain rooted in the past; in the latter case, material which is deliberately suppressed to protect France's public image.

Daeninckx's text reveals the obstacles facing the emergence of unpalatable facts of the past, but does it ultimately represent the victory of the 'truth' of history? After all, the conventions of *polar* dictate the need for closure: crimes must be solved and the truth must out.[12] Accordingly, the text does indeed come to the generically-expected conclusion. In a gesture of poetic licence the criminal Veillut dies at the hands of his own hit-man, and Cadin exposes Veillut's motives and modus operandi. But *Meurtres pour mémoire* is not simply an example of fictional wish-fulfilment. The tidy ending is, firstly, subverted by the suggestion of a future public cover-up of Veillut's crimes (213). Furthermore, readers familiar with the series in which Cadin features will know that his attempts to reveal the truth of the past wilfully masked by those in power will lead to his eventual downfall. By the last of the Cadin series, *Le Facteur fatal* (1990), Cadin's constant interference with those in high places has resulted in his resignation from the police force, and the text closes on his

9 'it's not in the interests [of governments] that certain ghosts reappear' .
10 'Don't mess about trying to get them to resurface: they'll be like Dracula, they'll use your blood to come back to life'.
11 'it was like speaking to a brick wall; one of the living dead'.
12 On the question of closure, see Forsdick, op. cit.

suicide. Significantly, Cadin's taking of his own life is immediately preceded by his request that a former colleague read a short story of his own composition – a tale based, significantly, on the fatal return of repressed memories.

Meurtres pour mémoire points both to the dangers of acting out and to the deliberate suppression of the past by those in power, but is Daeninckx himself guilty of acting out, repeating the French state's masking of the violence of the Algerian conflict? For Donadey, the fact that Thiraud son and father die because they uncover crimes committed under the Vichy regime:

> means that the 1961 massacre remains overshadowed in the plot by events related to Vichy. While Daeninckx's novel deals with the erasure of French memory, it has little to say about immigrant memory and thus unwittingly participates in the continued silencing of the October 1961 massacre.[13]

Although the text opens with a focus on named and partially characterised young French Algerians and on their attempts to forge an identity in France, it is true that after the representation of the demonstration of 17 October 1961 these Algerian characters are expunged from the plot, and equally true that the reader might all too easily forget that the eponymous murders extend beyond those of the two French characters whose deaths are the only ones investigated by Cadin. Donadey's condemnation is, however, perhaps a little harsh. It should be noted that, for some commentators, the trial of Papon, a man who served not only under Vichy but also under the Fourth and Fifth Republics, was not just the indictment of one individual; rather, the case put the French nation itself and its Republican credentials on trial.[14] This interrogation of national identity and its integrity is highlighted in the text by the thematisation of marginality, and an insistent emphasis on the exclusion of the Other – both Jew *and*

---

13   A. Donadey, 'Anamnesis and National Reconciliation', 50.
14   See Richard J. Golsan (ed.), *The Papon Affair: Memory and Justice on Trial* (New York and London: Routledge, 2000), xi–xiii. For a discussion of Papon's career after Vichy, see V. Kelly, 'Papon's Transition after World War II', ibid., 35–72.

Algerian.[15] The opening section of the text points to the marginali-
sation of the French Algerian population, geographically and symbolically relegated to the margins of Paris. Kaïra, representing the
younger generation, notes that for her elders Nanterre constitutes their
entire universe, and that most women never venture beyond this
peripheral location, in spite of the fact that the Champs Elysées (centre
of Paris, itself centre of the *métropole*, itself centre of the former
empire) is a mere ten minutes away by bus (21). The demonstration of
17 October 1961 is represented as a symbolic challenge to the centre
('cette guerre prenait corps au centre de Paris', (28)); Kaïra opti-
mistically suggests that the 'place de l'Étoile' might thereafter be
renamed 'place du Croissant et de l'Étoile' (25).[16] Bertrand's partner,
Claudine, later adds an historical dimension to the issue by pointing
out to Cadin that the construction and exclusion of the Other is a long
tradition: whereas in a previous era criminal activity in Paris was
blamed on members of the working-class inhabiting the outskirts of
the city, now, in the climate of so-called 'insécurité', the role of
scapegoat has devolved to immigrants (133–4).

Daeninckx makes the point that France's capital city – and by
extension French national identity – has traditionally functioned by
excluding the Other, a point which is further reinforced by repeated
highlighting of the parallel between Jews and Algerians. We thus find,
for example, the casual racist and anti-Semitic comments of a taxi-
driver (88). Furthermore, after reading of the deportation of Jews
under Vichy, Cadin has a dream in which Jews and Algerians are
conflated as victims of the state: train wagons filled with hundreds of
Algerians covered in blood are replaced in an oneiric dissolve by
thousands of children's voices shouting 'Pitchipoï' (182), the fictitious
name attributed by Jewish deportees to their unknown destination:

---

15   For a discussion of France's republican tradition and the exclusion of Jews and
     North African immigrants, see E. Benbassa, *La République face à ses min-
     orités. Les Juifs hier, les Musulmans aujourd'hui* (Paris: mille et une nuits,
     2003). For a critique of potential conflations of the Algerian War and Vichy
     regime see R. Golsan's 'Memory's *bombes à retardement*: Maurice Papon,
     crimes against humanity, and 17 October 1961', *Journal of European Studies*
     28 (1998), 153–72, and Forsdick's response (op. cit.).
16   'This war was taking shape in the centre of Paris'; 'Crescent and Star Square'.

Auschwitz.[17] The exclusion of both Jews and Algerians is further accentuated by an apparently secondary plot-line which throws up a minor mystery to be solved by Cadin: the summoning of members of the higher echelons of Toulouse society to the *préfecture*, there to be placed on file as part of an anti-terrorism campaign. The solution to the problem is a simple one – a clerical error has resulted in letters of thanks for contributions to police funds being placed in the wrong envelopes – but two points are indirectly made. Firstly, readers are reminded that both Jews and Algerians were submitted to a similarly sinister bureaucratic process under Vichy and in the years of the Algerian conflict (an issue also raised in Huston's text); secondly, the fortuitous alignment of the city 'notables' with a terrorist element suggests an indirect (and blackly humorous) indictment of those in positions of power.

Where Daeninckx's text takes the demonstration of 17 October 1961 as its starting point – both literally, and inasmuch as the conflict provides a springboard for a more generalised exploration of the exclusionary construction of French identity – Sebbar's *La Seine était rouge* (1999) focuses more specifically on the demonstration, the impact of the Algerian conflict on second generation immigrants, and France's colonial past. The teleology of the *polar* is replaced by a contrapuntal structure: sections set in Paris in 1996 charting the movements of the principal characters alternate with a diverse range of accounts given by (fictional) eye-witness participants in, or observers of, the events of October 1961. The text centres on Amel, a sixteen-year-old girl born in France to Algerian parents and whose grandfather helped organise the October 1961 demonstration in which her mother (then aged seven) and grandmother also participated. Amel is joined on a literal and metaphorical journey of discovery by two other representatives of the second generation: Louis, French, aged

---

17   The text suggests – incorrectly – that 'Pitchipoï' was the name given by the Jews to Drancy (178). Daeninckx, it should be noted, models Roger Thiraud's investigations into Drancy and the reconstitution of deportation lists on the work of Serge Klarsfeld (see the latter's *Le Mémorial de la déportation des Juifs de France* (New York: Beate Klarsfeld Foundation, 1978)).

twenty-five, son of French *porteurs de valises*;[18] and Omer, twenty-seven years old, an Algerian journalist who has come to France illegally after threats on his life.

Amel and Louis both seek 'the truth' about the Algerian conflict, and more particularly the demonstration of 17 October 1961 in which their parents – or, in Amel's case, grandparents – were directly involved, and for them both the events of the past are represented as key to their sense of personal identity. A French-born child of Algerian immigrants, Amel is typically situated astride two cultures. She has a map of Algeria pinned to her bedroom wall but has never left France. Her inability to learn Arabic induces feelings of guilt, and she distances herself from her grandparents' religious beliefs (17). Although Amel accepts her official status as French, she rejects the Algerian Omer's construction of her identity, rebutting his pronominal generalisation which equates 'vous' with all French nationals and excludes her Algerian heritage: 'Encore "vous"... Jusqu'à quand? J'ai des papiers français, d'accord, mais je suis pas tous les Français' (116).[19] Just as in *Meurtres pour mémoire* truth is both constantly deferred and represented as something which remains hidden with potentially dangerous consequences, so for Amel the 'truth' of the Algerian conflict is kept from her by her mother and grandmother: 'Des secrets, ma fille, des secrets, ce que tu ne dois pas savoir, ce qui doit être caché, ce que tu apprendras, un jour, quand il faudra' (13); 'un jour de malheur' (13).[20]

Louis also wishes to learn more of the struggle in which his mother was involved. Like Amel, he objects to Omer's sweeping designation of 'the French': '"Qui? 'Vous'?" Louis hurle. "Qu'est-ce que tu veux dire par là? 'Vous... vous...' Explique-toi"' (29–30).[21] Omer admits no differentiation in his definition of French identity; for

18   Those who supported the *Front de libération nationale*, often by transporting funds.
19   '"You're using that word 'you' again... Give it a rest. I've got French papers, okay, but I don't represent all the French people"'.
20   'Secrets, my girl, secrets, things that you musn't know, things that have to stay hidden, that you'll learn about, one day, when the time is right'; 'a terrible day'.
21   '"You who?", screamed Louis. "What do you mean by that? You... You... Explain yourself"'.

him, 'the French' remain fixed as those who fought against Algeria, but Louis is all too aware that as *porteurs de valises* his parents were regarded by many as traitors to France (30). Just as Amel seeks to situate herself between French and Algerian identities, so Louis's desire to explore the past is directly related to his own unformulated sense of self. Where members of the previous generation such as his parents took a stand, his own life lacks a clear sense of purpose and direction: 'je dois savoir, pas tout, mais comprendre un peu... Je ne sais plus ce que ça veut dire être révolutionnaire, aujourd'hui' (26–7).[22] For Louis, 'truth' initially equates to the experiences of his parents. In response to his mother's question – 'Quelle vérité?' – he replies 'ce que vous avez pensé, vécu, souffert... votre vie quoi...' (26).[23] This limited stance is challenged both by his mother, who points out that her testimony would represent only one, subjective point of view, and by Omer, who counters Louis's validation of the eye-witness – 'chacun son histoire, son regard...' – with an absolutist stance: '"Oui, mais la vérité historique?"' (26). For Omer, however, 'the truth' is quite simply his version of the truth – 'sa vérité historique' (30) – as Louis dubs it in a tellingly oxymoronic formulation.[24]

Answers to both Amel's and Louis's questions are provided when the latter decides to make a documentary film of the events of October 1961. Like Inspector Cadin in *Meurtres pour mémoire*, Louis facilitates the emergence of a range of eye-witnesses who have hitherto kept their silence. This proactive move takes him beyond his initial conception of 'the truth' as his parents' perspective on the events of October 1961, as he records a series of oral testimonies given by Amel's mother, but also, amongst others, café and bookshop owners who witnessed the demonstration, a *harki*, a policeman, and an Algerian rescued from the Seine, thereby gaining a multiple per-

---

22   'I need to know, not everything, I just need to understand a little... I don't know
     what being a revolutionary means today'.
23   'What truth?'; 'what you thought, what you lived through, suffered... your life
     in other words'.
24   'everyone has his own story, his own perspective'; 'Yes, but what about the
     historical truth?'; 'his historical truth'.

spective on past events. Watched several times by Amel and Omer, Louis's film is the trigger for the young girl's decision to follow the route taken by the demonstrators of 1961 from Nanterre to the centre of the capital, accompanied by Omer. Although Amel, like Bernard in *Meurtres pour mémoire*, thereby engages in an act of repetition, hers is more a process of working through than acting out; a knowing and willed assumption of the role of secondary witness. By the close of their trajectory through Paris she and Omer have each gained a measure of understanding of their relative perspectives and Amel has reached some sense of resolution: 'Je dirai que "le jour dit" est arrivé, que je l'ai vécu, j'ai appris la vérité, pas toute la vérité, que ce jour n'a pas été un jour de malheur' (125).[25]

Sebbar's text reveals how members of a post-conflict generation seeking to consolidate a sense of personal identity may learn from both a willed assumption of the past and from each other. Furthermore, where in Daeninckx, 'the truth' was uncovered by the historian working largely from archival material, the disparate – and indeed often antagonistic – perspectives of the various participants in, and observers of, the demonstration of 17 October 1961 in *La Seine était rouge* suggest that 'the truth' of the past can be located in the collected memory of eye-witnesses.[26] Indeed in its valorisation of eye-witness testimony Sebbar's text might be described as a typical product of what has been regarded as the new social imperative of the witness, a 'memory culture' which has arisen in the last decade of the twentieth-century.[27] Critics of this memory culture have pointed to some of its pitfalls: excessive, and often anachronistic, focus on the past may preclude an ethical, future-oriented stance; witnesses,

---

25   'I'll say that "the right time" arrived, that I lived through it, that I learned the truth, not all the truth, and that it wasn't a terrible day'.

26   For a discussion of the role of collective memory in Sebbar's text, see J. Hiddleston, 'Cultural memory and amnesia: the Algerian War and "second-generation" immigrant literature in France', *Journal of Romance Studies* 3.1, 2003, 59–71. The term 'collected' memory is used here to suggest disparate and potentially conflicting points of view.

27   See A. Wieviorka, *L'Ère du témoin* (Paris: Plon, 1998); T. Todorov, *Les Abus de la mémoire* (Paris: Arléa, 1998); E. Conan and H. Rousso, *Vichy: un passé qui ne passe pas* (Paris: Gallimard, 1996).

moreover, are inevitably caught up in attempts to consolidate their own identities (their testimonies tell us more about themselves and the present than the past). Although Sebbar's work does reveal, via its principal characters, that a search for personal identity is indeed at stake when the second generation seeks to explore the past, nevertheless, as we will see shortly, of the three texts in question it is only Huston's which demonstrates how memory may be used in the interests of an ethical future.

Like *Meurtres pour mémoire*, *La Seine était rouge* extends the question of personal identity to consider the construction of France's national identity: Sebbar's representation of the events of October 1961 is seen to form part of a long history of exclusion which sits badly with France's Republican ideals. Unlike *Meurtres pour mémoire*, however, the Jewish dimension is granted a significantly reduced status in Sebbar's text. Papon's role under the Vichy régime is mentioned, but on only two occasions. Amel's mother describes him briefly as the man currently in the news responsible for instigating the curfew for Algerians in 1961 and for having sent Jews to Nazi camps (42); Mourad, an Algerian cook working in a bistro run by a *pied-noir*, points out that it is only Papon's involvement in the deportation of the Jews which has led to a renewed interest in the demonstration of 1961 (103). One might also note that Amel's reference to Brigitte Bardot's ('BB's') attack on Muslims (for what 'BB' perceives as their 'barbaric' slaughter of animals for hallal meat) is accompanied by Amel's somewhat barbed observation that Bardot offers no objections to similar acts performed by Jews (65–6). Rather than focusing on Drancy and the deportation of the Jews, *La Seine était rouge* invokes Vichy via the prison of La Santé and plaques commemorating the execution of members of the Resistance in their fight against the occupying forces. By juxtaposing these plaques with hand-written notices which equate the French with the Nazis and the Algerians with the Resistance (30), Omer (and Sebbar) make the point that France's national image is constructed in a highly selective and exclusionary manner. Sebbar's focus on France's revolutionary past and Republican tradition is linked not to the emancipation of the Jews or to their subsequent betrayal under Vichy, but to France's colonial history. Louis's growing fascination with Bonaparte's Egyptian campaign serves as a reminder that France's revolutionary principles, enshrined in the slogan 'LIBERTÉ ÉGALITÉ FRATERNITÉ' inscribed above the prison of La Santé (29), and embodied in the various statues of Marianne encountered by Amel and Omer (55–6, 68), did not extend to France's empire. Amel, Louis and Omer, significantly, end their metaphoric and literal journey through Paris in Orly airport, and thence in Alexandria, as they return to the roots of France's colonialist past, and, it is implied, envisage future investigations.[28]

As with the two previous works, the problematic construction of personal identity and the often exclusionary nature of the French Republican tradition are key issues in Huston's *L'Empreinte de l'ange* (1998). Set in Paris between 1957 and 1964, Huston's text unfolds against the background of the Algerian conflict, with the demonstration of 17 October 1961 represented briefly towards the close of the main body of the work, which fast-forwards to the 1990s in the epilogue. Huston's text is based on the familiar topos of the love triangle, and features three principal characters, each with a very different background, and all of whom were children during World War II: flautist Rafaele, member of a wealthy French family with landed interests in Algeria; Saffie, a German immigrant whom he employs as a maid then marries almost immediately; and András, a Hungarian Jew who becomes Saffie's lover shortly after the birth of her child Emil.

A young child during World War II, Saffie is herself a victim of severe trauma, first witnessing the horrific death of her best friend in the rubble of the Allied bombings, then raped by Russian soldiers also responsible for the torture and rape of her mother, who subsequently committed suicide. The dangers of acting out and the transmission of trauma sketched out in *Meurtres pour mémoire* via the characters Bernard and Roger Thiraud take on a more extreme form in Huston's text. Settled in France as a young teenager, Saffie was informed in graphic detail by her French teacher of SS soldiers' murdering Jewish

28   See M. O'Riley, 'Cultural memory and the legacy of World War II in Assia Djebar, Leïla Sebbar, and Tahar Ben Jelloun', *Dalhousie French Studies*, 63 (2003), 147–61 (p.155–7).

babies by smashing their heads against walls (111). When Saffie discovers that she is pregnant, her first thought is to attempt deliberately to miscarry the child. In her imagination an SS soldier killing babies – tellingly described as 'suspendu hors du temps'[29] – fades into an image of her baby son Emil (112–13). Like Mme Thiraud in *Meurtres pour mémoire*, Saffie's trauma is such that present identities are frozen in time as she projects a former generation's guilt onto her innocent son. Indeed it is the birth of the third generation Emil and his mother's inability to accept both his and her own identity in the present which drives the plot, as Saffie finds herself situated between two men, husband and lover, who can be read as representatives of radically different attitudes to past conflict and to the formulation and assumption of personal identity in relation to that conflict.

Wholly oblivious to his wife's past, Rafaele is equally unaware of her present post-traumatic condition. For him, the present is best lived in a condition of blissful ignorance. In terms of the epistemological reading of the text, lover András, by contrast, represents a drive to knowledge and an ethical commitment to the future. It is thanks to his influence that Saffie talks openly of her past for the first time, thereby instigating a gradual process of working through. For András, the past must be willingly and wittingly assumed, then acted upon. Though he initially hesitates over whether to inform Saffie that his immediate and extended family was murdered by the Nazis, denial of the past is ultimately not an option he will entertain. András asks himself a series of crucial questions:

> De *quelles* vérités se doit-on d'être au courant, et lesquelles peut-on se permettre d'ignorer? Puis-je me foutre de ce qui s'est passé ce matin mais à l'autre bout du monde – ou alors ici même, mais en l'an deux mille? (180)[30]

The answer to these questions, which challenge the reader of the text, is that what has happened in the past, and is happening now, must be articulated, and Saffie learns the whole truth of András's past. Further-

---

29 'suspended in a timeless moment'.
30 '*Which* truths is it our duty to be aware of, and which ones is it permissible to ignore? Is it okay for me not to give a damn about what happened this morning but at the other end of the world – or right here, but in the year two thousand?'

more, knowledge of the past, for András, brings with it responsibility for the future via direct political engagement with the present. András's political commitment represents precisely the sort of ethical engagement in the future mapped out by Todorov in his discussion of memory and identity. For Todorov, a distinction must be drawn between recalled past events as 'literal' or 'exemplary'. 'Literal' memory is best described as intransitive. The recall of past events serves to establish or bolster the identity (often as victim) of individuals or groups and to establish blame. Exemplary memory is transitive in nature. Groups or individuals use their memories to conceptualise past events as examples of a broader category and to apply that insight to new situations. For Todorov, memory should thus be used to respond to present injustices; to promote engagement in the present.[31]

Where characters in the previous two texts sought above all to secure a sense of personal identity from their investigations into the past, András looks to the future. His and Rafaele's diametrically opposed stances are embodied in their reactions to the Algerian conflict. András challenges Saffie's ignorance of the latter, an ignorance which she defends by stating that *the* war – in other words the war in which she was personally involved – is over. For András, however, the Algerian war is part of a cycle of violence which characterises France's attempt to consolidate its national image:

> Entre 40 et 44 la France se laisse enculer par l'Allemagne, elle a honte alors en 1946 elle commence la guerre à l'Indochine. En 1954 elle la perd, les Viets l'enculent, elle a honte alors trois mois après elle commence la guerre à l'Algérie (166).[32]

As with the two previous texts, France's stance is represented in the light of the failings of the Republican ethos. András points out that in

---

31   See Todorov, *Les Abus de la mémoire*, especially 30–3.
32   'Between 1940 and 1944 France lets itself be shafted by the Germans, and it's so ashamed that in 1946 it starts a war in Indochina. In 1954 it loses that war, the Vietnamese shaft the country, and it's so ashamed that three months later it starts a war with Algeria' (166). P. Dine makes a similar point in his 'Memorial boundaries and textual transgressions: the narrative politics of France's Algerian War', *Yearbook of European Studies*, 15, 2000, 71–82 (p.72).

choosing France as his adopted country upon leaving Hungary he was following his mother's dream. Paris was, for her, 'La Ville Lumière dans le pays des Lumières' (178).[33] The dream, however, proved illusory for the second generation, and when Saffie notes that she too chose France because of its reputation as the land of freedom, András's response is a dismissive '– Ha!' (178-9).

Where Daeninckx could be accused of emphasising the Jewish dimension at the cost of understating the Algerian case, and Sebbar of taking the opposite stance, Huston's position is more inclusive. For András, the Vichy regime and the Algerian war form part of a single continuum. The announcement of the curfew for French Algerians (which triggered the October demonstration) in his eyes immediately brings to mind the curfew imposed on the Jews under Vichy (274). Any day now, András suggests, the French will force its Algerian population to collect and wear crescent moons just as the Jews were obliged to identify themselves via the Star of David (275).[34] Developing a point made more obliquely in *Meurtres pour mémoire*, Huston (via András) observes that both Jews and Algerians were forced to register their presence in local *préfectures*, and that the same exclusionary mentality is at work in both conflicts: 'Tu comprends, Saffie? *ça continue!* Les ratonnades, c'est les mêmes Scheißköpfe qui les font! Les gens qui torturent à (*sic*) Algérie, ils ont appris leur métier ici, avec la Gestapo!' (277–8).[35] András's point of view is backed up in this case by that of the third-person narrator, who

33 'The city of the Enlightenment in the land of the Enlightenment'.
34 Einaudi cites similar words uttered on 30 October 1961 by Eugène Claudius-Petit, vice-president of the French National Assembly: '"Faudra-t-il donc voir prochainement, car c'est la pente fatale, la honte du croissant jaune après avoir connu celle de l'étoile jaune?"'. ('Are we going to have to witness, because this is the slippery slope, the shame of the yellow crescent after having been through that of the yellow star?'). J.-L. Einaudi, *La Bataille de Paris*, 305.
35 'Do you understand, Saffie? *It's still happening.* The round-ups of Algerians are being carried out by the same shitheads! The people torturing in Algeria learned their trade here, with the Gestapo!'. See also the final section of G. Mattei's *La Guerre des Gusses* (Paris: Ballard 1982), which draws a similar parallel between treatment of the Jews and the Algerians. This section, focusing on the October demonstration is, unaccountably, omitted from the 2001 Aube edition of Mattei's text.

observes that Algerians died during and after the demonstration by drowning 'avec ou sans balle dans la tête, comme le père d'András', and that those found hanged died 'étranglés, comme la mère de Saffie' (288).[36] The link between past and present is further stressed when Saffie speaks for the first time of her discovery, aged eighteen, that her father's work directly implicated him in Nazi 'medical' experiments conducted in Auschwitz: as she speaks, she is standing on a flyover, her gaze fixed on Nanterre and its immigrant population (269).

In sharp contrast to András and an increasingly politically-aware Saffie, Rafaele can see no further than his own self. Where András opts to devote himself to an attempt to prevent a repetition of history, becoming a *porteur de valises* and helping to organise the demonstration of 17 October 1961, Rafaele, who is caught up in the violent police repression of the demonstration, limits his response to one of personal affront: he loses his precious flute in the fracas (284). His inability, or unwillingness, to engage in a broader socio-political context is such that the close of the text sees him effectively murdering his own son. When Emil refuses to discuss his mother's relationship with András, Rafaele, in a moment of blind anger, pushes him off a train. The fact that Emil dies with his head crushed should not be lost on the reader: ironically, Rafaele has taken on the symbolic role of the SS, killing the next generation (319).

Huston's text ultimately warns of the dangers both of ignoring the past and of placing one's personal life and identity ('histoires') over and above socio-political events ('Histoire'). In order to bring that message home, the author regularly interrupts the diegesis with statements reminding the reader of events taking place on the world stage. Whilst references to the bloody progress of the Algerian conflict dominate, mention is also made of (inter alia) Mao Ze-dong's Hundred Flowers campaign, the rumblings of the Cold War, Pol Pot, and the construction of the Berlin Wall, all of which, inevitably, serve both to contextualise and to relativise the life and trials of individual characters. The epilogue, finally, brings matters closer to home for the

---

36 'with or without a bullet in the head, like András's father'; 'strangled, like Saffie's mother'.

French reader with a reference to the disaffected grandchildren of Algerian immigrants, still relegated to the outskirts of Paris, and beginning to revolt against their conditions and bleak future prospects. The message of the text is clear: look to the past and the personal by all means, but use that knowledge wisely, by striving to prevent future conflict and exclusion. The final words of the text, appropriately enough, address the reader with a warning for the future:

> Et c'est la fin?
> Oh! non. Je vous assure que non.
> Il suffit d'ouvrir les yeux: partout, autour de vous, cela continue (328).[37]

Each of the three texts under discussion engages with issues of personal and national identity and trauma precipitated by periods of international conflict, but their approaches are filtered through very different socio-cultural prisms. Daeninckx's *Meurtres pour mémoire* appeared at a time when the Vichy years were already at the forefront of French national consciousness, but when the traumatic reper- cussions of the Algerian War had yet to be faced. As such, this prescient text represents one of the first cultural products to both engage with, and influence, the emergence of the Algerian conflict into the French national consciousness. Sebbar's *La Seine était rouge*, published well into the period characterised as the 'return of the repressed' of the Algerian conflict, also constitutes a typical product of a contemporary 'memory culture' which revalorises the status of the eye-witness and collected memory. As with Daeninckx's text, however, the exploration of past conflict is represented primarily as a means to shore up a post-conflict generation's sense of personal identity, and the work ends on a note of uncertainty as to the future. Tellingly, it falls to the Canadian-born Huston to engage with a future- oriented, ethical, concept of memory as a means of breaking a potentially endless cycle of violence. As well as problematising both national and individual identity and addressing the traumatic repercus- sions of international conflict, all three texts constitute cultural *lieux de mémoire* in which past conflict remains immanent. Their existence

37   'And is that the end? Oh no! I can assure you it's not. You just need to open
      your eyes: everywhere, all around you, it's still going on'.

bears witness to issues of national and personal trauma, and to the need of individual subjects to exorcise a past still largely unavowed at the national level of political institutions and official historiography.

DAVID PLATTEN

Violence and the Saint: Political Commitment in the Fiction of Jean Amila

This essay seeks to evaluate selected works of Jean Amila, a writer whose fiction speaks of the relationship of the state to the individual in terms of conflict and violence. Amila was a beacon of the 'néo-polar' school of French crime writing that achieved some notoriety during the 1970s. This was a time when polemicists from both ends of the political spectrum wrote crime stories published in the *Série Noire*, expressing the disillusionment and despondency felt by many in the aftermath of the student uprisings of May 1968. For the best part of a decade, the French crime novel became, extraordinarily, a site of resistance to the perceived violence of the State. However, Amila's work, which spans the period from 1942 up to his death in 1995, has a wider resonance; he is now recognised as one of the finest exponents of a distinctively French twist on the noir genre. The American noir, from Hammett and Chandler through to Ellroy, reflects the image of a society based entirely on the corruption of power, in which the very notion of the individual acting autonomously within a clear frame-work of moral reference is obsolete. By way of contrast, French noir writers retain the ideal of the republican citizen, as they subliminally revisit the Dreyfus Affair, constructing scenarios in which human rights enshrined in the Constitution are threatened by malevolent institutional forces.

The 'néo-polar' is typified by novels such as Jean Vautrin's *Billy ze Kick* (1974) and Jean-Patrick Manchette's *Fatale* (1977), bitter statements on, respectively, urban deprivation and the failure of cap-italism. On the strength of their and others' writings, it has left its distinctive mark on French literary history.[1] In the guise of a popular cultural form, the 'néo-polar' represents a powerful, collectivist attack on the ravages of transnational capitalism and its deleterious effects on the individual and communities alike. Also targeted are those re-actionary elements of the political establishment in France that came to the fore during the Occupation and then the Algerian War, with writers like Manchette constantly highlighting the commonalities be-tween the capitalist system and the interests of the nation-state. His archetypal hero is Gerfaut in *Le petit bleu de la côte Ouest* (1976), a marketing manager for an American company, who is pictured at the beginning and end of the novel driving in the early hours of the morning in a drunken state around the Paris ring-road, listening to jazz – a cultured, successful man transformed into a hamster on a wheel.[2] As the 'néo-polar' has developed, however, what might have been a transient, reactive phenomenon has become, over time, a robust, durable counter-culture. The example of the original band of 'néo-polar' activists inspired a second wave of campaigning crime novelists over recent decades, including Didier Daeninckx, who in the course of a dozen novels exposes various government-sanctioned crimes, and others like Jean-Bernard Pouy and Jean-Claude Izzo, who train their literary guns on the influence over the body politic of the lepéniste Far Right.

The crucial distinction that sets Amila apart from his peers, especially those like Manchette, Vautrin, Pierre Siniac and ADG most associated with the 'néo-polar', is also at the hub of his fictional

---

1   For detailed analyses of the political, cultural, and literary significance of the 'néo-polar', see 'Le Polar: entre Critique Sociale et Désenchantement', in *Mouvements* 15/16 (mai-juin-juillet-août 2001), 5–117, and Margaret Atack, *May 68 in French Fiction and Film* (Oxford: Oxford University Press, 1999), 123–42 ('Le néo-polar: behind enemy lines').

2   Jean-Patrick Manchette, *Le petit bleu de la côte Ouest* (Paris: Gallimard, Série Noire, 1976): 'La raison pour laquelle Georges file ainsi sur le périphérique avec des réflexes diminués et en écoutant cette musique-là, il faut la chercher surtout dans la place de Georges dans les rapports de production' (8); 'The reason why George is heading around the ring-road in this way, with his reactions dulled and listening to that music, must be sought in the position he occupies in the relations of production'.

project. The others were essentially political onlookers: Manchette a teacher, translator, and journalist; Vautrin a film-maker; Siniac and ADG, for different reasons, recluses. Amila also worked in the cinema and for the press, but at lower levels, as a dialogue writer on screen-plays, and as a door-stepping journalist. Information on his later life is, possibly for reasons that will become apparent below, difficult to ascertain. Our most reliable source remains the literary *œuvre*, im-aginative texts that offer a window on the author's world. What they reveal are facets of a self traversed by politics, in which content appears to transcend form. In comparison with the experiential ac-counts of the Spanish Civil War given by André Malraux in *L'Espoir* and George Orwell in *Homage to Catalonia*, where the distance between the events and the recording of those events is strategically maintained, Amila's politics are immanent to the stories he tells. The narrative of events obviates the requirement for concomitant political analysis. Significantly, the form of his novels, naturalistic and accessible, reflects this notion of a subject totally immersed in the world of politics, of which the novel-writing enterprise is an extension. It is a project that in some ways echoes Sartre's clarion call to the principle of committed literature articulated in his 1946 essay *Qu'est-ce que la littérature?* Sartre argues that the decision to write is in itself a political act, '[...] la littérature vous jette dans la bataille' ('literature launches you into battle').[3] From the perspective of Amila's work, Sartre's terms are inverted; here it is the battle that takes on a literary dimension.

After an initial discussion on the formation of Amila's political consciousness, this essay will explore his treatment of the conflict between the State and the individual, or rather national interests and individual rights, in three separate arenas. *La Lune d'Omaha* (1964) shows how war memorials propagate a distorted, mythical version of history, functioning as part of an official discourse that obliterates the private memories and trauma of the soldiers who served. *Contest-Flic* (1972), a seminal novel of the 'néo-polar', is a fictional account of a true crime, in which justice is sacrificed to the clandestine interests of

---

3   Jean-Paul Sartre, *Qu'est-ce que la littérature?* (Paris: Gallimard, Idées, 1967), 82.

the State. Finally, *Le Boucher des Hurlus* (1982) relates the devastating impact on the protagonist's childhood of nationalistic militarism during World War I.[4]

The template of the dissident political radical was imprinted on Amila's psyche from an early age. The chain of events that led to him being effectively orphaned at the age of eight seems to have played a key role in the evolution of his political temperament. Most accounts describe how, toward the latter stages of the Great War, his father was shot for 'desertion', and how, on hearing this news his mother broke down and was admitted to a psychiatric institution where she spent the next two years, a situation which inevitably resulted in her young son being sent to an orphanage. This early history informs Amila's semi-autobiographical novel, *Le Boucher des Hurlus*. However, it is at odds with a profile of the writer posted on an authoritative web-site, where it is claimed that his father survived the war only to elope with a nurse, and that it was his elopement which triggered the mother's psychiatric disorder and the child's admission to the orphanage.[5] Whatever the truth of the affair, it seems that, in Amila's mind's eye, this (his own) childhood trauma was interpreted as a political event. In *Le Boucher des Hurlus* the misery of the 'orphaned' child is transmuted into a microscopic reflection of the misery of the trenches. Even if, as it has been rumoured, the father did desert his wife and child rather than the French army, it could be argued that it was the experience of war which destroyed, as it so often did, the affective links between a soldier at the front and the family awaiting his return. The family breakdown is thus inextricably linked to the father's experience of war, most easily expressed from Amila's point of view as a simple collocation: his childhood trauma stemmed from his father's trauma, which stemmed in turn from the trauma of the Great War. In psychological terms this childhood experience of World War I seems to have triggered a coping mechanism within Amila which

---

4   Jean Amila, *La Lune d'Omaha* (Paris: Gallimard, Série Noire, 1964); *Contest-Flic* (Paris: Gallimard, Série Noire, 1972); *Le Boucher des Hurlus* (Paris: Gallimard, Série Noire, 1982).

5   'A l'ombre du polar', http://www.polars.org/article (consulted 31 October 2006).

endowed him with a mental capacity to leapfrog the complex middle ground between the personal and the political, to switch from the small to the big picture, from parochial squabbles to world war, in the blink of an eyelid, or in one metaphorical instant. It is precisely this capacity which is denied to the characters in his novels, who tend to be ordinary people pitched into political situations over which they have little or no influence.

Amila was born into an age of ideologies, when the search for alternative solutions to a bourgeois capitalist system seen as having engendered war, economic depression and fascism took on the utmost urgency. Collectively, however, his novels are a potpourri of different historical periods, milieus and character types, suggesting that, at least in his literary universe, he transcends the confines of a single political ideology. On the other hand, 'noir' specialists like Jean-Paul Schweighaeuser, pointing to the seam of social critique that runs through his fictional oeuvre, see Amila as a left-wing anarchist.[6] More broadly, he may be considered as a writer who incarnates what Edgar Morin has recently described, in a philosophical volte-face, as 'le principe hologrammique' ('the hologrammic principle').[7] Rather than conceiving of the totality as the sum of its constituent parts, Morin suggests that each disparate element carries within it the totality in a reduced form. Thus, society in its entirety is in the individual, and the individual contains within him or herself the totality of the universe that surrounds him and of which he is a part. In Amila's novels, the local scenes always form part of a broader canvas; they are the big picture in miniature.

His first novel, *Les Coups*, published in 1942 under his real name, Jean Meckert, is a good example of Amila's aptitude for depicting the political world in microcosm. In this instance the dark narrative of a doomed love affair involving Félix and Pauline, he an

6   See Jean-Paul Schweighaeuser, 'Du roman de voyou au roman engagé', in, *Les Temps Modernes* 595: *Roman noir: pas d'orchidées pour les T.M.* (August– October 1997), 100–21.

7   Morin develops the concept of 'le principe hologrammique' in a recent volume of his sociological opus, *La Méthode*. See Edgar Morin, *Ethique. La Méthode*, vol.VI (Paris: Seuil, 2004).

orphaned, itinerant, unemployed labourer and she the daughter of petit bourgeois parents, reads as a Marxist parable on the division of the social classes. Under intolerable pressure brought to bear by the constant jibes and condescending remarks of his in-laws, Félix cracks, and the love relationship degenerates into violence, as he repeatedly beats his wife. This futile response functions on two levels: firstly it translates Félix's inability to perceive the political causes of his distress and thus to channel his anger into revolutionary fervour; secondly, in classic Marxist terms, it alerts the reader to the inevitable disintegration of bourgeois capitalism as it spirals into class conflict and violence. The story is delivered in a popular vernacular, reminiscent of Céline, but the limited scope of the novel places it within the genre of 'la littérature prolétarienne' ('proletarian literature') associated with the Breton writer Louis Guilloux, which had become popular during the inter-war years. Two further novels dealing with similar themes in similar ways – *Nous avons les mains rouges* (1947) and *Je suis un monstre* (1949) – sold few copies and were quickly forgotten.

Having been co-opted into the *Série Noire* by its founder Marcel Duhamel, Amila became the second French author to appear in the series when *Y'a pas de Bon Dieu!* was published under the name of John Amila in 1950. The anglicisation of Amila's first name indicates both the fascination with American culture that gripped France at this time and Duhamel's chief marketing ploy, which was to bring the hard-boiled genre of American crime writing to a wider French audience.[8] With its portrayal of a flawed hero, Pastor Wiseman, and its plot in which the people of the imaginary town of Mowalla are deceived and exploited by the invisible forces of capitalism, *Y'a pas de Bon Dieu!* is earnest in its political orientation. However, Amila's debt to Dashiell Hammett, and especially to the latter's novel *Red Harvest*, is heavy, and the requirement to write a novel in French set

8   J. Amila, *Y'a pas de Bon Dieu!* (Paris: Gallimard, Série Noire, 1950). For an
     informative discussion on the cultural significance of the early French-language
     contributions to the *Série Noire*, see Claire Gorrara, 'Cultural Intersections: the
     American Hard-Boiled Detective Novel and Early French Roman Noir', *Modern Language Review* 98.3 (July 2003), 590–601.

in an imaginary projection of a small mid-western American town, a novel which purports to be the translation of an American original, is both a constraint on artistic freedom and suggestive of a cultural schizophrenia. At this point it is as if Amila is in limbo, waiting for the cultural climate in France to change, waiting for his moment which would come with the rise to prominence of the 'néo-polar' in the late 1960s and early 1970s. Nevertheless, in the meantime, he produces a major work, in which he deals again with American and French relations, but this time on his own terms and on his own turf.

La Lune d'Omaha was published in 1964, nearly twenty years after the D-Day landings. It is the first crime novel to deal extensively, and in a sophisticated manner, with the key post-war themes of memory, place and identity. The plot is ingeniously simple. One of the team of gardeners at the military cemetery on the cliff-tops over-looking Omaha Beach dies, leaving a substantial inheritance. An American GI, who had deserted in 1944 having refused to rejoin what was left of his regiment after the massacre on Omaha beach, now returns to the area to claim the inheritance. In law the relationship between the two men is that of father to son. The gardener, Amédée Delouis, had forged a wedding certificate and sold to the family who had been sheltering the GI a new 'French' identity which he could adopt. Thereby the latter became Georges Delouis rather than George Hutchins, the name on a tombstone at Omaha of the American GI, missing presumed dead. On his return, a melodrama is played out in a pared down theatrical setting, between Delouis/Hutchins, his wife, and the real family of the deceased gardener, which reaches its dénouement on Omaha beach, as the dogs guarding the cemetery howl under a full moon.

Amila may, by an act of imagination, have crossed the Atlantic with *Y'a pas de Bon Dieu!*, but the situation is reversed abruptly with the first sentence of *La Lune d'Omaha*, as the GIs, huddled in their landing craft, nauseous and fearful, glimpse France for the first time: 'On ne voyait rien que le ciel bas, sauf quand la barque piquait du nez; alors on distinguait la plage lointaine en rideau grisâtre. La France!'

(7).[9] Failure and success in overcoming cultural differences will be reflected through two survivors of the Normandy landings. Sergeant Reilly, who is stationed permanently at the Omaha Memorial Cemetery, patrolling the seventy hectares donated by the French government to the USA, would seem to epitomise the war hero. In reality he is a lonely, drunken cuckold, whose young French wife leaves him and whose attempts to converse in French make of him a figure of fun. By contrast, Hutchins has assumed his new identity so completely that the faintest trace of an accent is not sufficient in itself for him to be unmasked.[10] Yet both men are depicted as victims.

La Lune d'Omaha marks an important stage in the development of the 'roman noir' in France that recognises the influence of the American pioneers whilst drawing also on its own literary heritage – the term 'roman noir' was originally applied to the popular gothic novels of the nineteenth century – as it engages fully with aspects of French culture and history. Indeed it is possible to argue that the plot of this novel enacts the cultural tension created by French credentials being given to an American import, but whatever the symbolism of the cultural intersections – the ironies, the reversals, and the sense that a point is being made about the strength or otherwise of the authentically 'French' roman noir – my contention is that Amila's priorities lie elsewhere. *La Lune d'Omaha* is essentially a novel about representation. It questions our fascination with the business of commemoration. The reader is frequently reminded of the visibility of the memorial statue just beyond the gates to the cemetery, which, as in the following example, seems to dominate the horizons of the characters:

9   'We could see nothing other than the low sky, except when the boat pitched forward; then we could make out the beach in the distance enveloped in a greyish curtain. France!'

10   'Il y avait quelque chose d'indéfinissable, une certaine façon de liquider les "r" et de moduler dans les graves, un peu comme un comédien. Vague idée d'accent étranger, à peine perceptible' (*La Lune d'Omaha*, 86); 'There was an indefinable quality, a certain way of suppressing the 'r' sounds and deepening the voice, a bit like an actor would. The vague sense of a foreign accent, scarcely perceptible'.

Par-dessus la haie de roses pompons, on voyait le haut du portique du Mémorial et la grande statue de bronze de bonhomme à poil qui avait l'air de sauter du tremplin pour tenter la figure de plongeon dite 'coup de pied à la lune'. C'était sans doute censé représenter l'âme du Combattant s'envolant vers les cieux.[11]

The narrator's statement is ironic; it is not clear how the figure of a naked diver in mid-plunge is supposed to convey the spirit of a dying soldier. Moreover, if the shape of the memorial is inadequate for the purpose of commemoration, the ubiquitous inscriptions carved into the memorial, on the tombstones and in the remembrance chapel, constitute a dizzying replication of empty concepts, described ultimately by the enlightened Captain Mason as an 'Enfer de majuscules' (246) ('Inferno of capital letters').

The literal trappings of commemoration thus define a mythology of war rather than the reality of what happened on Omaha Beach in June 1944. However, thanks to the ingenious narrative design of *La Lune d'Omaha*, Amila can bring to life a simple, dead metaphor: that men are led into war like cattle to the slaughterhouse. The narrator describes the prevailing attitude on the landing craft: 'Chacun pour soi, dans la morne résignation du troupeau de bêtes qu'on conduit à l'abattoir' (8–9).[12] In this respect the supposedly glorious D-Day landings match the widely criticised trench warfare of World War I. The corpses bobbing in the waves are likened to 'pantins grotesques et disloqués' (20) ('grotesque, dislocated puppets'); the soldiers have been manipulated like puppets, their disempowerment evident in death as in life. The textual metaphor of the soldiers as cattle becomes a literal element of the story, when the hapless Sergeant Reilly is informed by the priest, speaking in a pronounced local dialect, that the immaculate lawns and white headstones of the cemetery cover a mass grave containing bovine carcasses as well as the remains of American

---

11   'Above the hedge of button roses, the top of the portico of the Memorial could be seen, and the large bronze statue of a naked man who looked as if he was jumping off a springboard in an attempt to produce the dive that goes by the name of the "moon kick". It was clearly supposed to represent the soul of the Combatant rising heavenward'. Ibid., 47.

12   'Each man for himself, in the dismal resignation of the herd of animals being led to the slaughterhouse'.

GIs: '[...] voilà des bêtes à cornes sous des croix de chrétiens' (63) ('there are beasts with horns beneath Christian crosses'). The outraged Reilly, already teetering on the verge of paranoia on account of his own linguistic shortcomings, recalls the 'moo-ing' quality of the locals' pronunciation of 'Omaha': 'Brusquement il se souvint de la curieuse manière qu'avaient les gens de par ici de prononcer Omaha, en le traînant, en le veulant jusqu'à en faire un meuglement: Omeu-heuuu!...' (65).[13] Like a bull in a china shop – Amila uses the verb 'foncer', normally applied to a charging bull – he rushes to alert his superior Mason to this discovery. The latter chooses an appropriate analogy with which to dismiss Reilly's complaint: 'Pas plus d'importance, sergent, que de saigner du nez dans un abattoir' (70) ('No more significant, Sergeant, than a nose-bleed in a slaughterhouse').

The bovine metaphor extends further into the text. As Georges and his wife Janine discuss tactics prior to their bid for the Delouis inheritance, they decide to 'prendre le taureau par les cornes' (112) ('take the bull by the horns'). The cliché allows for a subliminal comparison of, on the one hand, the bullish Reilly's blindness to the political realities of war and its aftermath with, on the other, the indifference to the war, and to the sacrifices made by those who fought in it, shown by the legatees who are consumed by their venality. Henceforth the narrative coils itself around the figure of the craven bourgeois wife, bound by her family and, in the case of Janine, by her devotion to the husband that she has in effect bought. They, like Reilly and the soldiers tending the cemetery, live in closed worlds.

Such a capacity for self-absorption and detachment replicates a more general 'repli sur soi' ('withdrawal into the self'). In the immediate post-war years the majority of the French population was naturally inclined to embrace de Gaulle's paternalism and shut out the painful memories of the Occupation. However, *La Lune d'Omaha* looks to a future beyond this time. It is an early intervention in the debate on the 'devoir de mémoire' ('duty to memory') which has

---

13 'Suddenly he remembered the curious way in which the local people pronounced Omaha, dragging out the sounds, so as to make a moo-ing noise: Omeuheuuu!...'

grown exponentially in France, and across the world, notably with regard to the commemoration of the Holocaust.[14] In the clear-sighted perspective of Captain Mason in the novel, which Amila appears to endorse, the war cemetery mirrors society at large. It represents our failure to learn from war, and therefore its commemorative function can only be to legitimise the violence, the loss of men and the human misery. He notes that no generals died in the D-Day landings; one was eventually found nine months later, killed by friendly fire in the Normandy campaign, and laid to rest alongside the fallen of Omaha Beach. However, Mason is comparable to the other characters in the novel for, like them, he exists in his own world, in the self-imposed isolation of his own cultural island. His house is presented as a sanctuary for the classical arts, sheltered from the vulgarity on its doorstep. On the last page of the novel he is described as an intellectual, 'donc un futile' (246) ('therefore a person of no consequence'). Mason's critique of war as a reflection of society may be well-founded, but his voice is unlikely to carry far. The 'futility' of his intervention thus applies to all those disengaged apostles of reason who refuse to dirty their hands with politics.

Amila's engagement with the politics of commemoration in *La Lune d'Omaha* blossoms with his role as a leading light of the 'néopolar' into a full-scale resistance against state oppression. However, his best-known work of the period is built on the same shifting sands of time and blurring between reality and fiction that we find in *La Lune d'Omaha*.

Contest-flic is the second of a series of three novels – the other are *La Nef des dingues* and *Terminus Iéna*[15] – that feature Edouard Magne, also known as Géronimo or Doudou, a hippy detective working out of the Quai des Orfèvres. Whilst on holiday, Magne becomes embroiled in the investigation of the murder of a family of German

---

14   Significant contributions to the discussion on the 'devoir de mémoire' include Marc Augé, *Les Formes de l'Oubli* (Paris: Payot, 1998); Paul Ricœur, *La Mémoire, l'Histoire, l'Oubli* (Paris: Seuil, 2000); and Tzvetan Todorov, *Les Abus de la Mémoire* (Paris: Arléa, 1998).

15   Jean Amila, *La Nef des dingues* (Paris: Gallimard, Série Noire, 1971); *Terminus Iéna* (Paris: Gallimard, Série Noire, 1972).

campers in the Basses-Alpes. Suspicions centre on the Bellone family, who live in a farmhouse near to where the bodies are found, and whose witness statements are not consistent with each other. Magne, however, teams up with Hilda, a young German journalist, and they pursue some more politically sensitive leads; the murdered father was a professor of biochemistry and expert on munitions. Ten days into the case, after several long interrogations, Donatien, the patriarch of the Bellone household, confesses to the murders. At the same time a car driven by Magne's chief suspect, a gangster in the pay of the West German Secret Services, plunges mysteriously into a ravine. Although forensic evidence comes to light which seems to support the confession of Donatien, Magne is convinced that the confession is part of a state-sponsored cover-up and the old man, who is communist to boot, a convenient scapegoat. He muses that it is always the Secret Services who 'règlent tout [...] au nom de quelque défense subtile du territoire' (171) ('sort it all out [...] in the name of some subtle defence of the realm').

However, *Contest-flic* is not simply a dreyfusard contestation of the concept of the 'national interest': it is also a trenchant critique of the power and sensationalism of the modern media. Overnight the small Alpine town of Colmar is transformed into the 'global village' of the telecommunications age. Reverting to a familiar refrain, Amila emphasises how the Bellone family are reduced to the status of exhibits in a zoo, animals in a cage baited by the investigating authorities and the journalists. As the daughter-in-law Sophie exclaims despairingly: 'On n'est pas des bêtes fauves dans la cage! Tout le monde vient nous voir, comme au zoo!' (15).[16] The impact of the mass media on the fortunes of the family is catastrophic:

> Tout cet immense théâtre, avec des journalistes aux premières loges, la France et le monde entier comme témoins plus lointains, avait été préparé pour confondre ces paysans bas-alpins qui paraissaient s'en foutre éperdument (43).[17]

16   'We are not wild animals in a cage! Everyone is coming to see us, as if we are in a zoo!'.
17   'All this immense theatre, with the journalists in the box seats and France and the whole world up in the gods, had been staged in order to confuse these peasants from the foothills of the Alps who seemed not to give a damn'.

This dismal portrayal of Debord's 'société du spectacle' looks forward to a world in which the spectator has become less a citizen and more a parasite, feeding on a diet of reality shows designed to stimulate a collective Schadenfreude. At the same time the progressive politics of Magne, alias 'Géronimo', with his long hair, headband, and passion for justice, is presented as a viable alternative to the docility of the consumer society. His non-conformism is reflected in the resourcefulness and independence of mind of the young journalist Hilda, 'gamine pure, page blanche où tout restait continuellement à inventer' (57) ('a pure kid, a blank page on which everything was still to be invented'), and as the couple make love beneath a painting of Napoleon, 'l'immonde ex-futur Empereur des Français' (159) ('the disgusting ex-future Emperor of the French'), Amila's faith in the prospect of political solutions to society's ills is symbolically reaffirmed. However, such optimism is curtailed when the novel is read in context. The scenario of *Contest-flic* is not original. Rather the novel is a Trojan horse which allows Amila to smuggle a small cast of fictional characters, recognizably imbued with the spirit of the late 1960s and operating within the discourse of their time, into a real-life crime case that gripped the French nation nearly two decades earlier. In all its major aspects the narrative of *Contest-flic* tracks that of a *cause célèbre*, the brutal murders in the Basses Alpes in August 1952 of Sir Jack Drummond, a British nutrition expert, his wife, and his daughter, that was originally termed 'l'affaire de Lurs' but quickly became known as 'l'affaire Dominici'. The case continues to generate controversy to the present day; in 2001 Alain Dominici, grandson of the late Gaston who 'confessed' to the murders, published an open letter to the Ministre de la Justice, Marylise Lebranchu, asking for a review of the trial. However, what primarily interests Amila, like Giono and Barthes before him, is the social, cultural, and above all political ramifications of the Dominici affair.[18] *Contest-flic* does not provide new angles on the case: rumours of Drummond's involvement

18   For a comprehensive discussion of the social, political, and cultural ramifications of 'l'affaire Dominici', see Margaret Atack, 'L'Affaire Dominici: Rural France, the State, and the Nation', *French Cultural Studies* 12.3 (October 2001), 285–301.

in espionage were rife at the time of the trial. What it does provide is a powerful new frame of cultural reference. The Zeitgeist of the hippy age serves to illuminate the possible ways in which the truth of the Dominici affair may have been forever occluded by authoritarian forces masquerading as the arbiters of justice. Thus, the notoriety of the affair lies precisely in its political nature. In this respect *Contest-flic* sounds a warning to the reader. At the end of the novel Hilda's story is 'killed' by her editor, and her political ardour extinguished with it: 'En quelques instants elle avait mûri, était devenue "intelligente", jeunesse perdue, cerveau déjà spécialisé, obsédé par la conquête d'une place au soleil dans la meute' (181).[19] She has, in the jargon, 'sold out'. In Amila's scale of values, such a withdrawal from civic and political involvement was not to be contemplated.

Jean Amila's literary career marks the course of his 'engagement', of the evolution of an identity in which the political and the personal are entwined. His penultimate novel, *Le Boucher des Hurlus* stands at both the beginning and end of this journey. It has been hailed as one of the finest examples of crime writing in the French language.[20] Whereas previously, in novels like *La Lune d'Omaha* and *Contest-flic*, Amila depicts ordinary characters whose lives are spun in the maelstrom of international politics, in *Le Boucher des Hurlus* the tone is more intimate, the violence close at hand, and the writing more intense.

The main character is an eight-year-old boy, Michou Lhozier, who is generally referred to as 'le môme'. The story is set in the

19 'In a few brief moments she had matured, had become "intelligent", lost her youth, her brain already that of a specialist, obsessed by emerging one day from the pack and winning her place in the sun'.
20 A noted specialist in French noir fiction describes it in the following terms: 'Jean Amila imprègne de toute la force de son immense talent ce roman sans fard, plus vrai que nature, et il nous offre l'un des plus terribles morceaux de bravoure du roman noir français'. ('Jean Amila brings the full force of his immense talent to bear on this unvarnished novel, truer than reality, and in so doing offers us one of the most terrifying examples of bravura to be found in French crime writing'.) See Robert Deleuse, 'Petite histoire du roman noir français', in *Les Temps Modernes*, 595 (August–October 1997), 53–87 (p.79–80).

weeks following the armistice that finally ended World War I. The boy's father, a left-wing sympathiser, has been shot along with a group of others who refused to 'go over the top' at Perthes-les-Hurlus, a strategically insignificant vantage-point about 15 to 20 km south-west of Verdun. The mother and child, eking out a living in a Parisian suburb, are subjected to unremitting abuse and harassment on account of the father's lack of patriotism. Their principal antagonist is their poisonous neighbour, 'la mère Venin'. One day when 'la mère Venin' jabs at Michou's mother's face with the tip of her umbrella, the latter retaliates, raining blows on her assailant, and is subsequently committed to a psychiatric institution on public order offences. (Amila uses the ironic expression 'troubler la paix', meaning 'a breach of the peace'.) The boy breaks out of the orphanage to which he has been sent and leads three older boys on a mission to the 'régions dévastées' ('devastated regions'), the war zone east of Châlons-sur-Marne, where his father met his death. There they find a framed photograph of the general who ordered the shootings, 'le boucher des Hurlus' ('the butcher of the Hurlus'). This photograph exists in counterpoint to the framed photograph of Michou's father which hung on the wall of his mother's flat, one of numerous structural parallels within the text. The boys simulate the ritual killing of the general by piercing the image of his chest with a hairpin. On their return to Paris, 'le môme' uses a revolver stolen from a dozing soldier to shoot the old woman who persecuted his mother, and they burn down the building in which Michou used to live before returning to the orphanage.

Although the orphans' journey to the front line verges on the burlesque – at one point the boys find themselves in the company of a team of prostitutes complete with domineering 'Madame' who are on their way to service the soldiers still on duty in the war zone – it is presented in terms of a military expedition. Preparations start in the orphanage which, in any case, resembles an army barracks. The boys eat their broth, 'le dîner pisse d'âne' ('the donkey's piss dinner'), out of billycans. When they first arrive, their heads are shaved and coated with iodine allegedly to protect them from Spanish influenza. Out on the streets their raising of their caps, which would have been a near-involuntary gesture of politeness, inspires revulsion and pity in those they encounter; more importantly, the yellow 'helmets' of their scalps bind them together in a common, regimental identity. This children's crusade would read as merely a pastiche of the standard military-epic plotline, familiar from Hollywood blockbusters such as *The Guns of Navarone* or *Where Eagles Dare*, were it not for the single-minded, earnest determination that sets 'le môme' apart from his contemporaries. His desire to exact direct reprisals is a consequence of what the narrator perceives to be the inverted moral order supported by those who sought to justify the war. Thus, the kind army captain and affable infantrymen who accompany the orphans to the front are:

> fabriqués, on ne pouvait leur en vouloir, tout 'verlans' de langage et pensée, parlant de sublime sacrifice et de Gloire immortelle là où il n'y avait que honteux charcutage, à trente obus par décimètre carré sur l'immense hachoir des Hurlus (172).[21]

Of course, these sections echo the pronouncements of writers in the 1920s like Hemingway who felt that, in the new reality of the massacre in the trenches, words such as 'glory' and 'sacrifice' had lost their conceptual value. Or like Céline, whose hero Bardamu fantasises that, if the officers and soldiers were all summarily liquidated, he and the few other survivors could take the place of the generals and enjoy the fanfare and trappings of a glorious homecoming.[22]

This kind of valedictory statement hints at an intriguing feature of the novel, which concerns dislocations and discontinuities at the level of the narrative voice. There is clearly an attempt to give an undiluted presentation of this world through the mind's eye of an eight-year old boy, living in difficult conditions at the end of World War I; the colloquial dialects of the period, for example, are faithfully captured. Near the beginning, the mother's fight with the neighbour and her subsequent arrest both happen off-stage. In the latter case, the boy is shut in his room and hears his mother's pleas. His restricted

21   '[...] fabricated, you can't blame them for it, all back-to-front in what they say and think, speaking of sublime sacrifice and immortal glory when there was only shameful butchery, of the order of thirty shells per square decimetre across the huge chopping board of the Hurlus'.

22   Louis-Ferdinand Céline, *Voyage au bout de la nuit* (1932) (Paris: Gallimard, Folio, 1979), 29–30.

perspective on the event merely serves to heighten the effect of the underlying violence which erupts later, when the neighbour and her husband try to smother him in his own eiderdown. In addition, Amila is sensitive to the ways in which hunger modulates the behaviour of his characters. The hunger of the orphans is omnipresent. When 'le môme' is asked by the teacher at the orphanage to give an example of a regular '-er' verb, he replies – 'Manger, M'Sieur. J'ai pas mangé, c'était pas bon' (43). ('To eat, sir. I haven't eaten, it wasn't good'.) Amila characterises one of the band of four, 'le grand Aristide', as in the throes of puberty. He is therefore always desperately hungry, so that when they enter the Gare de l'Est, it is he who is transfixed by the large sign spelling out the word 'BUFFET'. Hunger on the scale experienced by the orphans is, it is suggested, a form of violence perpetrated by the state on its own citizens.

The most momentous event in the novel occurs when the four orphans witness a large mound of human bones on the recently va-cated battlefield. This delayed representation of the carnage serves to encapsulate the horror of the war just as effectively as the unmediated, experiential accounts of the soldiers who returned from the front. Joanna Bourke argues convincingly in her book, *An Intimate History of Killing*, that the mechanical, technological nature of warfare in the twentieth century puts such a distance between opponents that the soldier rarely perceives the immediate consequences of his actions. The suffering he witnesses is uniquely that of himself or of his comrades.[23] By contrast, when in *Le Boucher des Hurlus* a group of children encounter the pile of bones, the effect is jarring. However, even here the scene is scrutinised by an analytical eye. The narrator observes that amidst the tangled mass of clavicles, femurs and pelvises, there are few skulls, thereby implying that the skulls had already, for some reason, been removed. This precise observation establishes a parallel with the killing fields of Cambodia, an event

---

23 Bourke makes the distinction between seeing men dying and seeing them being killed: 'The long-distant and indirect character of "area attacking weapons" such as shrapnel, bombs, and gas meant that while people could regularly be seen dying, it was rarer to see them being killed'. Joanna Bourke, *An Intimate History of Killing* (London: Granta, 1999), 6.

contemporaneous with the writing of *Le Boucher des Hurlus* and lodged in our global consciousness via the totemic image of the victims' skulls, displayed on shelves in Phnom Penh for posterity. Thus, Amila's retrospective evocation of the mound of bones at Verdun also looks forward into our more immediate past. For the reader of today it is superimposed over the other familiar images of horror and atrocity, from the Nazis' emaciated victims to the Cambodian and Rwandan genocides.

If we pause to consider the theme of violence and the way it is used in the crime genres, we can see how Amila's approach makes of his novels a special case. When Marcel Duhamel launched the Série Noire in 1945, he aimed to exploit public delectation in the representation of gratuitous violence:

> Que le lecteur non prévenu se méfie: les volumes de la Série noire ne peuvent pas sans danger être mis entre toutes les mains. L'amateur d'énigmes à la Sherlock Holmes n'y trouvera pas son compte [...]. Le détective sympathique ne résout pas toujours le mystère. Parfois il n'y a pas de mystère. Et quelquefois même, pas de détective du tout. Mais alors?... Alors, il reste de l'action, de l'angoisse, de la violence – sous toutes ses formes et plus particulièrement les plus honnies du tabassage et du massacre... Il y a aussi de l'amour - préférablement bestial – de la passion désordonnée, de la haine sans merci...[24]

Duhamel recognises that in nearly all crime fiction, including the quaint 'drawing room' whodunit, the crime is fetishised. In its classical form the crime novel or short story is engineered to recover the 'absent' narrative of the murder in all its details. In Poe's 'The Murders in the Rue Morgue', the state of the victim's bodies is repeatedly described: Madame L'Espanaye's corpse is discovered in

---

24   Quoted in Boileau-Narcejac, *Le Roman Policier* (Paris: PUF, 1994), 85. ('The unaware reader should beware: books published in the Série Noire should not be left around for anyone to read. The fan of Sherlock Holmes type puzzles will not find what he is looking for here [...]. The nice detective doesn't always solve the mystery. Sometimes there isn't any mystery, sometimes not even a detective. What is there then? Well, there is drama, suffering, and violence in all its conceivable forms, especially the nastiest kinds of beatings and slaughter... There is also love – preferably of the baser kind – uncontrolled passions, hatred without mercy...').

the back yard 'with her throat so entirely cut that, upon an attempt to raise her, the head fell off'', and that of her daughter dragged 'head downward' from the chimney, 'it having been thus forced up the narrow aperture for a considerable distance'.[25] Likewise, Agatha Christie gives precise details of the gruesome effects of strychnine poisoning in *The Mysterious Affair at Styles*. In neither of the above examples is the violence gratuitous – unlike the many violent episodes in the fiction of James Hadley Chase and Peter Cheyney that Duhamel was promoting – but its representation is direct and immediate. For some contemporary noir novelists the unmediated representation of extreme violence is a condition of their commitment to a new form of literary realism. Thus in the opening chapter of his novel *Moloch* Thierry Jonquet describes in distressing close-up a crime scene featuring the charred bodies of a group of children who have been tortured and murdered.[26] Such episodes raise ethical issues with which Didier Daeninckx seems to wrestle in *Meurtres pour Mémoire*, his story of the confrontations between protesting Algerians and the French riot police on 17 October 1961, in which the war criminal Maurice Papon, who was at the time the Prefect of Police in Paris, was implicated. Daeninckx feels bound to represent in the most graphic terms what happened at 'la bataille de Paris', in order to show the extent to which the French government suppressed the historical evidence. At the same time he is aware that in so doing he risks causing distress and offence to relatives of the victims. Daeninckx squares this particular circle by staging a literary recreation of the 'battle', which is narrated from the point of view of the victims.[27] These victims are named, fictional characters, whose separate lives have, up to this point, monopolised the narrative. They are also representatives of a 'forgotten' people whom Daeninckx attempts to rescue from historical oblivion.

Novels such as *Meurtres pour mémoire* have been incorporated into the polemical debate that has dominated the politics of memory

25   Edgar Allan Poe, *Selected Tales* (Oxford: Oxford University Press, 1980), 113.
26   Thierry Jonquet, *Moloch* (Paris: Gallimard, Folio Policier, 1998).
27   Didier Daeninckx, *Meurtres pour mémoire* (Paris: Gallimard, Folio, 1984), 27–33.

and the issue of commemorating the Holocaust, a debate in which intellectuals like Claude Lanzmann have rejected photographic evidence and other forms of representation as means of conveying the truth of the camps in favour of written or filmed testimony. Amila, whose fiction is grounded in traumatic historical events, elides the issue; he differs from nearly all other crime writers for whom the direct portrayal of violence is a necessary part of their mission in that, in his fiction, violence tends to be evoked metonymically. We can see this in the persistent return to the military cemetery in *La Lune d'Omaha*, in the characters' fixation with the place, and in the emblematic permanence of the memorial that rarely dips below the skyline. The killing of the gangster in *Contest-Flic*, who is overcome by cyanide fumes, occurs behind the closed doors of a lift, and in a comic reprise Magne, who is waiting for the lift to arrive, sends it back down to pick up the two thugs who have been sent to get him, and they suffer the same fate. The avenging of the father's death in *Le Boucher des Hurlus* is a pure simulacrum, and in Amila's last novel, *Au Balcon d'Hiroshima*, there is no attempt to represent the appalling after-effects of the dropping of the atomic bomb on Hiroshima. Although it would be inaccurate to claim that descriptions of violence and violent acts are entirely absent or expunged from the text of Amila's fiction, the balance of evidence suggests that the reader of his novels is in the presence of a writer whose instincts are to lead us quickly away from the physical reality of violence in order to prioritise its political context. His work betrays a constant awareness of the fundamental dignity of the individual human being which may go so far as to temper his radical politics. It transpires that this reluctance to entertain graphic descriptions of violence and death, whilst working within a genre predisposed to dealing with just these aspects, has conferred a kind of purity on a man whose discretion and respect for others has led to him being revered as a kind of secular saint among crime writers.[28] This saintliness was to encounter something like its own martyrdom in a Parisian underground car park in 1974.

---

28   Patrick Pécherot offers a concise portrait of a self-effacing crusader: 'La conscience en bandoulière [...], la résistance quand d'autres se taisent et l'anonymat quand ils se pavanent' ('Wearing his conscience slung over his

Some time in 1971 a French reconnaissance aircraft flying over remote Polynesian outcrops in preparation for the imminent testing of a French atomic bomb out in the Pacific detects a human presence on one of the islands. The French nuclear programme in the Pacific is immediately suspended for six months. In 1972 Jean Amila publishes a novel entitled *La Vierge et le Taureau*, which apparently contains information identifying him as the Polynesian interloper. The novel is withdrawn from all bookshops within days of its publication and the entire print run confiscated. In 1974, having received numerous death threats, Amila is attacked and savagely beaten in the car park beneath his Parisian apartment. For weeks he languishes comatose in hospital. He recovers, but has suffered a total amnesia. However, with the help of his sister, he relearns to read and write and makes a triumphant literary return, firstly with *Le Pigeon des Faubourgs*, then *Le Boucher des Hurlus*, and finally *Au Balcon d'Hiroshima*.[29]

The precise details of this story depend on which source you consult, but it appears to be true, in which case it puts the final stages of Amila's literary career in a different light.[30] Of the three novels published after the assault, *Le Boucher des Hurlus* is the most intriguing because it takes us back to a time prior to the event; *Le Pigeon des faubourgs* is a parochial affair, a 'crime passionnel' with political undertones that takes place in the working-class Parisian district of the Faubourg Saint-Antoine near to the Bastille, and *Au Balcon d'Hiroshima* is the story of an escalating quarrel between criminal rivals over

shoulder [...], resistance when others don't speak up and anonymity when they show off') (http://www.pecherot.com: note on Amila consulted 31 October 2006). This reputation is borne out by the rapt notices accorded to Amila in various study guides on the French *roman noir* and by the numerous dedications at the front of novels or, as is the case with a recent Daeninckx text, *12 rue Meckert*, encrypted in the title.

29   Jean Amila, *Le Pigeon des faubourgs* (Paris: Gallimard, Série Noire, 1981); *Au Balcon d'Hiroshima* (Paris: Gallimard, Série Noire, 1986).

30   A version of events is given in Deleuse, 'Petite histoire du roman noir français' (74), and the plot of *Nazis dans le Métro*, Daeninckx's contribution to the Le Poulpe collection, is generated by a vicious attack in analogous circumstances perpetrated by unknown assailants on André Sloga, a fictional writer with deep-seated political convictions. See Daeninckx, Didier, *Le Poulpe. Nazis dans le métro* (Paris: Éditions Baleine, 1996).

the division of the booty from a heist, which is presented as an allegory of the conflict between America and Japan in World War II. Amila's riposte to the physical violence he suffered was to create, in *Le Boucher des Hurlus*, a novel that takes its reader to the core of his political identity. In this context the parallelism of the dual time-scale is paramount. Michou's father is shot for his revolt against militaristic nationalism, and his son undertakes a symbolic gesture of protest in rectification of the injustice. In Amila's life during the 1970s and 1980s, he is beaten nearly to death as punishment for a similar revolt, and it is the writing of a novel, some years later, which represents his (again, the son's) symbolic protest and revenge against his oppressors. Seen in this light, the act of writing the novel is also, like the content of the text, an act of commemoration of his father, and a more authentic and subtle one than the statue at Omaha Beach: in fact it is a counter-gesture to the statue, in its active dissidence rather than passive, bovine acceptance.

Le Boucher des Hurlus is a novel of jagged edges and a notable discordance of tone. The narrator's language is extensively filtered through the perspective of Michou, the eight-year old protagonist, but the literary gloss applied to the perspective of the orphans is sometimes out of keeping with this angle of vision.[31] Moreover, while there is frequent, at times eccentric, recourse in the narrative to a Christian rhetoric,[32] the narrator, in keeping with the mantra of Michou's

---

31 For example, the description (211–3) of the fire taking hold of the building in which 'le môme' used to live, which is observed by the orphans from their vantage-point in a nearby church spire, is littered with extended similes. The initial flames are personified – '[...] on aurait même cru que le feu bâillait, se réveillait, qu'il se mettait sur le cul et se frottait les yeux [...]' ('you might even have thought that the fire was yawning, coming awake, sitting up on its arse and rubbing its eyes') – and the boys' vantage-point in the spectacle is compared to sitting in the audience at the opening night of an opera for which they had composed the music.

32 When one of the gang of boys narrowly evades a suspicious baker without revealing the gun he has concealed in his waistband, he is described as braying like 'le fameux chameau qui passe par le trou d'une aiguille' (*Le Boucher des Hurlus*, 221) ('the famous camel who passes through the eye of the needle'). It may have been a great escape, but it is difficult to see in what way the boy's

anarcho-syndicalist father, 'Ni Dieu ni maître' ('Neither God nor master'), feels obliged to provide his reader with a sermon on the absurdity of religious (specifically Christian) indoctrination, on which the novel closes.

Amila can be forgiven for wanting to punch home his atheism – he would no doubt have objected strongly to being described as a 'saint' among crime writers – but, in narratological and linguistic terms, *Le Boucher des Hurlus* remains an untidy novel. Be that as it may, those sections that lack harmony are compensated by the eerie sense of witness found in others, when the novel functions as a literary time capsule taking its reader back to an era on the brink of modernity, when the puzzling quiescence of the French population during the War hardened and splintered shortly after it, in the face of stark ideological alternatives. Given the circumstances, one could indeed speculate that this peculiar, fractured act of remembrance could only have come about as a consequence of the damage inflicted on Amila's brain by the unknown thugs in the underground car park.

In its autobiographical aspect *Le Boucher des Hurlus* brings us full circle. Amila's father may or may not have been condemned for refusing to fight on the front line, but there is no doubt that his mother was sectioned, and that as a small boy he was sent to an orphanage. However, this novel should not be read simply as a polemical fiction on the horror of World War I that draws on the childhood experiences of its author. It does not form part of a campaign for the rehabilitation of those who were shot for desertion or cowardice in the trenches. Rather it is an extraordinary verbal riposte to state violence, to the unknown agents who pulverised his body and to those whose orders they followed, and a vindication of a political ideology, that of a radical, engaged pacifist with anarchist tendencies, which remained with Amila throughout his life. *Le Boucher des Hurlus* affords us a unique insight into the formation of a political conscience at the dawn of the most turbulent century in the history of Europe. As Olivier Mongin has eloquently surmised: 'Qui sommes-nous? Un peuple dont

sense of relief is commensurate with a divine injunction to divest oneself of all material belongings and lead a pure, spiritual existence.

l'histoire a commencé à se défaire dans les tranchées de Verdun...'.[33]
Like the saint, Amila's good works will achieve posthumous recognition. The elasticity of point of view and shifting of temporal frames so conspicuous in *Le Boucher des Hurlus* are techniques that he honed throughout his novelistic career in order to encourage his reader to make comparisons between different times and epochs, and thus to learn lessons from history. Consequently, the reader may be inclined to look sympathetically on Amila's politics of commitment. The pseudonym, Amila, invites us to do so: it is a contraction of 'Amilanar', or 'Ami, l'anar', the anarchist is your friend.

33   Olivier Mongin, 'Temps de provocation', *Esprit* (January 1992), 3–4. ('Who are we? A people whose history began to unravel in the trenches of Verdun'.)

Notes on Contributors

KIRSTEEN ANDERSON is Senior Lecturer in French, Queen Mary, University of London. Her past research has centred on Valéry and on twentieth-century French ethical writing (Camus, Ponge, Barthes and Irigaray). At present she is exploring connections between Simone Weil's thinking on force and Foucault's theorising of power. A further strand of investigation focuses on the imagination in both creative and critical writing, its connection with intelligence and its role in intellectual and professional development. Significant publications include *Paul Valéry and the Voice of Desire* (Legenda, 2000) and a translation from the Italian of Luce Irigaray's 'Democracy Begins between Two' (Athlone, 2000).

DERVILA COOKE lectures at Oxford Brookes University. She has also taught at University College Dublin and at NUI Maynooth, and held an IRCHSS Research Fellowship at Trinity College Dublin from 2004–2006. Her most recent research project involved a study of the contemporary *flâneur* in Paris, in literature, photography and film. Her doctoral thesis examined Patrick Modiano's biographical fiction, and was published in adapted form as *Present Pasts: Patrick Modiano's (Auto)Biographical Fictions* (Rodopi, 2005).

TOBY GARFITT is Fellow and Tutor in French at Magdalen College, Oxford. He has worked extensively on French literature between the wars, as well as the contemporary writers Sylvie Germain and Andrei Makine, and has just completed a biography of Camus's mentor Jean Grenier. Publications include a study of Mauriac's *Thérèse Desqueyroux* (Grant and Cutler, 1991/1997), *Sylvie Germain: rose des vents et de l'ailleurs* (L'Harmattan, 2003), and *Daniel Halévy, Henri Petit, et les Cahiers Verts* (Peter Lang, 2003).

200

DAVID GASCOIGNE is Senior Lecturer (Research) in French at the University of St Andrews. He has published widely in the field of post-1960 fiction (Jean-Marie Le Clézio, Patrick Grainville, Amélie Nothomb, Michel Rio), including a book on the novels of Michel Tournier (Oxford: Berg, 1996). His recent book, *The Games of Fiction: Georges Perec and modern French ludic narrative* (Peter Lang, 2006), is a wide-ranging study of Perec's fiction in the context of the sub-genre of ludic narrative from Roussel to Ricardou, the *nouveau roman* and Oulipo.

MAIRÉAD HANRAHAN is Professor of French at UCL. She has published extensively on the writing of Jean Genet, including her book *Lire Genet: Une Poétique de la différence* (1997) and *Genet*, a Special Number she edited for the journal *Paragraph* (2004). She has also written widely on a range of other twentieth-century authors, including Marguerite Duras, Djuna Barnes and Hélène Cixous. She is currently finalising a book entitled *The Events of Writing: The Fiction of Hélène Cixous*.

MARGARET-ANNE HUTTON is Reader in French at the University of Nottingham. Her publications include books on Michel Tournier, Christiane Rochefort, and most recently, the testimonial accounts of French women deported to Nazi concentration camps (Routledge, 2005) as well as articles and book chapters on a wide range of contemporary (post-1980) French writers. She is currently working on a monograph which explores post-1980 fictional representations of the Occupation.

ALAN MORRIS is Senior Lecturer in French Studies at the University of Strathclyde. His research interests include the Occupation and its legacy, the *œuvre* of Patrick Modiano, and the French detective novel. He is the author of *Collaboration and Resistance Reviewed: Writers and the 'Mode Rétro' in Post-Gaullist France* (Berg, 1992) and of two separate books on Patrick Modiano (Berg, 1996 and Rodopi, 2000).

DAVID PLATTEN is Senior Lecturer in French and Head of Department at the University of Leeds. He has published widely in the fields of modern and contemporary French literature and film, including books and articles on Tournier, Djian, Verne, Artaud, Pennac, and, more recently, on various *noir* writers, as well as on themes ranging from film in its social, political, and cultural contexts to utopianism. He is currently writing a book on French crime fiction, entitled *Outsiders, Radicals and Storytellers: French Crime Fiction in the Modern Era*. Future plans include work on a critical guide to popular French literature.

PETER READ is Professor of French at the University of Kent in Canterbury. He has published widely on the work of Apollinaire and related topics and has contributed essays on Picasso to major exhibition catalogues in the UK, France and USA. Books he has published include *Picasso et Apollinaire: les métamorphoses de la mémoire* (Paris, 1995); *Apollinaire et 'Les Mamelles de Tirésias': la revanche d'Eros* (Rennes, 2000); a translation and critical edition of Apollinaire's *The Cubist Painters* (Berkeley/Los Angeles, 2004).

Index of Names

[Characters in italic indicate references that occur in footnotes only.]
Only the first editor has been listed in the case of edited volumes.

Cultural Identity Studies

Edited by
Helen Chambers

This series aims to publish new research (monographs and essays) into relationships and interactions between culture and identity. The notions of both culture and identity are broadly conceived; interdisciplinary and theoretically diverse approaches are encouraged in a series designed to promote a better understanding of the processes of identity formation, both individual and collective. It will embrace research into the roles of linguistic, social, political, psychological, and religious factors, taking account of historical context. Work on the theorizing of cultural aspects of identity formation, together with case studies of individual writers, thinkers or cultural products will be included. It focuses primarily on cultures linked to European languages, but welcomes transcultural links and comparisons. It is published in association with the Institute of European Cultural Identity Studies of the University of St Andrews.